The Continuing Dialogue

The Continuing Dialogue

MEN AND ISSUES

IN EARLY AMERICAN HISTORY

Richard D. Burns, Donald O. Dewey,

Eugene R. Fingerhut, and

Samuel T. McSeveney

Editors

PACIFIC  BOOKS

Publishers

Palo Alto, California

PREFACE

The Continuing Dialogue provides the readings for a one-semester "men and issues" course in United States history. Unlike the conventional survey approach, which seeks to sketch the broad sweep of American history, such a course necessarily emphasizes certain aspects of the nation's historical experience at the expense of others. Consequently, The Continuing Dialogue focuses on political, economic, and intellectual developments, while much less space is devoted to diplomacy and precious little to social history. Yet it should soon be clear that historical threads are interwoven, and that as one is untangled much is learned about the others.

As historians, we must seek to understand the past on its own terms, freeing ourselves from the prejudices of the present, or at least trying to understand the assumptions which color our view of that past. The use of primary sources should aid us in this attempt, for such materials enable historical figures to address the readers directly. The editors hope that these readings will give to students an acquaintance with a variety of historical personalities and epochs—men and periods significant in themselves and rich in their contributions to the nation's development. In addition, the reading of original sources confronts students with the invaluable, if sometimes trying, experience of evaluating the conflicting evidence from which historians seek to reconstruct the past.

This volume focuses on major and recurring themes in the American experience. Students should recognize the bewildering variety of problems which this nation has faced in the past, and which—since many are as yet unresolved—must be faced by present and future generations. We hope that students will realize that although our contemporaries (historians among them) celebrate the American consensus, vigorous and significant public controversies have also shaped the destiny of this nation. By relating these debates to contrasting, indeed competing, pairs of leaders, the editors do not wish to imply that historical choice is a simple, either-or matter. In each epoch studied, spokesmen representing a variety of viewpoints sought a national audience. At the same time, conflicting interests and ideas polarized around a few outstanding leaders. Those men and their ideas form The Continuing Dialogue.

v

Each section of readings is preceded by an introduction, which offers brief biographical sketches of the principal spokesmen and outlines the historical background of the issues confronting them. The annotated bibliography in each section is designed to direct students' attention to books dealing with general and special themes developed in the readings.

A companion volume, *The Continuing Dialogue: Men and Issues in Recent American History,* presents the thought of Andrew Carnegie and Henry George, Theodore Roosevelt and Woodrow Wilson, and Herbert Hoover and Franklin D. Roosevelt.

The present "men and issues" course can be taught with or without a survey history to accompany *The Continuing Dialogue.* If none is assigned, students may wish to consult a standard textbook for background information. Among worthwhile texts available in paperback editions, are: William Miller, *A History of the United States;* and, for sophisticated readers, Carl N. Degler, *Out of Our Past: The Forces That Shaped Modern America.* Praiseworthy two-volume, hardcover, texts include: Samuel Eliot Morison and Henry Steele Commager, *The Growth of the American Republic;* T. Harry Williams, Richard N. Current, and Frank Freidel, *A History of the United States* (a single-volume version of which is available as *American History: A Survey);* and Richard Hofstadter, William Miller, and Daniel Aaron, *The American Republic* (also available in one volume as *The United States: The History of the Republic).* Finally, John M. Blum, Bruce Catton, Edmund S. Morgan, Arthur Schlesinger, Jr., Kenneth M. Stampp, and C. Vann Woodward, *The National Experience: A History of the United States,* is an excellent one-volume text.

Among comprehensive works dealing with American political thought and intellectual history are: Alan P. Grimes, *American Political Thought;* Ralph H. Gabriel, *The Course of American Democratic Thought;* Merle Curti, *The Growth of American Thought;* Stow Persons, *American Minds: A History of Ideas;* and Vernon L. Parrington, *Main Currents of American Thought,* 3 volumes in paperback.

R. D. B.
D. O. D.
E. R. F.
S. T. McS.

November 5, 1963

ACKNOWLEDGMENTS

Thanks are due the following publishers for permission to reprint material for which they hold the copyright: Pocket Books, Inc., for passages from Richard B. Morris (ed.), *Basic Ideas of Alexander Hamilton;* Princeton University Press, for passages from Julian P. Boyd (ed.), *The Papers of Thomas Jefferson;* the University of Kentucky Press, for passages from James Hopkins (ed.), *The Papers of Henry Clay;* the University of Chicago Press, for passages from Paul M. Angle (ed.), *Created Equal;* Rutgers University Press, for passages from Paul M. Angle and Earl S. Miers (eds.), *The Living Lincoln,* and for passages from Roy P. Basler (ed.), *The Collected Works of Abraham Lincoln;* the Mississippi Department of Archives and History, for passages from Dunbar Rowland (ed.), *Jefferson Davis: Constitutionalist;* and Harper and Row, Publishers, Inc., for a passage from Henry Steele Commager, *Living Ideas in America.*

CONTENTS

The Continuing Dialogue

MEN AND ISSUES
IN EARLY AMERICAN HISTORY

Chapter I

FORMING THE REPUBLIC

ALEXANDER HAMILTON

and

THOMAS JEFFERSON

Introduction

American allegiance to the British Empire was not doubted until the dozen years which preceded the Revolution. Yet during these years this fidelity was re-examined and rejected on the basis of arguments which have been adopted by revolutionaries all over the world. The removal of British authority from America was the destructive part of the revolution. The constructive part was the formation of rules by which the former colonies were to govern themselves. For this task the revolutionaries built upon the foundations of logic and experience. The support was not rigid; there were differences of opinion. The break with Great Britain was all the revolution that some Americans envisioned. Others wished to use this opportunity to reform institutions. No matter what their goals, these men were products of their common experience, environment, and eighteenth-century philosophy. Alexander Hamilton and Thomas Jefferson were two of these creators who differed on many issues, such as the merits of an established aristocracy, tradition, landed and commercial wealth, and the goal of human perfectability. Their assumptions, arguments, and agreements were important factors in the formation of the republic. They and their allies established different guidelines by which America was to develop. Succeeding generations of Americans have returned to many of the alternatives offered by these men; this is the essence of the continuing dialogue.

Alexander Hamilton was born on the island of Nevis, British West Indies, probably in 1755. His mother and her legal husband were separated when Alexander was born, the natural son of a scion of the Scottish Hamiltons. Several times during his public career, Hamilton's illegitimacy was to be used as a basis for attacking him.

After an apprenticeship in a mercantile establishment on Saint Croix, he went to the mainland for a college education. His essay describing the effects of a Caribbean hurricane had caught the attention of his employer and his minister, and they sent him to the care of several families in the New York—New Jersey area, who helped the young immigrant enter King's College (later to be Columbia University) in 1773. While there he joined those who opposed the British colonial policy. He wrote two essays, "A

5

Full Vindication. . . ," defending the Continental Congress, and "The Farmer Refuted," a blistering denunciation of the Loyalist pamphleteer Samuel Seabury.

When the fighting began, Hamilton was commissioned as a captain in the Continental Army. He came to the attention of General George Washington during the frustrating campaigns in the middle states in 1776 and was invited to become aide-de-camp to the commander in chief. In this capacity Hamilton composed many orders issued over Washington's name, corresponded with state and Continental officials, and acted as Washington's personal representative on several missions. Therefore, he frequently observed Congress' inability to supply the army adequately and to conduct a vigorous war. In 1781 Hamilton resigned his position because of his desire to experience the glories of combat. This hope was fulfilled when he led a charge on the outposts of Cornwallis' camp at Yorktown, Virginia.

After the war Hamilton became a prominent lawyer in New York and defended several Loyalists when their property was confiscated by the state. He had married into the powerful and wealthy Schuyler family and was able to utilize his connections with the clique of New York aristocrats to rise to a prominent position in his profession. Throughout the 1780's Hamilton eagerly pressed for a stronger national government than that established by the Articles of Confederation. He was instrumental in convincing the New York government to send representatives to the Annapolis and Philadelphia conventions.

At the Philadelphia Convention he was one of three representatives from New York but had little influence. Although his comments on the floor were incisive and attracted attention, they were not adopted. During the ratification debate, Hamilton so exhausted himself that he became ill while fighting to persuade New York to accept the Constitution. He was the principal contributor to *The Federalist,* a series of essays advocating adoption of the Constitution. These essays written with the aid of James Madison —a few were penned by John Jay—have become the classic interpretation of the philosophy of the Constitution.

Washington appointed Hamilton as Secretary of the Treasury, and within two years of his appointment he suggested the economic program for which he has become famous. When it was criticized, Hamilton attacked his critics and organized a party to support his program and his concept of government and society; this was to be the Federalist Party.

In 1795, after six stormy years as a cabinet member, Hamilton retired to his law practice. Although his policy decisions enabled others to achieve great wealth, he left office in financial straits. Following his retirement, Hamilton's advice was repeatedly solicited by President Washington. During the administration of John Adams, Secretary of the Treasury Oliver Wolcott, Secretary of War James McHenry, and Secretary of State Timothy Pickering consulted with Hamilton without the knowledge of the President. Hamilton's control of the Federalist Party during the early years of Adams' administration was based solely on his personal abilities, for he had no official position.

After 1797, as the undeclared naval war with France threatened to embroil the United States in the general European conflict, Hamilton lost much of his influence over the party. He opposed President Adams' attempt to continue peace negotiations with France, partly because of the old antagonism between the two men as rival leaders of the Federalists. In the election of 1800, Hamilton was reduced to backstairs intrigue in his attempt to control his own party. The final decision in the presidential election was made by the House of Representatives, since the vote of the electoral college was inconclusive. There Hamilton used whatever influence he had to win the election of Jefferson over Aaron Burr: Jefferson was at least an honorable antagonist of Federalist ideals and a lesser evil than Burr, whom he regarded as an unscrupulous politician. The House finally elected Jefferson President after thirty-six ballots.

On July 11, 1804, Hamilton was killed in a duel with Burr, the political enemy whom he had so often antagonized on local New York issues, and whom he had helped to defeat in the races for President in 1800 and for governor of New York in 1804.

Thomas Jefferson was born in 1743 in western Virginia, where his father carved out a plantation on the fringe of settlement. His training followed the usual pattern for the son of a plantation owner: tutors, academy, the College of William and Mary, and practical business education by managing a plantation. By 1767 Jefferson had read law and been admitted to the bar. He was a member of the House of Burgesses in 1769, where he fell in with the anti-British group. In 1774 he wrote *A Summary View of the Rights of British North America*. As a delegate to the Second Continental Congress, Jefferson was one of the group most sympathetic to independence; he wrote the draft of the Declaration of Independence, which was accepted with several modifications by Congress.

Jefferson returned to Virginia soon after the acceptance of the Declaration. There he was instrumental in abolishing entail and primogeniture, separating church and state, and establishing a public school system. In 1779 he succeeded Patrick Henry as governor. During his two years in office, Virginia was invaded by the British and the government was constantly harassed. As governor, Jefferson was faced with many problems, not the least of which was his limited power under the state constitution, which made him unable to cope with hostile elements in the state legislature.

In 1783 Jefferson returned to Congress, where he was the first to suggest the decimal money system; he also proposed the Land Ordinance of 1784, intended to serve as the basis for national control of western land. His widely read *Notes on Virginia,* published in 1785, analyzed the virtues of his state's polity and economy. That year he was appointed minister to France by Congress. Like his predecessor, Benjamin Franklin, Jefferson's philosophic, scientific, and artistic talents made him a lion of salon society, and he became friendly with the writers who laid the intellectual basis for and carried out the early phases of the French Revolution.

Jefferson assumed the office of Secretary of State in March, 1790, some months after his return from France. By then Hamilton had already won approval of his funding plan. Jefferson agreed to throw his prestige behind the assumption plan if Hamilton would agree to do the same for the bill to establish the permanent national capital on the Potomac River. Later he broke with Hamilton over their political and economic views. With James Madison, he helped to organize those who opposed Hamilton's program into the Democratic-Republican Party. In 1793 Jefferson retired from the cabinet, partly because of his opposition to the policies of the administration.

He emerged from retirement in 1796 and was elected Vice-President. His election was due to the rapid rise of the Republican Party, which secured for him the second highest number of electoral votes. He supported President Adams' policy of avoiding war with France, but differed sharply with him over the Alien and Sedition Acts and the passage of high excise taxes to pay for the enlargement of the military and naval establishments. To counter the Alien and Sedition Acts, Jefferson and Madison wrote resolutions which denounced the acts as unconstitutional and suggested that the states, acting in concert, could void the laws. In 1800 Jefferson was chosen by the leaders of the Republican Party as their presidential candidate, with Aaron Burr as the vice-presidential candidate. Jefferson and Burr obtained more electoral votes than the Federalist candidates, Adams and Charles C. Pinckney, but since Jefferson and Burr each received the same number of votes, the decision went to the House of Representatives, where Jefferson won after protracted debate.

Jefferson's two administrations were notable for the war against the Barbary pirates (1801-1805), the Louisiana Purchase (1803), the Lewis and Clark (1804-1806) and Zebulon Pike (1806-1807) expeditions, the Burr treason trial (1807), and the attempt to keep the United States out of the Napoleonic Wars.

After retirement in 1809, Jefferson returned to his home at Monticello, where he developed plans to organize the University of Virginia and was its first rector. He died on July 4, 1826, the same day as John Adams.

Recommended Readings
(Titles followed by an asterisk are available in paperback editions)

John C. Miller, Alexander Hamilton: Portrait in Paradox, is the most readable and accurate short biography of Alexander Hamilton. Nathan Schachner. Alexander Hamilton,* is a well-balanced evaluation, but is marred by several factual errors. The most comprehensive biography to use modern methods and many previously untapped sources is Broadus Mitchell, Alexander Hamilton (2 vols). Richard B. Morris, ed., The Basic Ideas of Alexander Hamilton,* is an inexpensive and handy selection of the writings of Hamilton. Samuel McKee, Jr., ed., Alexander Hamilton's Papers on Public Credit, Finance and Commerce,* completely reproduces Hamilton's major economic proposals.

The best short biography of Thomas Jefferson is Gilbert Chinard, Thomas Jefferson: Apostle of Americanism.* Nathan Schachner, Thomas Jefferson (2 vols.), is more comprehensive. The definitive biography of Jefferson is Dumas Malone, Jefferson and His Time; three volumes have appeared in this balanced and judicious set. Several short selections of Jefferson's writings are available: Adrienne Koch and William Peden, eds., The Life and Selected Writings of Thomas Jefferson;* Edward Dumbald, ed., The Political Writings of Thomas Jefferson;* and Saul K. Padover, ed., Thomas Jefferson on Democracy.*

There are a number of volumes which evaluate the work of these two men. Louis Hacker, Alexander Hamilton in the American

Tradition, concludes that Hamilton's genius made modern America possible. A different view is Charles Wiltse, *The Jeffersonian Tradition in American Democracy.** John Tipple, *Hamilton/Jefferson: The New Order,** puts the ideas of the two men in the setting in which they acted. Several short sketches have value. Vernon Parrington, *Main Currents in American Thought,** Vol. I, is critical of Hamilton and laudatory of Jefferson. Adrienne Koch, *Power, Morals, and the Founding Fathers,** takes the same position, but is attuned more to intellectual differences than Parrington. Saul K. Padover, *The Genius of America,** attempts to be fair, in spite of a pro-Jefferson bias. Richard Hofstadter, *The American Political Tradition,** is critical of the Founding Fathers and Jefferson. George Rogers Taylor, ed., *Alexander Hamilton and the National Debt,** offers conflicting interpretations. Merrill D. Petersen, *The Jeffersonian Image in the American Mind,** is an able summary of Jefferson's importance.

Numerous books help to explain the scene in which Hamilton and Jefferson debated. Lawrence H. Gipson, *The Coming of the Revolution,** is a history of the causes of the war. Edmund Morgan, *The Birth of the Republic,** surveys the years from 1763 to the election of Washington. Merrill Jensen, *The New Nation,** looks with sympathy upon the Confederation period. Charles Beard, *An Economic Interpretation of the Constitution,** laid the groundwork for Jensen. A point-by-point denunciation of Beard's thesis is Robert Brown, *Charles Beard and the Constitution.** Forrest McDonald, *We, the People,** also attacks Beard and offers an alternative economic interpretation. The social life of the period is admirably described in Evarts B. Greene, *The Revolutionary Generation,* and the economic life in Curtis P. Nettels, *The Emergence of a National Economy.* John C. Miller, *The Federalist Era,** Joseph Charles, *The Origins of the American Party System,** and Noble Cunninghman, *The Jeffersonian Republicans,* and *The Jeffersonian Republicans in Power,* survey political development. Leonard White's *The Federalists* and *The Jeffersonians* describe the way in which these two groups viewed the problems of administering the government.

Natural Rights, Natural Law, and the Right of Revolution

THOMAS JEFFERSON

The *Summary View of the Rights of British America,* (Williamsburg, 1774), 5-23. When reprinted outside of Virginia the pamphlet helped to establish his reputation as a writer.

Resolved that it be an instruction to the said deputies, when assembled in general congress, with the deputies from the other states of British America, to propose to the said congress, that an humble and dutiful address be presented to his majesty, begging leave to lay before him, as chief magistrate of the British empire, the united complaints of his majesty's subjects in America; complaints which are excited by many unwarrantable encroachments and usurpations, attempted to be made by the legislature of one part of the empire, upon those rights which God and the laws have given equally and independently to all. To represent to his majesty that these his states have often individually made humble application to his imperial throne, to obtain, through its intervention, some redress of their injured rights, to none of which, was ever oven an answer condescended; humbly to hope that this their joint address, penned in the language of truth, and divested of those expressions of servility which would persuade his majesty that we are asking favours, and not rights, shall obtain from his majesty a more respectful acceptance. And this his majesty will think we have reason to expect when he reflects that he is no more than the chief officer of the people, appointed by the laws, and circumscribed with definite powers, to assist in working the great machine of government, erected for their use, and consequently subject to their superintendence. And in order that these our rights, as well as the invasions of them, may be laid more fully before his majesty, to take a view of them from the origin and first settlement of these countries.

. . . one of these conclusions must necessarily follow, either that justice is not the same thing in America as in Britain, or else, that the British parliament pay less regard to it here than there. But that we do not point out to his majesty the injustice of these acts, with intent to rest on that principle the cause of their nullity; but to shew that experience confirms the propriety of those political principles, which exempt us from the jurisdiction of the British parliament. The true ground on which we declare these acts void is, that the British parliament has no right to exercise authority over us.

That these exercises of usurped power have not been confined to instances alone, in which themselves were interested, but they have also intermeddled with the regulation of the internal affairs of the colonies. . . .

. . . It is now, therefore, the great office of his majesty, to resume the exercise of his negative power, and to prevent the passage of laws by any one legislature of the empire, which might bear injuriously on the rights and interests of another. Yet this will not excuse the wanton exercise of this power which we have seen his majesty practice on the laws of the American legislatures. For the most trifling reasons, and sometimes for no conceivable reason at all, his majesty has rejected laws of the most salutary tendency. . . .

. . . Only aim to do your duty, and mankind will give you credit where you fail. No longer persevere in sacrificing the rights of one part of the empire to the inordinate desires of another; but deal out to all equal and impartial right. Let no act be passed by any one legislature which may infringe on the rights and liberties of another. This is the important post in which fortune has placed you, holding the balance of a great, if a well poised empire. This, sire, is the advice of your great American council, on the observance of which may perhaps depend your felicity and future fame, and the preservation of that harmony which alone can continue both to Great Britain and America the reciprocal advantages of their connection. It is neither our wish nor our interest, to separate from her. We are willing, on our part, to sacrifice every thing which reason can ask to the restoration of that tranquility for which all must wish. On their part, let them be ready to establish union and a generous plan. Let them name their terms, but let them be just. Accept of every commercial preference it is in our power to give, for such things as we can raise for their use, or they make for ours. But let them not think to exclude us from going to other markets to dispose of those commodities which they cannot use, or to supply those wants which they cannot supply. Still less let it be proposed that our properties within our own territories shall be taxed or regulated by any power on earth but our own. The God who gave us life gave us liberty at the same time: the hand of force may destroy, but cannot disjoin them. This, sire, is our last, our determined resolution; and that you will be pleased to interpose with that efficacy which your earnest endeavours may ensure, to procure redress of these our great grievances, to quiet the minds of your subjects in British America, against any apprehensions of future encroachment, to establish fraternal love and harmony through the whole empire, and that that may continue to the latest ages of time, is the fervent prayer of all British America!

The original draft of the Declaration of Independence was written by Thomas Jefferson. The final version, which was accepted by the Continental Congress, included several changes. The footnote to the text below is one of the passages in Jefferson's draft which was deleted in the Congressional version. Worthington C. Ford *et al.*, eds., *Journals of the Continental Congress, 1774-1789* (Washington, D.C., 1906), V, 510-15.

The unanimous Declaration of the thirteen United States of America.

WHEN, in the Course of human events, it becomes necessary for one people to dissolve the political bands which have connected them with another, and to assume, among the Powers of the earth, the separate and equal station to which the Laws of Nature and of Nature's God entitle them, a decent respect to the opinions of mankind requires that they should declare the causes which impel them to the separation.

We hold these truths to be self-evident, that all men are created equal, that they are endowed by their Creator with certain unalienable Rights, that among these, are Life, Liberty, and the pursuit of Happiness. That to secure these rights, Governments are instituted among Men, deriving their just Powers from the consent of the governed. That, whenever any form of Government becomes destructive of these ends, it is the Right of the People to alter or to abolish it, and to institute new Government, laying its foundation on such Principles, and organizing its Powers in such form, as to them shall seem most likely to effect their Safety and Happiness. Prudence, indeed, will dictate that Governments long established should not be changed for light and transient causes; and, accordingly, all experience hath shewn, that mankind are more disposed to suffer, while evils are sufferable, than to right themselves by abolishing the forms to which they are accustomed. But, when a long train of abuses and usurpations, pursuing invariably the same Object, evinces a design to reduce them under absolute Despotism, it is their right, it is their duty, to throw off such Government, and to provide new Guards for their future Security.   Such has been the patient sufferance of these Colonies; and such is now the necessity which constrains them to alter their former Systems of Government. The history of the present King of Great Britain is a history of repeated injuries and usurpations, all having in direct object the establishment of an absolute Tyranny over these States. To prove this, let Facts be submitted to a candid world.

He has refused his Assent to Laws the most wholesome and necessary for the public good.

He has forbidden his Governors to pass Laws of immediate and pressing importance, unless suspended in their operation till his Assent should be obtained; and when so suspended, he has utterly neglected to attend to them.

He has refused to pass other Laws for the accommodation of large districts of People, unless those People would relinquish the right of Representation in the legislature; a right inestimable to them and formidable to tyrants only.

He has called together legislative bodies at places unusual, uncomfortable, and distant from the depository of their Public Records, for the sole Purpose of fatiguing them into compliance with his measures.

He has dissolved Representative Houses repeatedly, for opposing, with manly firmness, his invasions on the rights of the People.

He has refused for a long time, after such dissolutions, to cause others to be elected; whereby the Legislative Powers, incapable of Annihilation, have returned to the People at large for their exercise; the State remaining in the mean time exposed to all the dangers of invasion from without, and convulsions within.

He has endeavoured to prevent the Population of these States; for that purpose obstructing the Laws for Naturalization of Foreigners; refusing to pass others to encourage their migrations hither, and raising the conditions of new Appropriations of Lands.

He has obstructed the Administration of Justice, by refusing his Assent to Laws for establishing Judiciary Powers.

He has made Judges dependent on his Will alone, for the tenure of their offices, and the amount and payment of their salaries.

He has erected a multitude of New Offices, and sent hither swarms of Officers to harrass our People, and eat out their substance.

He has kept among us, in times of Peace, Standing Armies, without the Consent of our legislatures.

He has affected to render the Military independent of and superior to the Civil Power.

He has combined with others to subject us to a jurisdiction foreign to our constitution, and unacknowledged by our laws; giving his Assent to their Acts of pretended Legislation:

For quartering large bodies of armed troops among us:

For protecting them, by a mock Trial, from Punishment for any Murders which they should commit on the Inhabitants of these States:

For cutting off our Trade with all parts of the world:

For imposing Taxes on us without our Consent:

For depriving us, in many cases, of the benefits of Trial by Jury:

For transporting us beyond Seas to be tried for pretended offences:

For abolishing the free System of English Laws in a neighbouring province, establishing therein an Arbitrary government, and enlarging its Boundaries, so as to render it at once an example and fit instrument for introducing the same absolute rule into these Colonies:

For taking away our Charters, abolishing our most valuable Laws, and altering fundamentally the Forms of our Governments:

For suspending our own Legislatures, and declaring themselves invested with Power to legislate for us in all cases whatsoever.

He has abdicated Government here, by declaring us out of his protection, and waging War against us.

He has plundered our seas, ravaged our Coasts, burnt our towns, and destroyed the Lives of our People.

He is at this time transporting large Armies of foreign Mercenaries to compleat the works of death, desolation and tyranny, already begun with circumstances of Cruelty and perfidy scarcely paralleled in the most barbarous ages, and totally unworthy the Head of a civilized nation.

He has constrained our fellow Citizens, taken Captive on the high Seas, to bear Arms against their Country, to become the executioners of their friends and Brethren, or to fall themselves by their Hands.

He has excited domestic insurrections amongst us, and has endeavoured to bring on the inhabitants of our frontiers, the merciless Indian Savages, whose known rule of warfare, is an undistinguished destruction of all ages, sexes and conditions.[1]

In every stage of these Oppressions, We have Petitioned for Redress, in the most humble terms: Our repeated Petitions, have been answered only by repeated injury. A Prince, whose character is thus marked by every act which may define a Tyrant, is unfit to be the ruler of a free People.

Nor have We been wanting in attentions to our Brittish brethren. We have warned them from time to time of attempts by their legislature to extend an unwarrantable jurisdiction over us. We have reminded them of the circumstances of our emigration and settlement here. We have appealed to their native justice and magnanimity, and we have conjured them by the ties of our common kindred, to disavow these usurpations, which, would inevitably interrupt our connexions and correspondence. They too have been deaf to the voice of justice and of consanguinity. We must, therefore, acquiesce in the necessity, which denounces our Separation, and hold them, as we hold the rest of mankind, Enemies in War, in Peace Friends.

WE, THEREFORE, the Representatives of the UNITED STATES OF AMERICA, in General Congress assembled, appealing to the Supreme Judge of the World for the rectitude of our intentions, do, in the Name, and by Authority of the good People of these Colonies, solemnly publish and declare, That these United Colonies are, and of Right, ought to be FREE AND INDEPENDENT STATES; that they are Absolved from all Allegiance to the British Crown, and that all political connexion between them and the State of Great Britain, is and ought to be totally dissolved; and that, as Free and Independent States, they have full Power to levy War, conclude Peace, contract Alliances, establish Commerce, and to do all other Acts and Things which Independent States may of right

---

[1]He has incited treasonable insurrections of our fellow-citizens, with the allurements of forfeiture & confiscation of our property.

He has waged cruel war against human nature itself, violating it's most sacred rights of life and liberty in the persons of a distant people who never offended him, captivating & carrying them into slavery in another hemisphere or to incur miserable death in their transportation thither. This piratical warfare, the opprobrium of *infidel* powers, is the warfare of the *Christian* king of Great Britain. Determined to keep open a market where *Men* should be bought & sold, he has prostituted his negative for suppressing every legislative attempt to prohibit or to restrain this execrable commerce. And that this assemblage of horrors might want no fact of distinguished die, he is now exciting those very people to rise in arms among us, and to purchase that liberty of which he has deprived them, by murdering the people on whom he also obtruded them: thus paying off former crimes committed against the *Liberties* of one people, with crimes which he urges them to commit against the *lives* of another.

do.   And for the support of this Declaration, with a firm reliance
on the protection of divine Providence, we mutually pledge to each
other our Lives, our Fortunes, and our sacred Honour.

Jefferson wrote his Bill for Establishing Religious Freedom
in 1779 but it was not enacted until January 1786. By his
request Jefferson's tombstone cites what he considered his
three greatest contributions to the United States: this law,
the Declaration of Independence, and the establishment of
the University of Virginia.   William Waller Hening, *The
Statutes at Large;   Being a   Collection of All the Laws of
Virginia. . .,* X (Richmond, 1823), 86.

II. BE IT ENACTED BY THE GENERAL ASSEMBLY, That
no man shall be compelled to frequent or support any religious
worship, place, or ministry whatsoever, nor shall be enforced,
restrained, molested, or burthened in his body or goods, nor shall
otherwise suffer on account of his religious opinions or belief;
but that all men shall be free to profess, and by argument to
maintain, their opinions in matters of religion, and that the same
shall in no wise diminish, enlarge, or affect their civil capacities.
III. And though we well know that this assembly, elected by the
people for the ordinary purposes of legislation only, have no
power to restrain the acts of succeeding assemblies, constituted
with powers equal to our own, and that therefore to declare this
act to be irrevocable would be of no effect in law; yet we are
free to declare, and do declare, that the rights hereby asserted
are of the natural rights of mankind, and that if any act shall be
hereafter passed to repeal the present or to narrow its operation,
such act will be an infringement of natural right.

Letter to William Smith, November 13, 1787. Julian P. Boyd,
ed., *The Papers of Thomas Jefferson* (Princeton, N.J.,
1950-), XII, 356-57.

Wonderful is the effect of impudent and persevering lying.
The British ministry have so long hired their gazetteers to
repeat and model into every form lies about our being in anarchy,
that the world has at length believed them, the English nation has
believed them, the ministers themselves have come to believe
them, and what is more wonderful, we have believed them ourselves.   Yet where does this anarchy exist?   Where did it ever

exist, except in the single instance of Massachusets? And can history produce an instance of a rebellion so honourably conducted? I say nothing of it's motives. They were founded in ignorance, not wickedness. God forbid we should ever be 20. years without such a rebellion. The people can not be all, and always, well informed. The part which is wrong will be discontented in proportion to the importance of the facts they misconceive. If they remain quiet under such misconceptions it is a lethargy, the forerunner of death to the public liberty. We have had 13. states independant 11. years. There has been one rebellion. That comes to one rebellion in a century and a half for each state. What country before ever existed a century and half without a rebellion? And what country can preserve it's liberties if their rulers are not warned from time to time that their people preserve the spirit of resistance? Let them take arms. The remedy is to set them right as to facts, pardon and pacify them. What signify a few lives lost in a century or two? The tree of liberty must be refreshed from time to time with the blood of patriots and tyrants. It is it's natural manure. Our Convention has been too much impressed by the insurrection of Massachusets: and in the spur of the moment they are setting up a kite to keep the hen yard in order . . . .

ALEXANDER HAMILTON

"The Farmer Refuted," February 5, 1775. Henry Cabot Lodge, ed., *The Works of Alexander Hamilton* (New York, 1904), I, 61-76.

The first thing that presents itself is a wish, that "I had, explicitly, declared to the public my ideas of the *natural rights* of mankind. Man, in a state of nature (you say), may be considered as perfectly free from all restraint of *law* and *government;* and then, the weak must submit to the strong."

I shall, henceforth, begin to make some allowance for that enmity you have discovered to the *natural rights* of mankind. For, though ignorance of them, in this enlightened age, cannot be admitted as a sufficient excuse for you, yet it ought, in some measure, to extenuate your guilt. If you will follow my advice, there still may be hopes of your reformation. Apply yourself, without delay, to the study of the law of nature. I would recommend to your perusal, Grotius, Puffendorf, Locke, Montesquieu, and Burlemaqui.

I might mention other excellent writers on this subject; but if you attend diligently to these, you will not require any others.

There is so strong a similitude between your political principles and those maintained by Mr. Hobbes, that, in judging from them, a person might very easily *mistake* you for a disciple of his. His opinion was exactly coincident with yours, relative to man in a state of nature. He held, as you do, that he was then perfectly free from all restraint of *law* and *government*. Moral obligation, according to him, is derived from the introduction of civil society; and there is no virtue but what is purely artificial, the mere contrivance of politicians for the maintenance of social intercourse. But the reason he ran into this absurd and impious doctrine was, that he disbelieved the existence of an intelligent, superintending principle, who is the governor, and will be the final judge, of the universe.

As you sometimes swear by *Him that made you*, I conclude your sentiments do not correspond with his in that which is the basis of the doctrine you both agree in; and this makes it impossible to imagine whence this congruity between you arises. To grant that there is a Supreme Intelligence who rules the world and has established laws to regulate the actions of His creatures, and still to assert that man, in a state of nature, may be considered as perfectly free from all restraints of *law* and *government*, appears, to a common understanding, altogether irreconcilable.

Good and wise men, in all ages, have embraced a very dissimilar theory. They have supposed that the Deity, from the relations we stand in to Himself and to each other, has constituted an eternal and immutable law, which is indispensably obligatory upon all mankind, prior to any human institution whatever.

This is what is called the law of nature, "which, being coeval with mankind, and dictated by God himself, is, of course, superior in obligations to any other. It is binding over all the globe, in all countries, and at all times. No human laws are of any validity, if contrary to this; and such of them as are valid derive all their authority, mediately or immediately, from this original." —BLACK-STONE.

Upon this law depend the natural rights of mankind: the Supreme Being gave existence to man, together with the means of preserving and beautifying that existence. He endowed him with rational faculties, by the help of which to discern and pursue such things as were consistent with his duty and interest; and invested him with an inviolable right to personal liberty and personal safety.

Hence, in a state of nature, no man had any *moral* power to deprive another of his life, limbs, property, or liberty; nor the least authority to command or exact obedience from him, except that which arose from the ties of consanguinity.

Hence, also, the origin of all civil government, justly established, must be a voluntary compact between the rulers and the ruled, and must be liable to such limitations as are necessary for the security of the *absolute rights* of the latter; for what original title can any man, or set of men, have to govern others, except their own consent? To usurp dominion over a people in their own despite, or to grasp at a more extensive power than they are willing to intrust, is to violate that law of nature which gives every man a right to his personal liberty, and can therefore confer no obligation to obedience.

"The principal aim of society is to protect individuals in the enjoyment of those absolute rights which were vested in them by the immutable laws of nature, but which could not be preserved in peace without that mutual assistance and intercourse which is gained by the institution of friendly and social communities. Hence it follows, that the first and primary end of human laws is to maintain and regulate these *absolute rights* of individuals." — BLACKSTONE

If we examine the pretensions of Parliament by this criterion, which is evidently a good one, we shall presently detect their injustice. First, they are subversive of our natural liberty, because an authority is assumed over us which we by no means assent to. And, secondly, they divest us of that moral security for our lives and properties, which we are entitled to, and which it is the primary end of society to bestow. For such security can never exist while we have no part in making the laws that are to bind us, and while it may be the interest of our uncontrolled legislators to oppress us as much as possible.

To deny these principles will be not less absurd than to deny the plainest axioms. I shall not, therefore, attempt any further illustration of them. . . .

Admitting that the king of Great Britain was enthroned by virtue of an Act of Parliament, and that he is king of America because he is king of Great Britain, yet the Act of Parliament is not the *efficient cause* of his being the king of America. It is only the *occasion* of it. He is king of America by virtue of a compact between us and the kings of Great Britain. These colonies were planted and settled by the grants, and under the protection, of English kings, who entered into covenants with us, for themselves, their heirs, and successors; and it is from these covenants that the duty of protection on their part, and the duty of allegiance on ours, arise.

So that to disclaim the authority of a British Parliament over us does by no means imply the dereliction of our allegiance to British monarchs. Our compact takes no cognizance of the manner of their accession to the throne. It is sufficient for us that they are kings of England.

The most valid reasons can be assigned for our allegiance to the king of Great Britain, but not one of the least force or plausibility for our subjection to parliamentary decrees.

We hold our lands in America by virtue of charters from British monarchs, and are under no obligations to the Lords or Commons for them. Our title is similar, and equal, to that by which they possess their lands; and the king is the legal fountain of both.

This is one grand source of our obligation to allegiance. . . .

The best way of determining disputes and of investigating truth, is by descending to elementary principles.... By observing this method, we shall learn the following truths:—

That the existence of the House of Commons depends upon the people's right to a share in the legislature, which is exercised by means of electing the members of that House. That the end and intention of this right is to preserve the life, property, and liberty of the subject from the encroachments of oppression and tyranny.

That this end is accomplished by means of the *intimate connection* of interest between those members and their constituents, the people of Great Britain.

That with respect to the people of America there is no such *intimate connection* of interest, but the contrary, and therefore that end could not be answered to them; consequently, the *end* ceasing, the *means* must cease also.

The House of Commons derives all its power from its own real constituents, who are the people of Great Britain; and that, therefore, it has no power but what they *originally* had in themselves.

That they had no original right to the life, property, or liberty of Americans, nor any acquired from their own consent, and of course could give no authority over them.

That therefore the House of Commons has no such authority.

Representative Government and Democracy

THOMAS JEFFERSON

Letter to Edward Carrington, January 16, 1787. *Papers of Jefferson*, XI, 48-49.

The tumults in America, I expected would have produced in Europe an unfavorable opinion of our political state. But it has not. On the contrary, the small effect of those tumults seems to have given more confidence in the firmness of our governments. The interposition of the people themselves on the side of government has had a great effect on the opinion here. I am persuaded myself that the good sense of the people will always be found to be the best army. They may be led astray for a moment, but will soon correct themselves. The people are the only censors of their governors: and even their errors will tend to keep these to the true principles of their institution. To punish these errors too severely would be to suppress the only safeguard of the public liberty. The way to prevent these irregular interpositions of the people is to give them full information of their affairs thro' the channel of the public papers, and to contrive that those papers should penetrate the whole mass of the people. The basis of our governments being the opinion of the people, the very first object should be to keep that right; and were it left to me to decide whether we should have a government without newspapers, or newspapers without a government, I should not hesitate a moment to prefer the latter. But I should mean that every man should receive those papers and be capable of reading them. I am convinced that those societies (as the Indians) which live without government enjoy in their general mass an infinitely greater degree of happiness than those who live under European governments. Among the former, public opinion is in the place of law, and restrains morals as powerfully as laws ever did any where. Among the latter, under pretence of governing they have divided their nations into two classes, wolves and sheep. I do not exaggerate. This is a true picture of Europe. Cherish therefore the spirit of our people, and keep alive their attention. Do not be too severe upon their errors, but reclaim them by enlightening them. If once they become inattentive to the public affairs, you and I, and Congress, and Assemblies, judges and governors shall all become wolves. It seems to be the law of our general nature, in spite of individual exceptions; and experience declares that man is the only animal which devours his own kind, for I can apply no milder term to the governments of Europe, and to the general prey of the rich on the poor.

The *Anas* is a collection of autobiographical memoranda which Jefferson began compiling shortly after his return to the United States. Many of these memoranda were obviously designed to justify his policies. Andrew Lipscomb and Albert Bergh, eds., *The Writings of Thomas Jefferson* (Washington, D. C., 1905), I, 284-85.

Alexander Hamilton . . . declared in substance as follows: "I own it is my own opinion, though I do not publish it in Dan or Bershcba, that the present government is not that which will answer the ends of society, by giving stability and protection to its rights, and that it will probably be found expedient to go into the British form. However, since we have undertaken the experiment, I am for giving it a fair course, whatever my expectations may be. The success, indeed, so far, is greater than I had expected, and therefore, at present, success seems more possible than it had done heretofore, and there are still other and other stages of improvement which, if the present does not succeed, may be tried, and ought to be tried, before we give up the republican form altogether; for that mind must be really depraved, which would not prefer the equality of political rights, which is the foundation of pure republicanism, if it can be obtained consistently with order. Therefore, whoever by his writings disturbs the present order of things, is really blameable, however pure his intentions may be. . . ." This is the substance of a declaration made in much more lengthy terms, and which seemed to be more formal than usual for a private conversation between two, and as if intended to qualify some less guarded expressions which had been dropped on former occasions. Th: Jefferson has committed it to writing in the moment of A. Hamilton's leaving the room.

The *Anas*. *Writings of Jefferson*, I, 278-79.

. . . Hamilton was not only a monarchist, but for a monarchy bottomed on corruption. In proof of this, I will relate an anecdote, for the truth of which I attest the God who made me. Before the President set out on his southern tour in April, 1791, he addressed a letter of the fourth of that month, from Mount Vernon, to the Secretaries of State, Treasury and War, desiring that if any serious and important cases should arise during his absence, they would consult and act on them. And he requested that the Vice President should also be consulted. This was the only occasion on which that officer was ever requested to take part in a cabinet question. Some occasion for consultation arising, I invited those gentlemen (and the Attorney General, as well as I remember,) to dine with me, in order to confer on the subject. After the cloth was removed, and our question agreed and dismissed, conversation began on other matters, and by some circumstance, was led to the British constitution, on which Mr. Adams observed, "purge that constitution of its corruption, and give to its popular branch equality of representation, and it would be the most perfect constitution ever devised by the wit of man." Hamilton paused and said, "purge it of its corruption, and give to its popular branch equality of representation, and it would become an *impracticable* government: as it stands at present, with all its supposed defects, it is the most perfect government which ever existed." And this was assuredly the exact line which separated the political creeds of these two gentlemen. The one was for two hereditary branches and an honest elective one: the other, for an hereditary King, with a House of Lords and Commons corrupted to his will, and standing between him and the people.

Hamilton was, indeed, a singular character. Of acute understanding, disinterested, honest, and honorable in all private transactions, amiable in society, and duly valuing virtue in private life, yet so bewitched and perverted by the British example, as to be under thorough conviction that corruption was essential to the government of a nation.

Letter to Elbridge Gerry, January 26, 1799. *Writings of Jefferson*, X, 76-79.

I . . . wish an inviolable preservation of our present federal Constitution, according to the true sense in which it was adopted by the States, that in which it was advocated by its friends, and not that which its enemies apprehended, who therefore became its enemies; and I am opposed to the monarchising its features by the forms of its administration, with a view to conciliate a first transition to a President and Senate for life, and from that to an hereditary tenure of these offices, and thus to worm out the elective principle. I am for preserving to the States the powers not yielded by them to the Union, and to the legislature of the Union its constitutional share in the division of powers; and I am not for transferring all the powers of the States to the General Government, and all those of that government to the executive branch. I am for a government rigorously frugal and simple, applying all the possible savings of the public revenue to the discharge of the national debt; and not for a multiplication of officers and salaries merely to make partisans, and for increasing, by every device, the public debt, on the principle of its being a public blessing. I am for relying, for internal defence, on our militia solely, till actual invasion, and for such a naval force only as may protect our coasts and harbors from such depredations as we have experienced; and not for a standing army in time of peace, which may overawe the public sentiment; nor for a navy, which, by its own expenses and the eternal wars in which it will implicate us, will grind us with public burthens, and sink us under them. I am for free commerce with all nations; political connection with none; and little or no diplomatic establishment. And I am not for linking ourselves by new treaties with the quarrels of Europe; entering that field of slaughter to preserve their balance, or joining in the confederacy of kings to war against the principles of liberty. I am for freedom of religion, and against all manoeuvres to bring about a legal ascendancy of one sect over another: for freedom of the press, and against all violations of the Constitution to silence by force and not by reason the complaints or criticisms, just or unjust, of our citizens against the conduct of their agents. And I am for encouraging the progress of science in all its branches; and not for raising a hue and cry against the sacred name of philosophy; for awing the human mind by stories of raw-head and bloody bones to a distrust of its own vision, and to repose implicitly on that of others; to go backwards instead of forwards to look for improvement; to believe that government, religion, morality, and every other science were in the highest perfection in ages of the darkest ignorance, and that nothing can ever be devised more perfect that what was established by our forefathers.

First Inaugural Address, March 4, 1801. *Writings of Jefferson*, III, 318-22.

During the contest of opinion through which we have passed, the animation of discussion and of exertions has sometimes worn an aspect which might impose on strangers unused to think freely and to speak and to write what they think; but this being now decided by the voice of the nation, announced according to the rules of the constitution, all will, of course, arrange themselves under the will of the law, and unite in common efforts for the common good. All, too, will bear in mind this sacred principle, that though the will of the majority is in all cases to prevail, that will, to be rightful, must be reasonable; that the minority possess their equal rights, which equal laws must protect, and to violate which would be oppression. Let us, then, fellow citizens, unite with one heart and one mind. Let us restore to social intercourse that harmony and affection without which liberty and even life itself are but dreary things. And let us reflect that having banished from our land that religious intolerance under which mankind so long bled and suffered, we have yet gained little if we countenance a political intolerance as despotic, as wicked, and capable of as bitter and bloody persecutions. During the throes and convulsions of the ancient world, during the agonizing spasms of infuriated man, seeking through blood and slaughter his long-lost liberty, it was not wonderful that the agitation of the billows should reach even this distant and peaceful shore; that this should be more felt and feared by some and less by others; that this should divide opinions as to measures of safety. But every difference of opinion is not a difference of principle. We have called by different names brethren of the same principle. We are all republicans— we are all federalists. If there be any among us who would wish to dissolve this Union or to change its republican form, let them stand undisturbed as monuments of the safety with which error of opinion may be tolerated where reason is left free to combat it. I know, indeed, that some honest men fear that a republican government cannot be strong; that this government is not strong enough. But would the honest patriot, in the full tide of successful experiment, abandon a government which has so far kept us free and firm, on the theoretic and visionary fear that this government, the world's best hope, may by possibility want energy to preserve itself? I trust not. I believe this, on the contrary, the strongest government on earth. I believe it is the only one where every man, at the call of the laws, would fly to the standard of the law, and would meet invasions of the public order as his own personal concern. Sometimes it is said that man cannot be trusted with the government of himself. Can he then, be trusted with the government of others? Or have we found angels in the forms of kings to govern him? Let history answer this question.

Let us, then, with courage and confidence pursue our own federal and republican principles, our attachment to our union and representative government. Kindly separated by nature and a wide ocean from the exterminating havoc of one quarter of the globe; too high-minded to endure the degradations of the others; possessing a chosen country, with room enough for our descendants to the hundredth and thousandth generation; entertaining a due sense of our equal right to the use of our own faculties, to the acquisitions of our industry, to honor and confidence from our fellow citizens, resulting not from birth but from our actions and their sense of them; enlightened by a benign religion, professed, indeed, and practiced in various forms, yet all of them including honesty, truth, temperance, gratitude, and the love of man; acknowledging and adoring an over-ruling Providence, which by all its dispensations proves that it delights in the happiness of man here and his greater happiness hereafter; with all these blessings, what more is necessary to make us a happy and prosperous people? Still one thing more, fellow citizens—a wise and frugal government, which shall restrain men from injuring one another, which shall leave them otherwise free to regulate their own pursuits of industry and improvement, and shall not take from the mouth of labor the bread it has earned. This is the sum of good government, and this is necessary to close the circle of our felicities.

About to enter, fellow citizens, on the exercise of duties which comprehend everything dear and valuable to you, it is proper that you should understand what I deem the essential principles of our government, and consequently those which ought to shape its administration. I will compress them within the narrowest compass they will bear, stating the general principle, but not all its limitations. Equal and exact justice to all men, of whatever state or persuasion, religious or political; peace, commerce, and honest friendship, with all nations—entangling alliances with none; the support of the state governments in all their rights, as the most competent administrations for our domestic concerns and the surest bulwarks against anti-republican tendencies; the preservation of the general government in its whole constitutional vigor, as the sheet anchor of our peace at home and safety abroad; a jealous care of the right of election by the people—a mild and safe corrective of abuses which are lopped by the sword of the revolution where peaceable remedies are unprovided; absolute acquiescence in the decisions of the majority—the vital principle of republics, from which there is no appeal but to force, the vital principle and immediate parent of despotism; a well-disciplined militia—our best reliance in peace and for the first moments of war, till regulars may relieve them; the supremacy of the civil over the military authority; economy in the public expense, that labor may be lightly burdened; the honest payment of our debts and sacred preservation of the public faith; encouragement of agriculture, and of commerce as its handmaid; the diffusion of information and the arraignment of all abuses at the bar of public reason; freedom of religion; freedom of the press; freedom of person under the protection of the *habeas corpus;* and trial by juries impartially selected—these principles form the bright constellation which has gone before us, and guided our steps through an age of revolution and reformation. The wisdom of our sages and the blood of our heroes have been devoted to their attainment. They should be the creed of our political faith—the text of civil instruction—the touchstone by which to try the services of those we trust; and should we wander from them in moments of error or alarm, let us hasten to retrace our steps and to regain the road which alone leads to peace, liberty, and safety.

Letter to John Adams, October 28, 1813. *Writings of Jefferson,* XIII, 396-403.

. . . I agree with you that there is a natural aristocracy among men. The grounds of this are virtue and talents. Formerly, bodily powers gave place among the aristoi. But since the invention of gunpowder has armed the weak as well as the strong with missile death, bodily strength, like beauty, good humor, politeness and other accomplishments, has become but an auxiliary ground of distinction. There is also an artificial aristocracy, founded on wealth and birth, without either virtue or talents; for with these it would belong to the first class. The natural aristocracy I consider as the most precious gift of nature, for the instruction, the trusts, and government of society. And indeed, it would have been inconsistent in creation to have formed man for the social state, and not to have provided virtue and wisdom enough to manage the concerns of the society. May we not even say, that that form of government is the best, which provides the most effectually for a pure selection of these natural aristoi into the offices of government? The artificial aristocracy is a mischievous ingredient in government, and provision should be made to prevent its ascendency. On the question, what is the best provision, you and I differ; but we differ as rational friends, using the free exercise of our own reason, and mutually indulging its errors.   You think it best to put the pseudo-aristoi into a separate chamber of legislation, where they may be hindered from doing mischief by their coordinate branches, and where, also, they may be a protection to wealth against the agrarian and plundering enterprises of the majority of the people. I think that to give them power in order to prevent them from doing mischief, is arming them for it, and increasing instead of remedying the evil.   For if the co-ordinate branches can arrest their action, so may they that of the co-ordinates.   Mischief may be done negatively as well as positively.   Of this, a cabal in the Senate of the United States has furnished many proofs.   Nor do I believe them necessary to protect the wealthy; because enough of these will find their way into every branch of the legislation, to protect themselves.   From fifteen to twenty legislatures of our own, in action for thirty years past, have proved that no fears of an equalization of property are to be apprehended from them. I think the best remedy is exactly that provided by all our constitutions, to leave to the citizens the free election and separation of the aristoi from the pseudo-aristoi, of the wheat from the chaff.   In general they will elect the really good and wise.   In some instances, wealth may corrupt, and birth blind them; but not in sufficient degree to endanger the society. . . .

I have thus stated my opinion on a point on which we differ, not with a view to controversy, for we are both too old to change opinions which are the result of a long life of inquiry and reflection; but on the suggestions of a former letter of yours, that we ought not to die before we have explained ourselves to each other.   We acted in perfect harmony, through a long and perilous contest for our liberty and independence. A constitution has been acquired, which, though neither of us thinks perfect, yet both consider as competent to render our fellow citizens the happiest and the securest on whom the sun has ever shone.   If we do not think exactly alike as to its imperfections, it matters little to our country, which, after devoting to it long lives of disinterested labor, we have delivered over to our successors in life, who will be able to take care of it and of themselves.

Letter to Pierre Samuel Du Pont de Nemours, April 24, 1816. *Writings of Jefferson*, XIV, 487-92.

. . . We of the United States, you know, are constitutionally and conscientiously democrats.   We consider society as one of the natural wants with which man has been created; that he has been endowed with faculties and qualities to effect its satisfaction by concurrence of others having the same want; that when, by the exercise of these faculties, he has procured a state of society, it is one of his acquisitions which he has a right to regulate and control, jointly indeed with all those who have concurred in the procurement, whom he cannot exclude from its use or direction more than they him. We think experience has proved it safer, for the mass of individuals composing the society, to reserve to themselves personally the exercise of all rightful powers to which they are competent, and to delegate those to which they are not competent to deputies named, and removable for unfaithful conduct, by themselves immediately. Hence, with us, the people (by which is meant the mass of individuals composing the society) being competent to judge of the facts occurring in ordinary life, they have retained the functions of judges of facts, under the name of jurors; but being unqualified for the management of affairs requiring intelligence above the common level, yet competent judges of human character, they chose, for their management, representatives, some by themselves immediately, others by electors chosen by themselves. Thus our President is chosen by ourselves, directly in *practice*, for we vote for A as elector only on the condition he will vote for B, our representatives by ourselves immediately, our Senate and judges of law through electors chosen by ourselves. And we believe that this proximate choice and power of removal is the best security which experience has sanctioned for ensuring an honest conduct in the functionaries of society. . . .

[We] both consider the people as our children, and love them with parental affection. But you love them as infants whom you are afraid to trust without nurses; and I as adults whom I freely leave to self-government. . . .

But when we come to the moral principles on which the government is to be administered, we come to what is proper for all conditions of society. I meet you there in all the benevolence and rectitude of your native character; and I love myself always most where I concur most with you. Liberty, truth, probity, honor, are declared to be the four cardinal principles of your society. I believe with you that morality, compassion, generosity, are innate elements of the human constitution; that there exists a right independent of force; that a right to property is founded in our natural wants, in the means with which we are endowed to satisfy these wants, and the right to what we acquire by those means without violating the similar rights of other sensible beings; that no one has a right to obstruct another, exercising his faculties innocently for the relief of sensibilities made a part of his nature; that justice is the fundamental law of society; that the majority, oppressing an individual, is guilty of a crime, abuses its strength, and by acting on the law of the strongest, breaks up the foundations of society; that action by the citizens in person, in affairs within their reach and competence, and in all others by representatives, chosen immediately, and removable by themselves, constitutes the essence of a republic; that all governments are more or less republican in proportion as this principle enters more or less into their composition; and that a government by representation is capable of extension over a greater surface of country than one of any other form. These, my friend, are the essentials in which you and I agree; however, in our zeal for their maintenance, we may be perplexed and divaricate, as to the structure of society most likely to secure them.

In the Constitution of Spain, as proposed by the late Cortes, there was a principle entirely new to me, ... that no person, born after [a specified] day, should ever acquire the rights of citizenship until he could read and write. It is impossible sufficiently to estimate the wisdom of this provision. Of all those which have been thought of for securing fidelity in the administration of the government, constant ralliance to the principles of the Constitution, and progressive amendments with the progressive advances of the human mind, or changes in human affairs, it is the most effectual. Enlighten the people generally, and tyranny and oppressions of body and mind will vanish like evil spirits at the dawn of day. Although I do not, with some enthusiasts, believe that the human condition will ever advance to such a state of perfection as that there shall no longer be pain or vice in the world, yet I believe it susceptible of much improvement, and most of all, in matters of government and religion; and that the diffusion of knowledge among the people is to be the instrument by which it is to be effected.

Letter to John Taylor, May 28, 1816. *Writings of Jefferson*, XV, 19-23.

Indeed, it must be acknowledged, that the term *republic* is of very vague application in every language. . . . Were I to assign to this term a precise and definite idea, I would say, purely and simply, it means a government by its citizens in mass, acting directly and personally, according to rules established by the majority; and that every other government is more or less republican, in proportion as it has in its composition more or less of this ingredient of the direct action of the citizens. Such a government is evidently restrained to very narrow limits of space and population. I doubt if it would be practicable beyond the extent of a New England township. . . .

On this view of the import of the term *republic*, instead of saying, as has been said, "that it may mean anything or nothing," we may say with truth and meaning, that governments are more or less republican, as they have more or less of the element of popular election and control in their composition; and believing, as I do, that the mass of the citizens is the safest depository of their own rights and especially, that the evils flowing from the duperies of the people, are less injurious than those from the egoism of their agents, I am a friend to that composition of government which has in it the most of this ingredient. . . .

> Letter to Samuel Kercheval, July 12, 1816. *Writings of Jefferson*, XV, 39-43.

. . . I am not among those who fear the people. They, and not the rich, are our dependence for continued freedom. And to preserve their independence, we must not let our rulers load us with perpetual debt. We must make our election between *economy and liberty*, or *profusion* and *servitude*. If we run into such debts, as that we must be taxed in our meat and in our drink, in our necessaries and our comforts, in our labors and our amusements, for our callings and our creeds, as the people of England are, our people, like them, must come to labor sixteen hours in the twenty-four, give the earnings of fifteen of these to the government for their debts and daily expenses; and the sixteenth being insufficient to afford us bread, we must live, as they do now, on oatmeal and potatoes; have no time to think, no means of calling the mismanagers to account; but be glad to obtain subsistence by hiring ourselves to rivet their chains on the necks of our fellow sufferers. . . .[Private]fortunes are destroyed by public as well as by private extravagance. And this is the tendency of all human governments. A departure from principle in one instance becomes a precedent for a second; that second for a third; and so on, till the bulk of the society is reduced to be mere automatons of misery, to have no sensibilities left but for sinning and suffering. Then begins, indeed, the *bellum omnium in omnia*, which some philosophers observing to be so general in this world, have mistaken it for the natural, instead of the abusive state of man. And the fore horse of this frightful team is public dept. Taxation follows that, and in its train wretchedness and oppression.

Some men look at constitutions with sanctimonious reverence, and deem them like the ark of the covenant, too sacred to be touched. They ascribe to the men of the preceding age a wisdom more than human, and suppose what they did to be beyond amendment. I knew that age well; I belonged to it, and labored with it. It deserved well of its country. It was very like the present, but without the experience of the present; and forty years of experience in government is worth a century of book-reading; and this they would say themselves, were they to rise from the dead. I am certainly not an advocate for frequent and untried changes in laws and constitutions. I think moderate imperfections had better be borne with; because, when once known, we accommodate ourselves to them, and find practical means of correcting their ill effects. But I know also, that laws and institutions must go hand in hand with the progress of the human mind. As that becomes more developed, more enlightened, as new discoveries are made, new truths disclosed, and manners and opinions change with the change of circumstances, institutions must advance also, and keep pace with the times. We might as well require a man to wear still the coat which fitted him when a boy, as civilized society to remain ever under the regimen of their barbarous ancestors. It is this preposterous idea which has lately deluged Europe in blood. Their monarchs, instead of wisely yielding to the gradual change of circumstances, of favoring progressive accommodation to progressive improvement, have clung to old abuses, entrenched themselves behind steady habits, and obliged their subjects to seek through blood and violence rash and ruinous innovations, which, had they been referred to the peaceful deliberations and collected wisdom of the nation, would have been put into acceptable and salutary forms. Let us follow no such examples, nor weakly believe that one generation is not as capable as another of taking care of itself, and of ordering its own affairs. . . . And lastly, let us provide in our [state] Constitution for its revision at stated periods. What these periods should be, nature herself indicates. By the European tables of mortality, of the adults living at any one moment of time, a majority will be dead in about nineteen years. At the end of that period then, a new majority is come into place, or, in other words, a new generation. Each generation is as independent of the one preceding, as that was of all which had gone before. It has then, like them, a right to choose for itself the form of government it believes most promotive of its own happiness; consequently, to accommodate to the circumstances in which it finds itself, that received from its predecessors; and it is for the peace and good of mankind, that a solemn opportunity of doing this every nineteen or twenty years, should be provided by the Constitution; so that it may be handed on, with periodical repairs, from generation to generation, to the end of time, if anything human can so long endure. It is now forty years since the constitution of Virginia was formed. The same tables inform us, that, within that period, two-thirds of the adults then living are now dead. Have then the remaining third, even if they had the wish, the right to hold in obedience to their will, and to laws heretofore made by them, the other two-thirds, who, with themselves, compose the present mass of adults? If they have not, who has? The dead? But the dead have no rights. They are nothing; and nothing cannot own something. Where there is no substance, there can be no accident. This corporeal globe, and everything upon it, belong to its present corporeal inhabitants, during their generation. They alone have a right to direct what is the concern of themselves alone, and to declare the law of that direction; and this declaration can only be made by their majority. That majority, then, has a right to depute representatives to a convention, and to make the Constitution what they think will be the best for themselves.

ALEXANDER HAMILTON

Letter to Gouverneur Morris, May 19, 1777. *Works of Hamilton*, IX, 71-73. Hamilton here offers his views regarding the government of New York.

. . . That instability is inherent in the nature of popular government, I think very disputable; unstable democracy is an epithet frequently in the mouths of politicians; but I believe that from a strict examination of the matter, from the records of history, it will be found that the fluctuations of governments in which the popular principle has borne a considerable sway has proceeded from its being compounded with other principles; and from its being made to operate in an improper channel. Compound governments, though they may be harmonious in the beginning, will introduce different interests; and these interests will clash, throw the state into convulsions, and produce a change or dissolution.

When the deliberative or judicial powers are vested wholly or partly in the collective body of the people, you must expect error, confusion and instability. But a representative democracy, where the right of election is well secured and regulated, and the exercise of the legislative, executive and judiciary authorities is vested in select persons chosen really and not nominally by the people, will in my opinion be most likely to be happy, regular and durable. That complexity of your legislature will occasion delay and dilatoriness is evident and I fear may be attended with a much greater evil; as expedition is not very material in making laws, especially when the government is well digested and matured by time. The evil I mean is, that in time your Senate, from the very name and from the mere circumstances of its being a separate member of the legislature, will be liable to degenerate into a body purely aristocratical.

And I think the danger of an abuse of power from a simple legislature would not be very great in a government where the equality and fulness of popular representation is so wisely provided as in yours. . . .

Speech before the Constitutional Convention in Philadelphia. There is no transcript of the speech. There are, however, several references to it in notes made by participants in the Convention. The summary by Robert Yates, Hamilton's fellow delegate from New York, a foe of the Constitution and of Hamilton, is the first version. Below it is a brief of notes for the speech as it appears in Hamilton's papers. Both are printed in Richard B. Morris, ed., *The Basic Ideas of Alexander Hamilton* (New York, 1957) 126-27.

All communities divide themselves into the few and the many. The first are the rich and well born, the other the mass of the people. The voice of the people has been said to be the voice of God; and, however generally this maxim has been quoted and believed, it is not true to fact. The people are turbulent and changing; they seldom judge or determine right. Give, therefore, to the first class a distinct, permanent share in the government. They will check the unsteadiness of the second, and, as they cannot receive any advantage by a change, they therefore will ever maintain good government. Can a democratic assembly, who annually revolve in the mass of the people, be supposed steadily to pursue the public good? Nothing but a permanent body can check the imprudence of democracy. Their turbulent and uncontrolling disposition requires checks. . . .

Society naturally divides itself into two political divisions—
the very *few* and the *many,* who have distinct interests.

If government in the hands of the *few,* they will tyrannize
over the many.

If [in] the hands of the many, they will tyrannize over the
few.   It ought to be in the hands of both; and they should be
separated.

This separation must be permanent.

Representation alone will not do.

Demagogues will generally prevail.

And if separated, they will need a mutual check.

This check is a monarch.

Speech to the New York Convention held to consider the
Constitution, June 21, 1788. *Works of Hamilton,* II, 19-22.

. . . In my reasonings on the subject of government, I rely
more on the interests and opinions of men, than upon any speculative parchment provisions whatever. I have found that constitutions are more or less excellent, as they are more or less agreeable to the natural operation of things; I am therefore disposed
not to dwell long on curious speculations, or pay much attention
to modes and forms, but to adopt a system whose principles have
been sanctioned by experience, adapt it to the real state of our
country, and depend on probable reasonings for its operation and
result. . . . Sir, the general sense of the people will regulate the
conduct of their representatives. I admit that there are exceptions to this rule. There are certain conjunctures when it may be
necessary and proper to disregard the opinions which the majority
of the people have formed; but, in the general course of things, the
popular views, and even prejudices, will direct the actions of the
rulers.

All governments, even the most despotic, depend, in a great
degree, on opinion. In free republics it is most peculiarly the
case. In these the will of the people makes the essential principle
of the government, and the laws which control the community receive their tone and spirit from the public wishes. It is the
fortunate situation of our country, that the minds of the people
are exceedingly enlightened and refined. Here, then, we may
expect the laws to be proportionately agreeable to the standard
of a perfect policy, and the wisdom of public measures to consist with the most intimate conformity between the views of the
representative and his constituent.

It has been observed that a pure democracy, if it were practicable, would be the most perfect government. Experience has proved, that no position in politics is more false than this. The ancient democracies, in which the people themselves doliberated, never possessed one feature of good government. Their very character was tyranny; their figure deformity. When they assembled, the field of debate presented an ungovernable mob, not only incapable of deliberation, but prepared for every enormity. In these assemblies the enemies of the people brought forward their plans of ambition systematically. They were opposed by their enemies of another party; and it became a matter of contingency, whether the people subjected themselves to be led blindly by one tyrant or by another.

A brief outline for a speech to the New York Convention to consider the Constitution, June, 1788. *Works of Hamilton*, II, 91-3.

A. I. A republic, a word used in various senses.
Has been applied to aristocracies and monarchies.
1. To Rome, under the kings.
2. To Sparta, though a Senate for life.
3. To Carthage, though the same.
4. To United Netherlands, though Stadtholder, hereditary nobles.
5. To Poland, though aristocracy and monarchy.
6. To Great Britain, though monarchy, etc.
II. Again, great confusion about the words democracy, aristocracy, monarchy.
1. a. Democracy defined by some, Rousseau, etc., a government exercised by the collective body of the people.
b. Delegation of their power has been made the criterion of aristocracy.
2. Aristocracy has been used to designate governments.
a. Where an independent few possessed sovereignty.
b. Where the representatives of the people possessed it.
3. Monarchy, where sovereignty in the hands of a single man.
General idea—Independent in his situation; in any other sense would apply to State of New York.
III. Democracy in my sense, where the whole power of the government in the people.

      1. Whether exercised by themselves, or
      2. By their representatives, chosen by them either medi-
      ately or immediately and legally accountable to them.
  IV. Aristocracy, where whole sovereignty is permanently in
      the hands of a few for life or hereditary.
   V. Monarchy, where the whole sovereignty is in the hands of
      one man for life or hereditary.
  VI. Mixed government, where these three principles unite.

B. I. *Consequence*, the proposed government a *representative
    democracy.*
    1. House of Representatives directly chosen by the people
      for two years.
    2. Senate indirectly chosen by them for six years.
    3. President indirectly chosen by them for four years.
Thus legislative and executive representatives of the people.
    4. Judicial power, representatives of the people indirectly
      chosen during good behavior.
    5. All officers indirect choice of the people.
Constitution revocable and alterable by the people.

C. I. This representative democracy as far as is consistent with
    its genius has all the features of good government.
    These features are:
    1. An immediate and operative representation of the people,
      which is found in the House of Representatives.
    2. Stability and wisdom, which is found in the Senate.
    3. A vigorous executive, which is found in the President.
    4. An independent judicial, which is found in the Supreme
      Court, etc.
A separation of the essential powers of government. Ascer-
tain the sense of the maxim:
One department must not wholly possess the powers of another.
    = Montesquieu.
    = British Government. . . .

Letter to Edward Carrington, May 26, 1792. *Works of Hamilton*, IX, 532-35. Carrington was a Virginian friendly with
Jeffersonians and Hamiltonians alike, and Hamilton may have
wished this communication to reach his critics.

    . . . I am told that serious apprehensions are disseminated
in your State as to the existence of a monarchical party medi-
tating the destruction of State and republican government. If it

is possible that so absurd an idea can gain ground, it is necessary that it should be combated. I assure you, on my private faith and honor as a man, that there is not, in my judgment, a shadow of foundation for it. A very small number of men indeed may entertain theories less republican than Mr. Jefferson and Mr. Madison, but I am persuaded there is not a man among them who would not regard as both criminal and visionary any attempt to subvert the republican system of the country. Most of these men rather fear that it may not justify itself by its fruits, than feel a predilection for a different form; and their fears are not diminished by the factious and fanatical politics which they find prevailing among a certain set of gentlemen and threatening to disturb the tranquillity and order of the government.

As to the destruction of State governments, the great and real anxiety is to be able to preserve the national from the too potent and counteracting influence of those governments. As to my own political creed, I give it to you with the utmost sincerity. I am affectionately attached to the republican theory. I desire above all things to see the equality of political rights, exclusive of all hereditary distinction, firmly established by a practical demonstration of its being consistent with the order and happiness of society. As to State governments, the prevailing bias of my judgment is that if they can be circumscribed within bounds, consistent with the preservation of the national government, they will prove useful and salutary. If the States were all of the size of Connecticut, Maryland, or New Jersey, I should decidedly regard the local governments as both safe and useful. As the thing now is, however, I acknowledge the most serious apprehensions, that the government of the United States will not be able to maintain itself against their influence. I see that influence already penetrating into the national councils and preventing their direction. Hence, a disposition on my part towards a liberal construction of the powers of the national government, and to erect every fence, to guard it from depredations which is, in my opinion, consistent with constitutional propriety. As to any combination to prostrate the State governments, I disavow and deny it. From an apprehension lest the judiciary should not work efficiently or harmoniously, I have been desirous of seeing some national scheme of connection adopted as an amendment to the Constitution, otherwise I am for maintaining things as they are; though I doubt much the possibility of it, from a tendency in the nature of things towards the preponderancy of the State governments.

I said that I was affectionately attached to the republican theory. This is the real language of my heart, which I open to you in the sincerity of friendship; and I add that I have strong hopes of the success of that theory; but, in candor, I ought also to add that I am far from being without doubts. I consider its success as yet a problem. It is yet to be determined by experience whether it be consistent with that stability and order in government which are essential to public strength and private security and happiness.

On the whole, the only enemy which Republicanism has to fear in this country is in the spirit of faction and anarchy. If this will not permit the ends of government to be attained under it, if it engenders disorders in the community, all regular and orderly minds will wish for a change, and the demagogues who have produced the disorder will make it for their own aggrandizement. This is the old story. If I were disposed to promote monarchy and overthrow State governments, I would mount the hobby-horse of popularity; I would cry out "usurpation," "danger to liberty," etc., etc.; I would endeavor to prostrate the national government, raise a ferment, and then "ride in the whirlwind, and direct the storm." That there are men acting with Jefferson and Madison who have this in view, I verily believe; I could lay my finger on some of them. That Madison does not mean it, I also verily believe; and I rather believe the same of Jefferson, but I read him upon the whole thus: "A man of profound ambition and violent passions."

"Tully Papers," August 23—September 2, 1794. These papers were written for publication by Hamilton to obtain popular support for his policy of forceful suppression of the Whiskey Rebellion, if its leaders did not retreat from their opposition to the excise tax. *Works of Hamilton,* VI, 414-20.

Let us see then what is this question. It is plainly this—Shall the majority govern or be governed? shall the nation rule or be ruled? shall the general will prevail, or the will of a faction? shall there be government or no government? It is impossible to deny that this is the true and the whole question. No art, no sophistry can involve it in the least obscurity.

The Constitution *you* have ordained for yourselves and your posterity contains this express clause: "The Congress *shall have power* to lay and collect taxes, duties, imposts, and *excises,* to pay the debts, and provide for the common defence and general welfare of the United States."

. . . You have said, "The Congress *shall have power* to lay *excises*." They say, "The Congress *shall not have* this power." Or, what is equivalent—they shall not exercise it: for a *power* that may not be exercised is a nullity. Your representatives have said, and four times repeated it, "An excise on distilled spirits *shall* be collected." They say it *shall not* be collected. We will punish, expel, and banish the officers who shall attempt the collection. We will do the same by every other person who shall dare to comply with your decree expressed in the constitutional charter; and with that of your representatives expressed in the laws. The sovereignty shall not reside with you, but with us. . . .

If there is a man among us who shall affirm that the question is not what it has been stated to be, who shall endeavor to perplex it by ill-timed declamations against excise laws, who shall strive to paralyze the efforts of the community by invectives or insinuations against the government, who shall inculcate, directly or indirectly, that force ought not to be employed to compel the insurgents to a submission to the laws, if the pending experiment to bring them to reason (an experiment which will immortalize the moderation of the government) shall fail,—such a man is not a good citizen; such a man, however he may prate and babble republicanism, is not a republican; he attempts to set up the *will* of a part against the *will* of the whole, the *will* of a *faction* against the *will* of the *nation,* the pleasure of a *few* against *your* pleasure, the violence of a lawless combination against the sacred authority of laws pronounced under *your* indisputable commission. . . .

Government is frequently and aptly classed under two descriptions—a government of *force,* and a government of *laws;* the first is the definition of despotism—the last, of liberty. But how can a government of laws exist when the laws are disrespected and disobeyed? Government supposes control. It is that *power* by which individuals in society are kept from doing injury to each other, and are brought to co-operate to a common end. The instruments by which it must act are either the *authority* of the laws or *force.* If the first be destroyed, the last must be substituted; and where this becomes the ordinary instrument of government, there is an end to liberty!

Those, therefore, who preach doctrines, or set examples which undermine or subvert the authority of the laws, lead us from freedom to slavery; they incapacitate us for a *government of laws,* and consequently prepare the way for one of *force,* for mankind must have *government of one sort or another.* There are, indeed, great and urgent cases where the bounds of the Constitution are manifestly transgressed, or its constitutional authorities so exercised as to produce unequivocal oppression on the community, and to render resistance justifiable. But such cases can give no color to the resistance by a comparatively inconsiderable part of a community, of constitutional laws distinguished by no extraordinary features of rigor or oppression, and acquiesced in by the body of the community.

Such a resistance is treason against society, against liberty, against every thing that ought to be dear to a free, enlightened, and prudent people. To tolerate it, were to abandon your most precious interests. Not to subdue it, were to tolerate it. Those who openly or covertly dissuade you from exertions adequate to the occasion, are your worst enemies. They treat you either as fools or cowards, too weak to perceive your interest or your duty, or too dastardly to pursue them. They therefore merit and will, no doubt, meet your contempt. To the plausible but hollow harangue of such conspirators you cannot fail to reply, How long, ye Catilines, will ye abuse our patience?

Opinions on the United States Constitution

ALEXANDER HAMILTON

Letter to James Duane, September 3, 1780. *Works of Hamilton*, I, 213-39.

DEAR SIR:

Agreeably to your request, and my promise, I sit down to give you my ideas of the defects of our present system, and the changes necessary to save us from ruin. They may, perhaps, be the reveries of a projector, rather than the sober views of a politician. You will judge of them, and make what use you please of them.

The fundamental defect is a want of power in Congress. It is hardly worthwhile to show in what this consists, as it seems to be universally acknowledged; or to point out how it has happened, as the only question is how to remedy it. It may, however, be said, that it has originated from three causes: an excess of the spirit of liberty, which has made the particular States show a jealousy of all power not in their own hands,—and this jealousy has led them to exercise a right of judging in the last resort of the measures recommended by Congress, and of acting according to their own opinions of their propriety, or necessity; a diffidence, in Congress, of their own powers, by which they have been timid and indecisive in their resolutions, constantly making concessions to the States, till they have scarcely left themselves the shadow of power; a want of sufficient means at their disposal to answer the public exigencies, and of vigor to draw forth these means, which have occasioned them to depend on the States individually to fulfil their engagements with the army, the consequence of which has been to ruin their influence and credit with the army, to establish its dependence on each State separately, rather than on *them*, that is, on the whole collectively.

It may be pleaded that Congress had never any definite powers granted them, and of course could exercise none, could do nothing more than recommend. The manner in which Congress was appointed would warrant, and the public good required that they should have considered themselves as vested with full power *to preserve the republic from harm*. They have done many of the highest acts of sovereignty, which were always cheerfully

43

submitted to: The declaration of independence, the declaration of war, the levying of an army, creating a navy, emitting money, making alliances with foreign powers; appointing a dictator, etc. All these implications of a complete sovereignty were never disputed, and ought to have been a standard for the whole conduct of administration. Undefined powers are discretionary powers, limited only by the object for which they were given; in the present case the independence and freedom of America. The Confederation made no difference, for as it has not been generally adopted it had no operation. But from what I recollect of it, Congress have even descended from the authority which the spirit of that act gives them, while the particular States have no further attended to it than as it suited their pretensions and convenience. It would take too much time to enter into particular instances, each of which separately might appear inconsiderable, but united are of serious import. I only mean to remark, not to censure.

But the Confederation itself is defective, and requires to be altered. It is neither fit for war nor peace. The idea of an uncontrollable sovereignty, in each State over its internal police will defeat the other powers given to Congress, and make our union feeble and precarious. There are instances without number where acts, necessary for the general good, and which rise out of the powers given to Congress, must interfere with the internal police of the States; and there are many instances in which the particular States, by arrangements of internal police, can effectually, though indirectly, counteract the arrangements of Congress. You have already had examples of this, for which I refer to your own memory.

The Confederation gives the States, individually, too much influence in the affairs of the army. They should have nothing to do with it.   The entire formation and disposal of our military forces ought to belong to Congress. It is an essential cement of the union; and it ought to be the policy of Congress to destroy all ideas of State attachments in the army, and make it look up wholly to them.   For this purpose, all appointments, promotions, and provisions, whatsoever, ought to be made by them. It may be apprehended that this may be dangerous to liberty. But nothing appears more evident to me than that we run much greater risk of having a weak and disunited federal government, than one which will be able to usurp upon the rights of the people.

Already some of the lines of the army would obey their States in opposition to Congress, notwithstanding the pains we have taken to preserve the unity of the army. If any thing would hinder this it would be the personal influence of the General—a melancholy and mortifying consideration.

The forms of our State constitutions must always give them great weight in our affairs, and will make it too difficult to bend them to the pursuit of a common interest, too easy to oppose whatever they do not like, and to form partial combinations subversive of the general one. There is a wide difference between our situation and that of an empire under one simple form of government, distributed into counties, provinces or districts, which have no Legislatures, but merely magistratical bodies to execute the laws of a common sovereign. Here the danger is that the sovereign will have too much power, and oppress the parts of which it is composed. In our case, that of an empire composed of confederated States, each with a government completely organized within itself, having all the means to draw its subjects to a close dependence on itself, the danger is directly the reverse. It is that the common sovereign will not have power sufficient to unite the different members together, and direct the common forces to the interest and happiness of the whole. . . .

The Confederation, too, gives the power of the purse too entirely to the State Legislatures. It should provide perpetual funds, in the disposal of Congress, by a land tax, poll tax, or the like. All imposts upon commerce ought to be laid by Congress, and appropriated to their use. For, without certain revenues, a Government can have no power. That power which holds the pursestrings absolutely, must rule. This seems to be a medium which, without making Congress altogether independent, will tend to give reality to its authority.

Another defect in our system is want of method and energy in the administration. This has partly resulted from the other defect; but in a great degree from prejudice, and the want of a proper executive. Congress have kept the power too much in their own hands, and have meddled too much with the details of every sort. Congress is, properly, a deliberative corps, and it forgets itself when it attempts to play the executive. It is impossible such a body, numerous as it is, and constantly fluctuating, can ever act with sufficient decision or with system. Two thirds of the members, one half the time, cannot know what has gone before them, or what connection the subject in hand has to what has been transacted on former occasions. The members who have been more permanent, will only give information that promotes the side they espouse in the present case, and will as often mislead as enlighten. The variety of business must distract; and the proneness of every assembly to debate must at all times delay. . . .

I shall now propose the remedies which appear to me applicable to our circumstances, and necessary to extricate our affairs from their present deplorable situation. . . .

The first step must be to give Congress powers competent to the public exigencies. This may happen in two ways: one by resuming and exercising the discretionary powers I suppose to have been originally vested in them for the safety of the States, and resting their conduct on the candor of their countrymen and the necessity of the conjuncture; the other, by calling immediately a Convention of all the States, with full authority to conclude finally upon a General Confederation, stating to them beforehand, explicitly, the evils arising from a want of power in Congress, and the impossibility of supporting the contest as well on its present footing, that the delegates may come possessed of proper sentiments as well as proper authority to give efficacy to the meeting. Their commission should include a right of vesting Congress with the whole, or a portion, of the unoccupied lands, to be employed for the purpose of raising a revenue; reserving the jurisdiction to the States by whom they are granted.

The first plan, I expect, will be thought too bold an expedient by the generality of Congress; and, indeed, their practice hitherto has so riveted the opinion of their want of power, that the success of this experiment may very well be doubted.

I see no objection to the other mode that has any weight, in competition with the reasons for it. . . .

The Confederation, in my opinion, should give Congress complete sovereignty, except as to that part of internal police which relates to the rights of property and life among individuals, and to raising money by internal taxes. . . .

Paper credit never was long supported in any country, on a national scale, where it was not founded on a joint basis of public and private credit. . . .

We have seen the effects of it in America, and every successive experiment, proves the futility of the attempt. Our new money is depreciating almost as fast as the old though it has, in some States, as real funds as paper money ever had. The reason is that the moneyed men have not an immediate interest to uphold its credit. They may even, in many ways, find it their interest to undermine it. The only certain manner to obtain a permanent paper credit is to engage the moneyed interest immediately in it, by making them contribute the whole or part of the stock, and giving them the whole or part of the profits. . . .

And why can we not have an American Bank? Are our money men less enlightened to their own interest, or less enterprising in the pursuit? I believe the fault is in government, which does not exert itself to engage them in such a scheme. It is true the individuals in America are not very rich, but this would not prevent their instituting a bank; it would only prevent its being done with such ample funds as in other countries. Have they not sufficient confidence in the Government, and in the issue of the cause? Let the Government endeavor to inspire that confidence, by adopting the measures I have recommended, or others equivalent to them. Let it exert itself to procure a solid Confederation; to establish a good plan of executive administration; to form a permanent military force; to obtain, at all events, a foreign loan. If these things were in a train of vigorous execution, it would give a new spring to our affairs; government would recover its respectability, and individuals would renounce their diffidence. . . .

And, in future, my dear sir, two things let me recommend as fundamental rules for the conduct of Congress; to attach the army to them by every motive; to maintain an air of authority (not domineering) in all their measures with the States. The manner in which a thing is done has more influence than is commonly imagined. Men are governed by opinion: this opinion is as much influenced by appearances as by realities. If a Government appears to be confident of its own powers, it is the surest way to inspire the same confidence in others. If it is diffident, it may be certain there will be a still greater diffidence in others; and that its authority will not only be distrusted, controverted, but contemned.

Speech of June 18, 1787, in the Constitutional Convention, recorded by James Madison. Gaillard Hunt, ed., *The Writings of James Madison* (New York, 1900-10, III, 182-83.

Mr. Paterson's plan provides no remedy. If the powers proposed were adequate, the organization of Congress is such that they could never be properly and effectually exercised. The members of Congress being chosen by the states and subject to recall, represent all the local prejudices. Should the powers be found effectual, they will from time to time be heaped on them, till a tyrannic sway shall be established. The general power, whatever be its form, if it preserves itself, must swallow up the state powers. Otherwise, it will be swallowed up by them. It is against all the principles of good government to vest the requisite powers in such a body as Congress. Two sovereignties cannot co-exist within the same limits. Giving powers to Congress must eventuate in a bad government or in no government. The plan of

New Jersey, therefore, will not do. What, then, is to be done? Here he was embarrassed. The extent of the country to be governed discouraged him. The expense of a General Government was also formidable; unless there was such a diminution of expense on the side of the state governments as the case would admit. If they were extinguished, he was persuaded that great economy might be obtained by substituting a General Government. . . .

This view of the subject almost led him to despair that a republican government could be established over so great an extent. He was sensible, at the same time, that it would be unwise to propose one of any other form. In his private opinion, he had no scruple in declaring, supported as he was by the opinion of so many of the wise and good, that the British government was the best in the world; and that he doubted much whether anything short of it would do in America. He hoped gentlemen of different opinions would bear with him in this, and begged them to recollect the change of opinion on this subject which had taken place, and was still going on. It was once thought that the power of Congress was amply sufficient to secure the end of their institution. The error was now seen by every one. The members most tenacious of republicanism were as loud as any in declaiming against the vices of democracy. This progress of the public mind led him to anticipate the time when others as well as himself would join in the praise bestowed by Mr. Neckar on the British constitution, namely, that it is the only government in the world "which unites public strength with individual security. . . ."

Gentlemen differ in their opinions concerning the necessary checks, from the different estimates they form of the human passions. They suppose seven years a sufficient period to give the Senate an adequate firmness, from not duly considering the amazing violence and turbulence of the democratic spirit. When a great object of government is pursued which seizes the popular passions, they spread like wildfire and become irresistible. He appealed to the gentlemen from the New England states whether experience had not there verified the remark. As to the Executive, it seemed to be admitted that no good one could be established on republican principles. Was not this giving up the merits of the question; for can there be a good government without a good Executive? The English model was the only good one on this subject. The hereditary interest of the king was so interwoven with that of the nation, and his personal emolument so great, that he was placed above the danger of being corrupted from abroad, and, at the same time, was both sufficiently independent and sufficiently controlled to answer the purpose of the institution at home. One of the weak sides of republics was their being liable to foreign influence and corruption. Men of little character, acquiring great power, became easily the tools of intermeddling neighbors. . . .

What is the inference from all these observations? That we ought to go as far, in order to attain stability and permanency, as republican principles will admit. Let one branch of Legislature hold their places for life, or, at least, during good behavior. Let the Executive, also, be for life. He appealed to the feelings of the members present whether a term of seven years would induce the sacrifice of private affairs, which an acceptance of public trust would require, so as to ensure the services of the best citizens. On this plan we should have in the Senate a permanent will, a weighty interest, which would answer essential purposes. But is this a republican government? it will be asked. Yes, if all the magistrates are appointed and vacancies are filled by the people, or a process of election originating with the people. He was sensible that an Executive, constituted as he proposed, would have, in fact, but little of the power and independence that might be necessary. On the other plan of appointing him for seven years, he thought the Executive ought to have but little power. He would be ambitious, with the means of making creatures; and as the object of his ambition would be to *prolong* his power, it is probable that in case of a war he would avail himself of the emergency to evade or refuse a degradation from his place. An Executive for life has not this motive for forgetting his fidelity, and will therefore be a safer depository of power.

Speech of September 6, 1787, in the Constitutional Convention, recorded by James Madison. *Writings of Madison,* IV, 383.

Mr. Hamilton said that he had been restrained from entering into the discussions by his dislike of the Scheme of Govt. in General; but as he meant to support the plan to be recommended as better than nothing, he wished in this place to offer a few remarks. . . .

Speech of September 17, 1787, in the Constitutional Convention, recorded by James Madison. *Writings of Madison,* IV, 478.

Mr. Hamilton expressed his anxiety that every member should sign. A few characters of consequence, by opposing or even refusing to sign the Constitution, might do infinite mischief by kindling the latent sparks which lurk under an enthusiasm in favor of the Convention which may soon subside. No man's ideas were more remote from the plan than his were known to be; but is it possible to deliberate between anarchy and convulsion on one side, and the chance of good to be expected from the plan on the other.

The Federalist, No. 1, October 27, 1787.

To the People of the State of New York:
After an unequivocal experience of the inefficiency of the subsisting federal government, you are called upon to deliberate on a new Constitution for the United States of America. The subject speaks its own importance; comprehending in its consequences nothing less than the existence of the UNION, the safety and welfare of the parts of which it is composed, the fate of an empire in many respects the most interesting in the world. It has been frequently remarked that it seems to have been reserved to the people of this country, by their conduct and example, to decide the important question, whether societies of men are really capable or not of establishing good government from reflection and choice, or whether they are forever destined to depend for their political constitutions on accident and force. If there be any truth in the remark, the crisis at which we are arrived may with propriety be regarded as the era in which that decision is to be made; and a wrong election of the part we shall act may, in this view, deserve to be considered as the general misfortune of mankind. . . .

The Federalist, No. 84, May 28, 1788.

It has been several times truly remarked, that bills of rights are in their origin, stipulations between kings and their subjects, abridgments of prerogative in favor of privilege, reservations of rights not surrendered to the prince. Such was the MAGNA CHARTA, obtained by the Barons, sword in hand, from king John. . . . It is evident, therefore, that according to their primitive signification, they have no application to constitutions professedly founded upon the power of the people, and executed by their immediate representatives and servants. Here, in strictness, the people surrender nothing, and as they retain every thing, they have no need of particular reservations. "WE THE PEOPLE of the United States, to secure the blessings of liberty to ourselves and our posterity, do *ordain* and *establish* this constitution for the United States of America." Here is a better recognition of popular rights than volumes of those aphorisms which make the principal figure in several of our state bills of rights, and which would sound much better in a treatise of ethics than in a constitution of government.

But a minute detail of particular rights is certainly far less applicable to a constitution like that under consideration, which is merely intended to regulate the general political interests of the nation, than to a constitution which has the regulation of every species of personal and private concerns. If therefore the loud clamours against the plan of the convention on this score, are well founded, no epithets of reprobation will be too strong for the constitution of this state. But the truth is, that both of them contain all, which in relation to their objects, is reasonably to be desired.

I go further, and affirm that bills of rights, in the sense and in the extent in which they are contended for, are not only unnecessary in the proposed constitution, but would even be dangerous. They would contain various exceptions to powers which are not granted; and on this very account, would afford a colourable pretext to claim more than were granted. For why declare that things shall not be done which there is no power to do? Why for instance, should it be said, that the liberty of the press shall not be restrained, when no power is given by which restrictions may be imposed? I will not contend that such a provision would confer a regulating power; but it is evident that it would furnish, to men disposed to usurp, a plausible pretence for claiming that power. They might urge with a semblance of reason, that the constitution ought not to be charged with the absurdity of providing against the abuse of an authority, which was not given, and that the provision against restraining the liberty of the press afforded a clear implication, that a power to prescribe proper regulations concerning it, was intended to be vested in the national government. This may serve as a specimen of the numerous handles which would be given to the doctrine of constructive powers, by the vested indulgence of an injudicious zeal for bills of rights.

On the subject of the liberty of the press, as much has been said, I cannot forbear adding a remark or two: In the first place, I observe that there is not a syllable concerning it in the constitution of this state, and in the next, I contend that whatever has been said about it in that of any other state, amounts to nothing.

What signifies a declaration that "the liberty of the press shall
be inviolably preserved?" What is the liberty of the press? Who
can give it any definition which would not leave the utmost latitude
for evasion? I hold it to be impracticable; and from this, I infer,
that its security, whatever fine declarations may be inserted in
any constitution respecting it, must altogether depend on public
opinion, and on the general spirit of the people and of the government. And here, after all, as intimated upon another occasion,
must we seek for the only solid basis of all our rights.

There remains but one other view of this matter to conclude
the point. The truth is, after all the declamation we have heard,
that the constitution is itself in every rational sense, and to every
useful purpose, A BILL OF RIGHTS. The several bills of rights,
in Great-Britain, form its constitution, and conversely the con-
sitution of each state is its bill of rights. And the proposed constitution, if adopted, will be the bill of rights of the union. Is it one
object of a bill of rights to declare and specify the political privileges of the citizens in the structure and administration of the
government? This is done in the most ample and precise manner
in the plan of the convention, comprehending various precautions
for the public security, which are not to be found in any of the state
constitutions. Is another object of a bill of rights to define certain
immunities and modes of proceeding, which are relative to personal
and private concerns? This we have seen has also been attended
to, in a variety of cases, in the same plan. Adverting therefore to
the substantial meaning of a bill of rights, it is absurd to allege
that it is not to be found in the work of the convention. It may be
said that it does not go far enough, though it will not be easy to
make this appear; but it can with no propriety be contended that
there is no such thing. It certainly must be immaterial what mode
is observed as to the order of declaring the rights of the citizens,
if they are to be found in any part of the instrument which estab-
lishes the government. And hence it must be apparent that much
of what has been said on this subject rests merely on verbal and
nominal distinctions, which are entirely foreign from the substance
of the thing.

The Federalist, No. 85, May 28, 1788. This was the last
of Publius' essays.

I shall not dissemble that I feel an entire confidence in the
arguments which recommend the proposed system to your adoption,
and that I am unable to discern any real force in those by which

it has been opposed. I am persuaded that it is the best which our political situation, habits, and opinions will admit, and superior to any the revolution has produced.

. . . No advocate of the measure can be found, who will not declare as his sentiment, that the system, though it may not be perfect in every part, is, upon the whole, a good one; is the best that the present views and circumstances of the country will permit; and is such an one as promises every species of security which a reasonable people can desire.

I answer in the next place, that I should esteem it the extreme of imprudence to prolong the precarious state of our national affairs, and to expose the Union to the jeopardy of successive experiments, in the chimerical pursuit of a perfect plan. I never expect to see a perfect work from imperfect man. The result of the deliberation of all collective bodies must necessarily be a compound, as well of the errors and prejudices, as of the good sense and wisdom, of the individuals of whom they are composed. . . .

. . . It may be in me a defect of political fortitude, but I acknowledge that I cannot entertain an equal tranquility with those who affect to treat the dangers of a longer continuance in our present situation as imaginary. A nation without a national government is, in my view, an awful spectacle. The establishment of a Constitution, in time of profound peace, by the voluntary consent of a whole people, is a prodigy, to the completion of which I look forward with trembling anxiety.

Letter to Timothy Pickering, September 15, 1803. *Basic Ideas of Hamilton*, 131-32.

The highest-toned propositions which I made in the convention were for a President, Senate, and Judges during good behavior—a House of Representatives for three years. Though I would have enlarged the legislative power of the general government, yet I never contemplated the abolition of the State governments, but on the contrary, they were, in some particulars, constituent parts of my plan. This plan was, in my conception, conformable with the strict theory of a government purely republican, the essential criteria of which are that the principal organs of the executive and legislative departments be elected by the people, and hold their offices by a *responsible* and temporary or *defeasible* tenure. A vote was taken on the proposition respecting the executive. Five States were in favor of it, among these Virginia, and though, from the manner of voting—by delegations,—individuals were not distinguished, it was morally certain, from the known situation of the Virginia members (six in number, two of them, *Mason* and *Randolph,* professing popular doctrines), that *Madison* must have concurred in the vote of Virginia; thus, if I sinned against *republicanism,* Mr. Madison was not less guilty. I may truly then say that I never proposed either a President or Senate for life, and that I neither recommended nor meditated the annihilation of the State governments. And I may add that, in the course of the discussions in the convention, neither the propositions thrown out for debate, nor even those voted in the earlier stages of the deliberation, were considered as evidences of a definitive opinion in the proposer or voter. It appeared to me to be in some sort understood that, with a view to free investigation, experimental propositions might be made, which were to be received merely as suggestions for consideration. Accordingly, it is a fact that my final opinion was against an Executive during good behavior, on account of the increased danger to the public tranquillity incident to the election of a magistrate of this degree of permanency. In the plan of a constitution which I drew up while the convention was sitting, and which I communicated to Mr. Madison about the close of it, perhaps a day or two after, the office of President has no greater duration than for three years. This plan was predicated upon these bases: 1. That the political principles of the people of this country would endure nothing but republican government. 2. That in the actual situation of the country, it was in itself right and proper that the republican theory should have a fair and full trial. 3. That to such a trial it was essential that the government should be so constructed as to give all the energy and stability reconcilable with the principles of that theory.

These were the genuine sentiments of my heart, and upon them I acted. I sincerely hope that it may not hereafter be discovered that, through want of sufficient attention to the last idea, the experiment of republican government, even in this country, has not been as complete, as satisfactory, and as decisive as could be wished.

THOMAS JEFFERSON

Jefferson expressed his opinion of the Constitution in several letters to his friends in America while he was the American minister in Paris. The following are representative selections from these letters.

Letter to Edward Carrington, August 4, 1787. *Papers of Jefferson,* XI, 678-79.

. . . I am happy to find that the states have come so generally into the scheme of the Federal Convention, from which I am sure we shall see wise propositions. I confess I do not go as far in the reforms thought necessary as some of my correspondents in America; but if the Convention should adopt such propositions I shall suppose them necessary. My general plan would be to make the states one as to every thing connected with foreign nations, and several as to every thing purely domestic. But with all the imperfections of our present government, it is without comparison the best existing or that ever did exist. It's greatest defect is the imperfect manner in which matters of commerce have been provided for. It has been so often said, as to be generally believed, that Congress have no power by the confederation to enforce any thing, e.g. contributions of money. It was not necessary to give them that power expressly; they have it by the law of nature. . . .

I think it very material to separate in the hands of Congress the Executive and Legislative powers, as the Judiciary already are in some degree. This I hope will be done. The want of it has been the source of more evil than we have ever experienced from any other cause. Nothing is so embarrassing nor so mischievous in a great assembly as the details of execution. The smallest trifle of that kind occupies as long as the most important act of legislation, and takes place of every thing else. Let any man recollect, or look over the files of Congress, he will observe the most important propositions hanging over from week to week and month to month, till the occasions have past them, and the thing never done. I have ever viewed the executive details as the greatest cause of evil to us, because they in fact place us as if we had no federal head, by diverting the attention of that head from great to small objects; and should this division of power not be recommended by the Convention, it is my opinion Congress should make it itself by establishing an Executive committee.

Letter to James Madison, December 20, 1787. *Papers of Jefferson,* XII, 439-42.

I like much the general idea of framing a government which should go on of itself peaceably, without needing continual recurrence to the state legislatures. I like the organization of the government into Legislative, Judiciary and Executive. I like the power given the Legislature to levy taxes; and for that reason solely approve of the greater house being chosen by the people directly. For tho' I think a house chosen by them will be very illy qualified to legislate for the Union, for foreign nations &c. yet this evil does not weigh against the good of preserving inviolate the fundamental principle that the people are not to be taxed but by representatives chosen immediately by themselves. I am captivated by the compromise of the opposite claims of the great and little states, of the latter to equal, and the former to proportional influence. I am much pleased too with the substitution of the method of voting by persons, instead of that of voting by states; and I like the negative given to the Executive with a third of either house, though I should have liked it better had the Judiciary been associated for that purpose, or invested with a similar and separate power. There are other good things of less moment. I will now add what I do not like. First the omission of a bill of rights providing clearly and without the aid of sophisms for freedom of religion, freedom of the press, protection against standing armies, restriction against monopolies, the eternal and unremitting force of the habeas corpus laws, and trials by jury in all matters of fact triable by the laws of the land and not by the law of Nations. To say, as Mr. Wilson does that a bill of rights was not necessary because all is reserved in the case of the general government which is not given, while in the particular ones all is given which is not reserved might do for the Audience to whom it was addressed, but is surely gratis dictum, opposed by strong inferences from the body of the instrument, as well as from the omission of the clause of our present confederation which had declared that in express terms. It was a hard conclusion to say because there has been no conformity among the states as to the cases triable by jury, because some have been so incautious as to abandon this mode of trial, therefore the more prudent states shall be reduced to the same level of calamity. It would have been much more just and wise to have concluded the other way that as most of the states had judiciously preserved this palladium, those who had wandered should be brought back to it, and to have established general right instead of general wrong. Let me add that a bill of rights is what the people are entitled to against every government on earth, general or particular, and what no just government should refuse, or rest on inference. The second feature I dislike, and greatly dislike, is the abandonment in every instance of the necessity of rotation in office, and most particularly in the case of the President. Experience concurs with reason in concluding that the first magistrate will always be re-elected if the constitution permits it. He is then an officer for life. This once observed it becomes of so much consequence to certain nations to have a friend or a foe at the head of our affairs that they will interfere with money and with arms. A Galloman or an Angloman will be supported by the nation he befriends. If once elected, and at a second or third election outvoted by one or two votes, he will pretend false votes, foul play, hold possession of the reins of government, be supported by the states voting for him, especially if they are the central ones lying in a compact body themselves and separating their opponents: and they will be aided by one nation of Europe, while the majority are aided by another. . . .

. . . Smaller objections are the Appeal in fact as well as law, and the binding all persons Legislative, Executive and Judiciary by oath to maintain that constitution. I do not pretend to decide what would be the best method of procuring the establishment of the manifold good things in this constitution, and of getting rid of the bad. Whether by adopting it in hopes of future amendment, or, after it has been duly weighed and canvassed by the people, after seeing the parts they generally dislike, and those they generally approve, to say to them 'We see now what you wish. Send together your deputies again, let them frame a constitution for you omitting what you have condemned, and establishing the powers you approve. Even these will be a great addition to the energy of your government.'—At all events I hope you will not be discouraged from other trials, if the present one should fail of it's full effect.— I have thus told you freely what I like and dislike: merely as a matter of curiosity for I know your own judgment has been formed on all these points after having heard every thing which could be urged on them. I own I am not a friend to a very energetic government. It is always oppressive. The late rebellion in Massachusets has given more alarm than I think it should have done. Calculate that one rebellion in 13 states in the course of 11 years, is but one for each state in a century and a half. No country should be so long without one. Nor will any degree of power in the hands of government prevent insurrections. France with all it's despotism, and two or three hundred thousand men always in arms has had three insurrections in the three years I have been here in every one of which greater numbers were engaged than in Massachusets and a great deal more blood was spilt. . . .—After all, it is my principle that the will of the Majority should always prevail. If they approve the proposed Convention in all it's parts, I shall concur in it chearfully, in hopes that they will amend it whenever they shall find it work wrong. I think our governments will remain virtuous for many centuries; as long as they are chiefly agricultural; and this will be as long as there shall be vacant lands in any part of America. When they get piled upon one another in large cities, as in Europe, they will become corrupt as in Europe. Above all things I hope the education of the common people will be attended to; convinced that on their good sense we may rely with the most security for the preservation of a due degree of liberty.

Letter to Francis Hopkinson, March 13, 1789. *Papers of Jefferson*, XIV, 650.

. . . You say that I have been dished up to you as an anti-federalist, and ask me if it be just. My opinion was never worthy enough of notice to merit citing: but since you ask it I will tell it you. I am not a Federalist, because I never submitted the whole system of my opinions to the creed of any party of men whatever in religion, in philosophy, in politics, or in any thing else where I was capable of thinking for myself. Such an addiction is the last degradation of a free and moral agent. If I could not go to heaven but with a party, I would not go there at all. Therefore I protest to you I am not of the party of federalists. But I am much farther from that of the Antifederalists. I approved from the first moment, of the great mass of what is in the new constitution. . . .

Constitutional Crisis: The Bank Issue

THOMAS JEFFERSON

Cabinet opinion on the constitutionality of the Bank of the United States, February 15, 1791. *Writings of Jefferson*, III, 146-53.

I consider the foundation of the Constitution as laid on this ground: That "all powers not delegated to the United States, by the Constitution, nor prohibited by it to the States, are reserved to the States or to the people."... To take a single step beyond the boundaries thus specially drawn around the powers of Congress, is to take possession of a boundless field of power, no longer susceptible of any definition.

The incorporation of a bank, and the powers assumed by this bill, have not, in my opinion, been delegated to the United States, by the Constitution.

I. They are not among the powers specially enumerated: for these are: 1st.   A power to lay taxes for the purpose of paying the debts of the United States; but no debt is paid by this bill, nor any tax laid.   Were it a bill to raise money, its origination in the Senate would condemn it by the Constitution.

2d. "To borrow money." But this bill neither borrows money nor ensures the borrowing it.   The proprietors of the bank will be just as free as any other money holders, to lend or not to lend their money to the public.   The operation proposed in the bill, first, to lend them two millions, and then to borrow them back again, cannot change the nature of the latter act, which will still be a payment, and not a loan, call it by what name you please.

3d. To "regulate commerce with foreign nations, and among the States, and with the Indian tribes."   To erect a bank, and to regulate commerce, are very different acts.   He who erects a bank, creates a subject of commerce in its bills; so does he who makes a bushel of wheat, or digs a dollar out of the mines; yet neither of these persons regulates commerce thereby. To make a thing which may be bought and sold, is not to prescribe regulations for buying and selling.   Besides, if this was an exercise of the power of regulating commerce, it would be void, as extending as much to the internal commerce of every State, as to its external.

59

For the power given to Congress by the Constitution does not extend to the internal regulation of the commerce of a State, (that is to say of the commerce between citizen and citizen,) which remain exclusively with its own legislature; but to its external commerce only, that is to say, its commerce with another State, or with foreign nations, or with the Indian tribes. Accordingly the bill does not propose the measure as a regulation of trade, but as "productive of considerable advantages to trade." Still less are these powers covered by any other of the special enumerations.

II. Nor are they within either of the general phrases, which are the two following: —

1. To lay taxes to provide for the general welfare of the United States, that is to say, "to lay taxes for *the purpose* of providing for the general welfare." For the laying of taxes is the *power*, and the general welfare the *purpose* for which the power is to be exercised. They are not to lay taxes *ad libitum for any purpose they please;* but only *to pay the debts or provide for the welfare of the Union.* In like manner, they are not *to do anything they please* to provide for the general welfare, but only to *lay taxes* for that purpose. To consider the latter phrase, not as describing the purpose of the first, but as giving a distinct and independent power to do any act they please, which might be for the good of the Union, would render all the preceding and subsequent enumerations of power completely useless.

It would reduce the whole instrument to a single phrase, that of instituting a Congress with power to do whatever would be for the good of the United States; and, as they would be the sole judges of the good or evil, it would be also a power to do whatever evil they please.

It is an established rule of construction where a phrase will bear either of two meanings, to give it that which will allow some meaning to the other parts of the instrument, and not that which would render all the others useless. Certainly no such universal power was meant to be given them. It was intended to lace them up straitly within the enumerated powers, and those without which, as means, these powers could not be carried into effect. It is known that the very power now proposed *as a means* was rejected as *an end* by the Convention which formed the Constitution. A proposition was made to them to authorize Congress to open canals, and an amendatory one to empower them to incorporate. But the whole was rejected, and one of the reasons for rejection urged in debate was, that then they would have a power to erect a bank, which would render the great cities, where there were prejudices and jealousies on the subject, adverse to the reception of the Constitution.

2. The second general phrase is, "to make all laws *necessary* and proper for carrying into execution the enumerated powers." But they can all be carried into execution without a bank. A bank therefore is not *necessary*, and consequently not authorized by this phrase.

It has been urged that a bank will give great facility or convenience in the collection of taxes. Suppose this were true: yet the Constitution allows only the means which are *"necessary,"* not those which are merely "convenient" for effecting the enumerated powers. If such a latitude of construction be allowed to this phrase as to give any non-enumerated power, it will go to every one, for there is not one which ingenuity may not torture into a *convenience* in some instance *or other,* to *some one* of so long a list of enumerated powers. It would swallow up all the delegated powers, and reduce the whole to one power, as before observed. Therefore it was that the Constitution restrained them to the *necessary* means, that is to say, to those means without which the grant of power would be nugatory. . . .

Perhaps, indeed, bank bills may be a more *convenient* vehicle than treasury orders. But a little *difference* in the degree of *convenience*, cannot constitute the necessity which the constitution makes the ground for assuming any non-enumerated power.

Besides; the existing banks will, without a doubt, enter into arrangements for lending their agency, and the more favorable, as there will be a competition among them for it; whereas the bill delivers us up bound to the national bank, who are free to refuse all arrangement, but on their own terms, and the public not free, on such refusal, to employ any other bank. That of Philadelphia, I believe, now does this business, by their post-notes, which, by an arrangement with the treasury, are paid by any State collector to whom they are presented. This expedient alone suffices to prevent the existence of that *necessity* which may justify the assumption of a non-enumerated power as a means for carrying into effect an enumerated one. The thing may be done, and has been done, and well done, without this assumption; therefore, it does not stand on that degree of *necessity* which can honestly justify it.

It may be said that a bank whose bills would have a currency all over the States, would be more convenient than one whose currency is limited to a single State. So it would be still more convenient that there should be a bank, whose bills should have a currency all over the world. But it does not follow from this superior conveniency, that there exists anywhere a power to establish such a bank; or that the world may not go on very well without it.

Can it be thought that the Constitution intended that for a shade or two of *convenience*, more or less, Congress should be authorized to break down the most ancient and fundamental laws of the several States; such as those against Mortmain, the laws of Alienage, the rules of descent, the acts of distribution, the laws of escheat and forfeiture, the laws of monopoly? Nothing but a necessity invincible by any other means, can justify such a prostitution of laws, which constitute the pillars of our whole system of jurisprudence. Will Congress be too strait-laced to carry the Constitution into honest effect, unless they may pass over the foundation-laws of the State government for the slightest convenience of theirs?

The negative of the President is the shield provided by the Constitution to protect against the invasions of the legislature: 1. The right of the Executive. 2. Of the Judiciary. 3. Of the States and State legislatures. The present is the case of a right remaining exclusively with the States, and consequently one of those intended by the Constitution to be placed under its protection.

It must be added, however, that unless the President's mind on a view of everything which is urged for and against this bill, is tolerably clear that it is unauthorized by the Constitution; if the pro and the con hang so even as to balance his judgment, a just respect for the wisdom of the legislature would naturally decide the balance in favor of their opinion. It is chiefly for cases where they are clearly misled by error, ambition, or interest, that the Constitution has placed a check in the negative of the President.

Letter to Albert Gallatin, Secretary of the Treasury, December 13, 1803. *Writings of Jefferson*, X, 437-39.

From a passage in the letter of the President [of the bank], I observe an idea of establishing a branch bank of the United States in New Orleans. This institution is one of the most deadly hostility existing, against the principles and form of our Constitution. The nation is, at this time, so strong and united in its sentiments, that it cannot be shaken at this moment. But suppose a series of untoward events should occur, sufficient to bring into doubt the competency of a republican government to meet a crisis of great danger, or to unhinge the confidence of the people in the public functionaries; an institution like this, penetrating by its branches every part of the Union, acting by command and in phalanx, may, in a critical moment, upset the government. I deem no government safe which is under the vassalage of any self-constituted authorities, or any other authority than that of the nation, or its regular functionaries. What an obstruction could not this bank of the United States, with all its branch banks, be in time of war! It might dictate to us the peace we should accept, or withdraw its aids. Ought we then to give further growth to an institution so powerful, so hostile?. . . Now, while we are strong, it is the greatest duty we owe to the safety of our Constitution, to bring this powerful enemy to a perfect subordination under its authorities. The first measure would be to reduce them to an equal footing only with other banks, as to the favors of the government. But, in order to be able to meet a general combination of the banks against us, in a critical emergency, could we not make a beginning towards an independent use of our own money, towards holding our own bank in all the deposits where it is received, and letting the treasurer give his draft or note, for payment at any particular place, which, in a well-conducted government, ought to have as much credit as any private draft, or bank note, or bill, and would give us the same facilities which we derive from the banks?. . .

Letter to Colonel Charles Yancey, January 6, 1816. *Writings of Jefferson*, XIV, 381-426. An attempt to recharter the Bank of the United States called forth this denunciation of the institution.

Like a dropsical man calling out for water, water, our deluded citizens are clamoring for more banks, more banks. The American mind is now in that state of fever which the world has so often seen in the history of other nations. . . . We are now taught to believe that legerdemain tricks upon paper can produce as solid wealth as hard labor in the earth. It is vain for common sense to urge that *nothing* can produce but *nothing;* that it is an idle dream to believe in a philosopher's stone which is to turn everything into gold, and to redeem man from the original sentence of his Maker, "in the sweat of his brow shall he eat his bread.". . .

It is a litigated question, whether the circulation of paper, rather than of specie, is a good or an evil. In the opinion of England and of English writers it is a good; in that of all other nations it is an evil; and excepting England and her copyist, the United States, there is not a nation existing, I believe, which tolerates a paper circulation. The experiment is going on, however, desperately in England, pretty boldly with us, and at the end of the chapter, we shall see which opinion experience approves: for I believe it to be one of those cases where mercantile clamor will bear down reason, until it is corrected by ruin. In the meantime, however, let us reason on this new call for a national bank.

After the solemn decision of Congress against the renewal of the charter of the bank of the United States, and the grounds of that decision, (the want of constitutional power,) I had imagined that question at rest, and that no more applications would be made to them for the incorporation of banks. The opposition on that ground to its first establishment, the small majority by which it was overborne, and the means practised for obtaining it, cannot be already forgotten. The law having passed, however, by a majority, its opponents, true to the sacred principle of submission to a majority, suffered the law to flow through its term without obstruction. During this, the nation had time to consider the constitutional question, and when the renewal was proposed, they condemned it, not by their representatives in Congress only, but by express instructions from different organs of their will. . . .

At the time we were funding our national debt, we heard much about "a public debt being a public blessing;" that the stock representing it was a creation of active capital for the aliment of commerce, manufactures and agriculture. This paradox was well adapted to the minds of believers in dreams, and the gulls of that size entered *bona fide* into it. But the art and mystery of banks is a wonderful improvement on that. It is established on the principle that *"private* debts are a public blessing." That the evidences of those private debts, called bank notes, become active capital, and aliment the whole commerce, manufactures, and agriculture of the United States. Here are a set of people, for instance, who have bestowed on us the great blessing of running in our debt about two hundred millions of dollars, without our knowing who they are, where they are, or what property they have to pay this debt when called on; nay, who have made us so sensible of the blessings of letting them run in our debt, that we have exempted them by law from the repayment of these debts beyond a given proportion, (generally estimated at one-third). And to fill up the measure of blessing, instead of paying, they receive an interest on what they owe from those to whom they owe; for all the notes, or evidences of what they owe, which we see in circulation, have been lent to somebody on an interest which is levied again on us through the medium of commerce. . . .

It is said that our paper is as good as silver, because we may have silver for it at the bank where it issues. This is not true. One, two, or three persons might have it; but a general application would soon exhaust their vaults, and leave a ruinous proportion of their paper in its intrinsic worthless form. It is a fallacious pretence, for another reason. The inhabitants of the banking cities might obtain cash for their paper, as far as the cash of the vaults would hold out, but distance puts it out of the power of the country to do this. A farmer having a note of a Boston or Charleston bank, distant hundreds of miles, has no means of calling for the cash. And while these calls are impracticable for the country, the banks have no fear of their being made from the towns; because their inhabitants are mostly on their books, and there on sufferance only, and during good behavior.

ALEXANDER HAMILTON

Cabinet opinion on the constitutionality of the Bank of the United States, February 23, 1791. *Works of Hamilton*, III, 445-58. Hamilton regarded the national bank as a necessary adjunct to his economic system, for it would make capital available for investment in the American economy and would provide a uniform currency for interstate commerce.

The Secretary of the Treasury having perused with attention the papers containing the opinions of the Secretary of State and the Attorney-General, concerning the constitutionality of the bill for establishing a national bank, proceeds, according to the order of the President, to submit the reasons which have induced him to entertain a different opinion.

. . . In entering upon the argument, it ought to be premised that the objections of the Secretary of State and the Attorney-General are founded on a general denial of the authority of the United States to erect corporations. The latter, indeed, expressly admits, that if there be anything in the bill which is not warranted by the Constitution, it is the clause of incorporation.

Now it appears to the Secretary of the Treasury that this *general principle* is *inherent* in the very *definition* of government, and *essential* to *every* step of the progress to be made by that of the United States, namely: That every power vested in a government is in its nature *sovereign, and includes,* by *force* of the *term,* a right to employ all the *means* requisite and fairly applicable to the attainment of the *ends* of such power, and which are not precluded by restrictions and exceptions specified in the Constitution, or not immoral, or not contrary to the *essential ends* of political society.

This principle, in its application to government in general, would be admitted as an axiom; and it will be incumbent upon those who may incline to deny it, to prove a distinction, and to show that a rule which, in the general system of things, is essential to the preservation of the social order, is inapplicable to the United States.

The circumstance that the powers of sovereignty are in this country divided betweeen the National and State governments, does not afford the distinction required. It does not follow from this, that each of the portion of *powers* delegated to the one or to the other, is not sovereign with *regard to its proper objects*. It will only *follow* from it, that each has sovereign power as to *certain things*, and not as to *other things*. To deny that the Government of the United States has sovereign power, as to its declared purposes and trusts, because its power does not extend to all cases, would be equally to deny that the State governments have sovereign power in any case, because their power does not extend to every case. The tenth section of the first article of the Constitution exhibits a long list of very important things which they may not do. And thus the United States would furnish the singular spectacle of a *political society* without *sovereignty*, or of a *people governed*, without *government*.

If it would be necessary to bring proof to a proposition so clear, as that which affirms that the powers of the Federal Government, as to *its objects*, were sovereign, there is a clause of its Constitution which would be decisive. It is that which declares that the Constitution, and the laws of the United States made in pursuance of it, and all treaties made, or which shall be made, under their authority, shall be the *supreme law of the land.* The power which can create the *supreme law of the land* in *any case*, is doubtless *sovereign* as to such case.

This general and indisputable principle puts at once an end to the *abstract* question, whether the United States have power to erect a *corporation;* that is to say, to give a *legal* or *artificial capacity* to one or more persons, distinct from the *natural.* For it is unquestionably incident to *sovereign power* to erect corporations, and consequently to *that* of the United States, in *relation* to the *objects* intrusted to the management of the government. The difference is this: where the authority of the government is general, it can create corporations in *all cases;* where it is confined to certain branches of legislation, it can create corporations *only* in those cases. . . . It shall also be shown that the power of incorporation, incident to the government in certain cases, does fairly extend to the particular case which is the object of the bill.

The first of these arguments is, that the foundation of the Constitution is laid on this ground: "That all powers not delegated to the United States by the Constitution, nor prohibited by it to the States, are reserved to the States, or to the people." Whence it is meant to be inferred, that Congress can in no case exercise any power not included in those enumerated in the Constitution. And it is affirmed, that the power of erecting a corporation is not included in any of the enumerated powers.

The main proposition here laid down, in its true signification, is not to be questioned. It is nothing more than a consequence of this republican maxim, that all government is a delegation of power. But how much is delegated in each case is a question of fact, to be made out by fair reasoning and construction, upon the particular provisions of the Constitution, taking as guides the general principles and general ends of governments.

It is not denied that there are *implied,* as well as *express powers,* and that the *former* are as effectually delegated as the *latter.* . . . It is conceded that *implied powers* are to be considered as delegated equally with *express ones.* Then it follows, that as a power of erecting a corporation may well be *implied* as any other thing, it may as well be employed as an *instrument* or *means* of carrying into execution any of the specified powers, as any other *instrument* or *means* whatever. The only question must be in this, as in every other case, whether the means to be employed, or, in this instance, the corporation to be erected, has a natural relation to any of the acknowledged objects or lawful ends of the government. Thus a corporation may not be erected by Congress for superintending the police of the city of Philadelphia, because they are not authorized to *regulate* the *police* of that city. But one may be erected in relation to the collection of taxes, or to the trade with foreign countries, or to the trade between the States, or with the Indian tribes; because it is the province of the Federal Government to *regulate* those objects, and because it is incident to a general *sovereign* or *legislative* power to *regulate* a thing, to employ all the means which relate to its regulation to the best and greatest advantage.

A strange fallacy seems to have crept into the manner of thinking and reasoning upon this subject. Imagination appears to have been unusually busy concerning it. An incorporation seems to have been regarded as some *great independent substantive thing;* as a political end of peculiar magnitude and moment; whereas it is truly to be considered as a *quality, capacity,* or *means* to an end. Thus a mercantile company is formed, with a certain capital, for the purpose of carrying on a particular branch of business. Here the business to be prosecuted is the end. The association in order to form the requisite capital, is the primary mean. Suppose that an incorporation were added to this, it would only be to add a new *quality* to that association, to give it an artificial capacity, by which it would be enabled to prosecute the business with more safety and convenience. . . .

Through this mode of reasoning respecting the right of employing all the means requisite to the execution of the specified powers of the government, it is to be objected, that none but necessary and proper means are to be employed; and the Secretary of State maintains, that no means are to be considered *necessary* but those without which the grant of the power would be *nugatory.* Nay, so far does he go in his restrictive interpretation of the *word,* as even to make the case of *necessity* which shall warrant the constitutional exercise of the power to depend on *casual* and *temporary* circumstances; an idea which alone refutes the construction. The *expediency* of exercising a particular power, at a particular time, must, indeed, depend on circumstances; but the constitutional right of exercising it must be uniform and invariable, the same today as tomorrow.

All the arguments, therefore, against the constitutionality of the bill derived from the accidental existence of certain State banks—institutions which happen to exist today, and, for aught that concerns the government of the United States, may disappear tomorrow—must not only be rejected as fallacious, but must be viewed as demonstrative that there is a *radical* source of error in the reasoning.

It is essential to the being of the national government, that so erroneous a conception of the meaning of the word *necessary* should be exploded.

It is certain, that neither the grammatical nor popular sense of the term requires that construction. According to both, *necessary* often means no more than *needful, requisite, incidental, useful,* or *conducive to.* It is a common mode of expression to say, that it is *necessary* for a government or a person to do this or that thing, when nothing more is intended or understood, than that the interests of the government or person require, or will be promoted by, the doing of this or that thing. The imagination can be at no loss for exemplifications of the use of the word in this sense. And it is the true one in which it is to be understood as used in the Constitution. The whole turn of the clause containing it indicates, that it was the intent of the Convention, by that clause, to give a liberal latitude to the exercise of the specified powers. The expressions have peculiar comprehensiveness. They are, "to make all *laws* necessary and proper for *carrying into execution* the *foregoing powers*, and *all other powers* vested by the Constitution in the *Government* of the United States, or in any department or officer thereof."

To understand the word as the Secretary of State does, would be to depart from its obvious and popular sense, and to give it a restrictive operation, an idea never before entertained. It would be to give it the same force as if the word *absolutely* or *indispensably* had been prefixed to it.

Such a construction would beget endless uncertainty and embarrassment. The cases must be palpable and extreme, in which it could be pronounced, with certainty, that a measure was absolutely necessary, or one, without which the exercise of a given power would be nugatory. There are a few measures of any government which would stand so severe a test. To insist upon it, would be to make the criterion of the exercise of any implied power, a *case of extreme necessity;* which is rather a rule to justify the overleaping of the bounds of constitutional authority, than to govern the ordinary exercise of it. . . .

But the doctrine which is contended . . . does not affirm that the National Government is sovereign in all respects, but that it is sovereign to a certain extent—that is, to the extent of the objects of its specified powers.

It leaves, therefore, a criterion of what is constitutional, and of what is not so. This criterion is the *end,* to which the measure relates as a *means. If the end* be clearly comprehended within any of the specified powers, and if the measure have an obvious relation to *that end,* and is not forbidden by any particular provision of the Constitution, it may safely be deemed to come within the compass of the national authority. There is also this further criterion, which may materially assist the decision: Does the proposed measure abridge a pre-existing right of any State or of any individual? If it does not, there is a strong presumption in favor of its constitutionality, and slighter relations to any declared object of the Constitution may be permitted to turn the scale.

Economic Development

ALEXANDER HAMILTON

First Report on the Public Credit, January 9, 1790. In this report Hamilton outlined his funding proposal and assumption plan. Although these two aspects of his financial program are sometimes considered separately, Hamilton considered them sufficiently connected to include them in one report. *Works of Hamilton*, II, 232-51.

To justify and preserve their confidence; to promote the increasing respectability of the American name, to answer the calls of justice; to restore landed property to its due value; to furnish new resources, both to agriculture and commerce; to cement more closely the union of the States, to add to their security against foreign attack; to establish public order on the basis of an upright and liberal policy;—these are the great and invaluable ends to be secured by a proper and adequate provision, at the present period, for the support of public credit. . . .

The advantage to the public creditors, from the increased value of that part of their property which constitutes the public debt, needs no explanation.

But there is a consequence of this, less obvious, though not less true, in which every other citizen is interested. It is a well-known fact, that, in countries in which the national debt is properly funded, and an object of established confidence, it answers most of the purposes of money. Transfers of stock or public debt are there equivalent to payments in specie; or, in other words, stock, in the principal transactions of business, passes current as specie. The same thing would, in all probability, happen here under the like circumstances. The benefits of this are various and obvious:

First. —Trade is extended by it, because there is a larger capital to carry it on, and the merchant can, at the same time, afford to trade for smaller profits; as his stock, which, when unemployed, brings him an interest from the Government, serves him also as money when he has a call for it in his commercial operations.

Secondly. —Agriculture and manufactures are also promoted by it, for the like reason, that more capital can be commanded to be employed in both; and because the merchant, whose enterprise in foreign trade gives to them activity and extension, has greater means for enterprise.

Thirdly. —The interest of money will be lowered by it; for this is always in a ratio to the quantity of money, and to the quickness of circulation. This circumstance will enable both the public and individuals to borrow on easier and cheaper terms.

And from the combination of these effects, additional aids will be furnished to labor, to industry, and to arts of every kind. But these good effects of a public debt are only to be looked for, when, by being well funded, it has acquired an adequate and stable value; till then, it has rather a contrary tendency. . . .

The Secretary has too much deference for the opinions of every part of the community not to have observed one, which has more than once made its appearance in the public prints, and which is occasionally to be met with in conversation. It involves this question: Whether a discrimination ought not to be made between original holders of the public securities, and present possessors, by purchase? Those who advocate a discrimination are for making a full provision for the securities of the former at their nominal value, but contend that the latter ought to receive no more than the cost to them, and the interest. And the idea is sometimes suggested of making good the difference to the primitive possessor.

In favor of this scheme it is alleged that it would be unreasonable to pay twenty shillings in the pound to one who had not given more for it than three or four. And it is added that it would be hard to aggravate the misfortune of the first owner, who, probably through necessity, parted with his property at so great a loss, by obliging him to contribute to the profit of the person who had speculated on his distresses.

The Secretary, after the most mature reflection on the force of this argument, is induced to reject the doctrine it contains, as equally unjust and impolitic; as highly injurious, even to the original holders of public securities; as ruinous to public credit.

It is inconsistent with justice, because, in the first place, it is a breach of contract—a violation of the rights of a fair purchaser. . . .

That the case of those who parted with their securities from necessity is a hard one, cannot be denied. But, whatever complaint of injury, or claim of redress, they may have, respects the Government solely. They have not only nothing to object to the persons who relieved their necessities, by giving them the current price of their property, but they are even under an implied condition to contribute to the reimbursement of those persons. They knew that, by the terms of the contract with themselves, the public were bound to pay to those to whom they should convey their title the sums stipulated to be paid to them; and that, as citizens of the United States, they were to bear their proportion of the contribution for that purpose. This, by the act of assignment, they tacitly engaged to do; and, if they had an option, they could not, with integrity or good faith, refuse to do it, without the consent of those to whom they sold.

But, though many of the original holders sold from necessity, it does not follow that this was the case with all of them. It may well be supposed that some of them did it either through want of confidence in an eventual provision, or from the allurements of some profitable speculation. How shall these different classes be discriminated from each other? How shall it be ascertained, in any case, that the money which the original holder obtained for his security was not more beneficial to him, than if he had held it to the present time, to avail himself of the provision which shall be made? How shall it be known whether, if the purchaser had employed his money in some other way, he would not be in a better situation than by having applied it in the purchase of securities, though he should now receive their full amount? And, if neither of these things can be known, how shall it be determined, whether a discrimination, independent of the breach of contract, would not do a real injury to purchasers; and, if it included a compensation to the primitive proprietors, would not give them an advantage to which they had no equitable pretension?

It may well be imagined, also, that there are not wanting instances in which individuals, urged by a present necessity, parted with the securities received by them from the public, and shortly after replaced them with others, as an indemnity for their first loss. Shall they be deprived of the indemnity which they have endeavored to secure by so provident an arrangement?

Questions of this sort, on a close inspection, multiply themselves without end, and demonstrate the injustice of a discrimination, even on the most subtile calculations of equity, abstracted from the obligation of contract.

The difficulties, too, of regulating the details of a plan for that purpose, which would have even the semblance of equity, would be found immense. It may well be doubted, whether they would not be insurmountable, and replete with such absurd as well as inequitable consequences, as to disgust even the proposers of the measure.

As a specimen of its capricious operation, it will be sufficient to notice the effect it would have upon two persons, who may be supposed, two years ago, to have purchased, each, securities, at three shillings in the pound, and one of them to retain those bought by him, till the discrimination should take place; the other, to have parted with those bought by him, within a month past, at nine shillings. The fomer, who had had most confidence in the Government, would, in this case, only receive at the rate of three shillings, and the interest; while the latter, who had less confidence, would receive, for what cost him the same money, at the rate of nine shillings, and his representative, standing in his place, would be entitled to a like rate. . . .

[Assumption]

The Secretary, concluding that a discrimination between the different classes of creditors of the United States cannot, with propriety, be made, proceeds to examine whether a difference ought to be permitted to remain between them and another description of public creditors—those of the States individually. The Secretary, after mature reflection on this point, entertains a full conviction that an assumption of the debts of the particular States by the Union, and a like provision for them as for those of the Union, will be a measure of sound policy and substantial justice. . . .

If all the public creditors receive their dues from one source, distributed with an equal hand, their interest will be the same. And, having the same interests, they will unite in the support of the fiscal arrangements of the Government—as these, too, can be made with more convenience where there is no competition. These circumstances combined will insure to the revenue laws a more ready and more satisfactory execution.

If, on the contrary, there are distinct provisions, there will be distinct interests, drawing different ways. That union and concert of views among creditors, which in every Government is of great importance to their security and to that of public credit, will not only not exist, but will be likely to give place to mutual jealousy and opposition. And from this cause the operation of the systems which may be adopted, both by the particular States and by the Union, with relation to their respective debts, will be in danger of being counteracted. . . .

The general principle of it seems to be equitable: for it appears difficult to conceive a good reason why the expenses for the particular defence of a part, in a common war, should not be a common charge, as well as those incurred professedly for the general defence. The defence of each part is that of the whole; and unless all the expenditures are brought into a common mass, the tendency must be to add to the calamities suffered, by being the most exposed to the ravages of war, and increase of burthens. . . .

Second Report on the Public Credit, January 20, 1795. *Works of Hamilton*, III, 298-300.

Credit is an *entire* thing. Every part of it has the nicest sympathy with every other part; wound one limb, and the whole tree shrinks and decays.

The security of each creditor is inseparable from the security of all creditors. The boundary between foreigner and citizen would not be deemed a sufficient barrier against extending the precedent of an invasion of the rights of the former to the latter. The most judicious and cautious would be most apt to reason thus, and would only look for stronger shades of apparent necessity or expediency to govern the extension. And, in affairs of credit, the opinion of the judicious and cautious may be expected to prevail. . . .

It is wisdom, in every case, to cherish whatever is useful, and guard against its abuse. It will be the truest policy of the United States to give all possible energy to public credit, by a firm adherence to its strictest maxims; and yet avoid the ills of an excessive employment of it by true economy and system in the public expenditures; by steadily cultivating peace; and by using sincere, efficient, and persevering endeavors to diminish present debts, prevent the accumulation of new, and secure the discharge, within a reasonable period, of such as it may be at any time matter of necessity to contract. It will be wise to cultivate and foster private credit by an exemplary observance of the principles of public credit, and to guard against the misuse of the former by a speedy and vigorous administration of justice, and by taking away every temptation to run in debt, founded in the hope of evading the just claims of creditors.

Hamilton is often described as one of the first American advocates of deficit financing. The following statements, one from each of his reports on Public Credit, show his views on a large public debt. *Works of Hamilton,* II, 283; III, 262.

. . . Persuaded, as the Secretary is, that the proper funding of the present debt will render it a national blessing, yet he is so far from acceding to the position, in the latitude in which it is sometimes laid down, that "public debts are public benefits"—a position inviting to prodigality and liable to dangerous abuse—that he ardently wishes to see it incorporated as a fundamental maxim in the system of public credit of the United States, that the creation of debt should always be accompanied with the means of extinguishment. This he regards as the true secret for rendering public credit immortal. And he presumes that it is difficult to conceive a situation in which there may not be an adherence to the maxim. At least, he feels an unfeigned solicitude that this may be attempted by the United States, and that they may commence their measures for the establishment of credit with the observance of it. . . .

To extinguish a debt which exists, and to avoid the contracting more, are ideas always favored by public feeling and opinion: but to pay taxes for the one or the other purpose, which are the only means of avoiding the evil, is always, more or less, unpopular. These contradictions are in human nature; and happy, indeed, would be the lot of a country that should ever want men ready to turn them to the account of their own popularity, or to some other sinister account.

Hence, it is no uncommon spectacle to see the same men clamoring for occasions of expense, when they happen to be in unison with the present humor of the community, whether well or ill directed, declaiming against a public debt, and for the reduction of it as an abstract thesis; yet vehement against every plan of taxation which is proposed to discharge old debts, or to avoid new, by the defraying expenses of exigencies as they emerge.

Report on a National Bank, December 13, 1790. *Works of Hamilton,* III, 389, 427-8.

It is a fact, well understood, that public banks have found admission and patronage among the principal and most enlightened commercial nations. They have successively obtained in Italy,

Germany, Holland, England, and France, as well as in the United States. And it is a circumstance which cannot but have considerable weight, in a candid estimate of their tendency, that after an experience of centuries, there exists not a question about their utility in the countries in which they have been so long established. Theorists and men of business unite in the acknowledgment of it. . . .

Considerations of public advantage suggest a . . . wish, which is—that the bank could be established upon principles that would cause the profits of it to redound to the immediate benefit of the State. This is contemplated by many who speak of a national bank, but the idea seems liable to insuperable objections. To attach full confidence to an institution of this nature, it appears to be an essential ingredient in its structure, that it shall be under a *private* not a *public* direction—under the guidance of *individual interest*, not of *public policy;* which would be supposed to be, and, in certain emergencies, under a feeble or too sanguine administration, would really be, liable to being too much influenced by *public necessity*. The suspicion of this would, most probably, be a canker that would continually corrode the vitals of the credit of the bank, and would be most likely to prove fatal in those situations in which the public good would require that they should be most sound and vigorous. It would, indeed, be little less than a miracle, should the credit of the bank be at the disposal of the government, if, in a long series of time, there was not experienced a calamitous abuse of it. It is true, that it would be the real interest of the government not to abuse it; its genuine policy to husband and cherish it with the most guarded circumspection, as an inestimable treasure. But what government ever uniformly consulted its true interests in opposition to the temptations of momentary exigencies? What nation was ever blessed with a constant succession of upright and wise administrators?

Report on Manufactures, December 5, 1791. *Works of Hamilton,* IV, 83-160.

To affirm that the labor of the manufacturer is unproductive, because he consumes as much of the produce of land as he adds value to the raw material which he manufactures, is not better founded than it would be to affirm that the labor of the farmer, which furnishes materials to the manufacturer, is unproductive, because he consumes an equal value of manufactured articles. Each furnishes a certain portion of the produce of his labor to the other, and each destroys a corresponding portion of the produce of the labor of the other. In the meantime, the maintenance of two citizens, instead of one, is going on; the State has two members instead of one; and they, together, consume twice the value of what is produced from the land.

If, instead of a farmer and artificer, there were a farmer only, he would be under the necessity of devoting a part of his labor to the fabrication of clothing and other articles, which he would procure of the artificer, in the case of there being such a person; and of course he would be able to devote less labor to the cultivation of his farm, and would draw from it a proportionately less product. The whole quantity of production, in this state of things, in provisions, raw materials, and manufactures, would certainly not exceed in value the amount of what would be produced in provisions and raw materials only, if there were an artificer as well as a farmer.

Again, if there were both an artificer and a farmer, the latter would be left at liberty to pursue exclusively the cultivation of his farm. A greater quantity of provisions and raw materials would, of course, be produced, equal, at least, as has been already observed, to the whole amount of the provisions, raw materials, and manufactures, which would exist on a contrary supposition. The artificer, at the same time, would be going on in the production of manufactured commodities, to an amount sufficient, not only to repay the farmer, in those commodities, for the provisions and materials which were procured from him, but to furnish the artificer himself with a supply of similar commodities for his own use. Thus, then, there would be two quantities or values in existence, instead of one; and the revenue and consumption would be double, in one case, what it would be in the other. . . .

It is now proper to proceed a step further, and to enumerate the principal circumstances from which it may be inferred that manufacturing establishments not only occasion a positive augmentation of the produce and revenue of the society, but that they contribute essentially to rendering them greater than they could possibly be without such establishments. These circumstances are: . . .

1. As to the division of labor

It has justly been observed, that there is scarcely any thing of greater moment in the economy of a nation than the proper division of labor. The separation of occupations causes each to be carried to a much greater perfection than it could possibly acquire if they were blended. . . .

2. As to an extension of the use of machinery, a point which, though partly anticipated, requires to be placed in one or two additional lights

The employment of machinery forms an item of great importance in the general mass of national industry. It is an artificial force brought in aid of the natural force of man; and, to all the purposes of labor, is an increase of hands, an accession of strength, unencumbered too by the expense of maintaining the laborer. May it not, therefore, be fairly inferred, that those occupations which give greatest scope to the use of this auxiliary, contribute most to the general stock of industrious effort, and, in consequence, to the general product of industry?

3. As to the additional employment of classes of the community not originally engaged in the particular business

This is not among the least valuable of the means by which manufacturing institutions contribute to augment the general stock of industry and production. In places where those institutions prevail, besides the persons regularly engaged in them, they afford occasional and extra employment to industrious individuals and families, who are willing to devote the leisure resulting from the intermissions of their ordinary pursuits to collateral labors, as a resource for multiplying their acquisitions or their enjoyments. The husbandman himself experiences a new source of profit and support from the increased industry of his wife and daughters, invited and stimulated by the demands of the neighboring manufactories.

Besides this advantage of occasional employment to classes having different occupations, there is another, of a nature allied to it, and of a similar tendency. This is the employment of persons who would otherwise be idle, and in many cases a burthen on the community, either from the bias of temper, habit, infirmity of body, or some other cause, indisposing or disqualifying them for the toils of the country. It is worthy of particular remark that, in general, women and children are rendered more useful, and the latter more early useful, by manufacturing establishments, than they would otherwise be. Of the number of persons employed in the cotton manufactories of Great Britain, it is computed that four sevenths nearly are women and children, of whom the greatest proportion are children, and many of them of a tender age. . . .

4. As to the promoting of emigration from foreign countries

Men reluctantly quit one course of occupation and livelihood for another, unless invited to it by very apparent and proximate advantages. Many who would go from one country to another,

if they had a prospect of continuing with more benefit the callings
to which they have been educated, will often not be tempted to
change their situation by the hope of doing better in some other
way. . . .

    5. As to the furnishing greater scope for the diversity of
        talents and dispositions, which discriminate men from
        each other

    This is a much more powerful means of augmenting the fund
of national industry, than may at first sight appear. It is a just
observation, that minds of the strongest and most active powers
for their proper objects, fall below mediocrity, and labor without
effect, if confined to uncongenial pursuits. And it is thence to be
inferred, that the results of human exertion may be immensely
increased by diversifying its objects. When all the different
kinds of industry obtain in a community, each individual can find
his proper element, and can call into activity the whole vigor of
his nature. And the community is benefited by the services of
its respective members, in the manner in which each can serve
it with most effect. . . .

    6. As to the affording a more ample and various field for
        enterprise

    This also is of greater consequence in the general scale of
national exertion than might, perhaps, on a superficial view be
supposed, and has effects not altogether dissimilar from those
of the circumstance last noticed. To cherish and stimulate the
activity of the human mind, by multiplying the objects of enterprise, is not among the least considerable of the expedients by
which the wealth of a nation may be promoted. Even things in
themselves not positively advantageous sometimes become so, by
their tendency to provoke exertion. Every new scene which is
opened to the busy nature of man to rouse and exert itself, is the
addition of a new energy to the general stock of effort. . . .

    7. As to the creating, in some instances, a new, and securing,
        in all, a more certain and steady demand for the surplus
        produce of the soil

    This is among the most important of the circumstances which
have been indicated. It is a principal means by which the establishment of manufactures contributes to an augmentation of the produce
or revenue of a country, and has an immediate and direct relation
to the prosperity of agriculture. . . .

    Considering how fast and how much the progress of new settle-
ments in the United States must increase the surplus produce
of the soil, and weighing seriously the tendency of the system which

prevails among most of the commercial nations of Europe, whatever dependence may be placed on the force of natural circumstances to counteract the effects of an artificial policy, there appear strong reasons to regard the foreign demand for that surplus as too uncertain a reliance, and to desire a substitute for it in an extensive domestic market.

To secure such a market there is no other expedient than to promote manufacturing establishments.   Manufacturers, who constitute the most numerous class, after the cultivators of land, are for that reason the principal consumers of the surplus of their labor. . . .

. . . The importations of manufactured supplies seem invariably to drain the merely agricultural people of their wealth. Let the situation of the manufacturing countries of Europe be compared, in this particular, with that of countries which only cultivate, and the disparity will be striking.   Other causes, it is true, help to account for this disparity between some of them; and among these causes, the relative state of agriculture; but between others of them, the most prominent circumstance of dissimilitude arises from the comparative state of manufactures. In corroboration of the same idea, it ought not to escape remark, that the West India Islands, the soils of which are the most fertile, and the nation which, in the greatest degree, supplies the rest of the world with the precious metals, exchange to a loss with almost every other country. . . .

One more point of view only remains, in which to consider the expediency of encouraging manufactures in the United States.

It is not uncommon to meet with an opinion, that, though the promoting of manufactures may be the interest of a part of the Union, it is contrary to that of another part. The Northern and Southern regions are sometimes represented as having adverse interests in this respect. Those are called manufacturing, these agricultural States; and a species of opposition is imagined to subsist between manufacturing and agricultural interests.

This idea of an opposition between those two interests is the common error of the early periods of every country; but experience gradually dissipates it.   Indeed, they are perceived so often to succor and befriend each other, that they come at length to be considered as one—a supposition which has been frequently abused, and is not universally true. Particular encouragements of particular manufactures may be of a nature to sacrifice the interests of landholders to those of manufacturers; but it is nevertheless a maxim, well established by experience, and generally acknowledged, where there has been sufficient experience, that the aggregate prosperity of manufactures and the aggregate prosperity of agriculture are intimately connected. In the course of the discussion which has had place, various weighty considerations have been adduced, operating in support of that maxim. Perhaps the superior steadiness of the demand of a domestic market, for the surplus produce of the soil, is, alone, a convincing argument of its truth.

Ideas of a contrariety of interests between the Northern and Southern regions of the Union are, in the main, as unfounded as they are mischievous. . . .

. . . If the Northern and Middle States should be the principal scenes of such establishments, they would immediately benefit the more Southern, by creating a demand for productions, some of which they have in common with the other States, and others, which are either peculiar to them, or more abundant, or of better quality, than elsewhere. These productions, principally, are timber, flax, hemp, cotton, wool, raw silk, indigo, iron, lead, furs, hides, skins, and coal; of these articles, cotton and indigo are peculiar to the Southern States, as are hitherto lead and coal; flax and hemp are, or may be, raised in greater abundance there than in the more Northern States; and the wool of Virginia is said to be of better quality than that of any other State. . . .

. . . it is proper, in the next place, to consider the means by which it may be effected, as introductory to a specification of the objects, which, in the present state of things, appear the most fit to be encouraged, and of the particular measures which it may be advisable to adopt, in respect to each.

In order to a better judgment of the means proper to be resorted to by the United States, it will be of use to advert to those which have been employed with success in other countries. The principal of these are:

1. Protecting duties—or duties on those foreign articles which are the rivals of the domestic ones intended to be encouraged

Duties of this nature evidently amount to a virtual bounty on the domestic fabrics; since, by enhancing the charges on foreign articles, they enable the national manufacturers to undersell all their foreign competitors. . . .

2. Prohibitions of rival articles, or duties equivalent to prohibitions

This is another and an efficacious mean of encouraging national manufactures; but, in general, it is only fit to be employed when a manufacture has made such progress, and is in so many hands, as to insure a due competition, and an adequate supply on reasonable terms. Of duties equivalent to prohibitions, there are examples in the laws of the United States; and there are other cases to which the principle may be advantageously extended, but they are not numerous. . . .

   3. Prohibitions of the exportation of the materials of manufactures

The desire of securing a cheap and plentiful supply for the national workmen, and where the article is either peculiar to the country, or of peculiar quality there, the jealousy of enabling foreign workmen to rival those of the nation with its own materials, are the leading motives to this species of regulation. It ought not to be affirmed that it is in no instance proper; but is, certainly, one which ought to be adopted with great circumspection, and only in very plain cases. . . .

   4. Pecuniary bounties

This has been found one of the most efficacious means of encouraging manufactures, and is, in some views, the best. . . .

   [Lay] a duty on foreign manufactures of the material, the growth of which is desired to be encouraged, and . . . apply the produce of that duty, by way of bounty, either upon the production of the material itself, or upon its manufacture at home, or upon both. In this disposition of the thing, the manufacturer commences his enterprise under every advantage which is attainable, as to quantity or price of the raw material; and the farmer, if the bounty be immediately to him, is enabled by it to enter into a successful competition with the foreign material. . . .

   5. Premiums

These are of a nature allied to bounties, though distinguishable from them in some important features.

Bounties are applicable to the whole quantity of an article produced, or manufactured, or exported, and involve a correspondent expense. Premiums serve to reward some particular excellence or superiority, some extraordinary exertion or skill, and are dispensed only in a small number of cases. . . .

   6. The exemption of the materials of manufactures from duty

The policy of that exemption, as a general rule, particularly in reference to new establishments, is obvious. It can hardly ever be advisable to add the obstructions of fiscal burthens to the difficulties which naturally embarrass a new manufacture; and where it is matured, and in condition to become an object of revenue, it is, generally speaking, better that the fabric, than the material, should be the subject of taxation. . . .

7. Drawbacks of the duties which are imposed on the materials of manufactures

It has already been observed, as a general rule, that duties on those materials ought, with certain exceptions, to be forborne. Of these exceptions, three cases occur, which may serve as examples. One, where the material is itself an object of general or extensive consumption, and a fit and productive source of revenue. Another, where a manufacture of a simpler kind, the competition of which, with a like domestic article, is desired to be restrained, partakes of the nature of a raw material, from being capable, by a further process, to be converted into a manufacture of a different kind, the introduction or growth of which is desired to be encouraged. A third, where the material itself is a production of the country, and in sufficient abundance to furnish a cheap and plentiful supply to the national manufactures. . . .

8. The encouragement of new inventions and discoveries at home, and of the introduction into the United States of such as may have been made in other countries; particularly those which relate to machinery

This is among the most useful and unexceptionable of the aids which can be given to manufactures. The usual means of that encouragement are pecuniary rewards, and, for a time, exclusive privileges. The first must be employed according to the occasion and the utility of the invention or discovery. For the last, so far as respects "authors and inventors," provision has been made by law. But it is desirable, in regard to improvements, and secrets of extraordinary value, to be able to extend the same benefit to introducers, as well as authors and inventors; a policy which has been practised with advantage in other countries. . . .

9. Judicious regulations for the inspections of manufactured commodities

This is not among the least important of the means by which the prosperity of manufactures may be promoted. It is, indeed, in many cases, one of the most essential. Contributing to prevent frauds upon consumers at home and exporters to foreign countries, to improve the quality and preserve the character of the national manufactures, it cannot fail to aid the expeditious and advantageous sale of them, and to serve as a guard against successful competition from other quarters. The reputation of the flour and lumber of some States, and of the potash of others, has been established by an attention to this point. And the like good name might be procured for those articles, wheresoever produced, by a judicious and uniform system of inspection throughout the ports of the

United States. A like system might also be extended with advantage to other commodities.

10. The facilitating of pecuniary remittances from place to place

[It] is a point of considerable moment to trade in general, and to manufacturers in particular, by rendering more easy the purchase of raw materials and provisions, and the payment for manufactured supplies. A general circulation of bank paper, which is to be expected from the institution lately established, will be a most valuable means to this end. . . .

11. The facilitating of the transportation of commodities

Improvements favoring this object intimately concern all the domestic interests of a community; but they may, without impropriety, be mentioned as having an important relation to manufactures. There is, perhaps, scarcely anything which has been better calculated to assist the manufacturers of Great Britain than the melioration of the public roads of that kingdom, and the great progress which has been of late made in opening canals. Of the former, the United States stand much in need; for the latter, they present uncommon facilities.

The symptoms of attention to the improvement of inland navigation, which have lately appeared in some quarters, must fill with pleasure every breast warmed with a true zeal for the prosperity of the country. These examples, it is to be hoped, will stimulate the exertions of the government and citizens of every State. There can certainly be no object more worthy of the cares of the local administrations; and it were to be wished that there was no doubt of the power of the National Government to lend its direct aid on a comprehensive plan. This is one of those improvements which could be prosecuted with more efficacy by the whole than by any part or parts of the Union. There are cases in which the general interest will be in danger to be sacrificed to the collision of some supposed local interests. Jealousies, in matters of this kind, are as apt to exist as they are apt to be erroneous.

THOMAS JEFFERSON

Notes on Virginia (1785). *Writings of Jefferson*, II, 228-30.

The political economists of Europe have established it as a

principle, that every State should endeavor to manufacture for itself; and this principle, like many others, we transfer to America,
without calculating the difference of circumstance which should
often produce a difference of result. In Europe the lands are
either cultivated, or locked up against the cultivator. Manufacture
must therefore be resorted to of necessity not of choice, to support the surplus of their people. But we have an immensity of
land courting the industry of the husbandman. Is it best then that
all our citizens should be employed in its improvement, or that
one half should be called off from that to exercise manufactures
and handicraft arts for the other? Those who labor in the earth are
the chosen people of God, if ever He had a chosen people, whose
breasts He has made His peculiar deposit for substantial and
genuine virtue. It is the focus in which he keeps alive that sacred
fire, which otherwise might escape from the face of the earth.
Corruption of morals in the mass of cultivators is a phenomenon
of which no age nor nation has furnished an example. It is the
mark set on those, who, not looking up to heaven, to their own
soil and industry, as does the husbandman, for their subsistence,
depend for it on casualties and caprice of customers. Dependence
begets subservience and venality, suffocates the germ of virtue,
and prepares fit tools for the designs of ambition. This, the natural
progress and consequence of the arts, has sometimes perhaps been
retarded by accidental circumstances; but, generally speaking, the
proportion which the aggregate of the other classes of citizens
bears in any State to that of its husbandmen, is the proportion
of its unsound to its healthy parts, and is a good enough barometer
whereby to measure its degree of corruption. While we have
land to labor then, let us never wish to see our citizens occupied
at a workbench, or twirling a distaff. Carpenters, masons,
smiths, are wanting in husbandry; but, for the general operations
of manufacture, let our workshops remain in Europe. It is better
to carry provisions and materials to workmen there, than bring
them to the provisions and materials, and with them their
manners and principles. The loss by the transportation of commodities across the Atlantic will be made up in happiness and
permanence of government. The mobs of great cities add just
so much to the support of pure government, as sores do to the
strength of the human body. It is the manners and spirit of a
people which preserve a republic in vigor. A degeneracy in these
is a canker which soon eats to the heart of its laws and constitution.

Letter to John Jay, August 23, 1785. *Papers of Jefferson*, VIII, 426-27. Jay was secretary for foreign affairs.

I shall sometimes ask your permission to write you letters, not official but private. The present is of this kind, and is occasioned by the question proposed in yours of June 14 'Whether it would be useful to us to carry all our own productions, or none?' Were we perfectly free to decide this question, I should reason as follows. We have now lands enough to employ an infinite number of people in their cultivation. Cultivators of the earth are the most valuable citizens. They are the most vigorous, the most independant, the most virtuous, and they are tied to their country and wedded to its liberty and interests by the most lasting bands. As long therefore as they can find emploiment in this line, I would not convert them into mariners, artisans, or any thing else. But our citizens will find emploiment in this line till their numbers, and of course their productions, become too great for the demand both internal and foreign. This is not the case as yet, and probably will not be for a considerable time. As soon as it is, the surplus of hands must be turned to something else. I should then perhaps wish to turn them to the sea in preference to manufactures, because comparing the characters of the two classes I find the former the most valuable citizens. I consider the class of artificers as the panders of vice and the instruments by which the liberties of a country are generally overturned. However we are not free to decide this question on principles of theory only. Our people are decided in the opinion that it is necessary for us to take a share in the occupation of the ocean, and their established habits induce them to require that the sea be kept open to them, and that that line of policy be pursued which will render the use of that element as great as possible to them. I think it a duty in those entrusted with the administration of their affairs to conform themselves to the decided choice of their constituents: and that therefore we should in every instance preserve an equality of right to them in the transportation of commodities, in the right of fishing, and in the other uses of the sea. But what will be the consequence? Frequent wars without a doubt. Their property will be violated on the sea, and in foreign ports, their persons will be insulted, emprisoned &c. for pretended debts, contracts, crimes, contraband &c. These insults must be resented, even if we had no feelings, yet to prevent their eternal repetition. Or in other words, our commerce on the ocean and in other countries must be paid for by frequent war. The justest dispositions possible in ourselves will

not secure us against it. It would be necessary that all other
nations were just also. Justice indeed on our part will save us
from those wars which would have been produced by a contrary
disposition. But how to prevent those produced by the wrongs
of other nations? By putting ourselves in a condition to punish
them. Weakness provokes insult and injury, while a condition to
punish it often prevents it. This reasoning leads to the necessity
of some naval force, that being the only weapo[n] with which
we can reach an enemy. I think it to our interest to punis[h] the
first insult: because an insult unpunished is the parent of many
oth[ers]. We are not at this moment in a condition to do it, but
we should put ourselv[es] into it as soon as possible. If a war
with England should take place it see[ms] to me that the first
thing necessary would be a resolution to abandon the carrying
trade because we cannot protect it. Foreign nations must in that
case be invited to bring us what we want and to take our productions in their own bottoms. This alone could prevent the loss
of those productions to us and the acquisition of them to our
enemy. Our seamen might be emploied in depredations on their
trade. But how dreadfully we shall suffer on our coasts, if we
have no force on the water, former experience has taught us.
Indeed I look forward with horror to the very possible case of war
with an European power, and think there is no protection against
them but from the possession of some force on the sea. Our
vicinity to their West India possessions and to the fisheries is
a bridle which a small naval force on our part would hold in the
mouths of the most powerful of these countries. I hope our land
office will rid us of our debts, and that our first attention then will
be to the beginning a naval force of some sort. This alone can
countenance our people as carriers on the water, and I suppose
them to be determined to continue such.

Letter to James Madison, September 6, 1789. *Papers of
Jefferson*, XV, 392-97.

. . . I set out on this ground, which I suppose to be self
evident, *'that the earth belongs in usufruct to the living'*: that
the dead have neither powers nor rights over it. The portion
occupied by any individual ceases to be his when himself ceases
to be, and reverts to the society. If the society has formed no
rules for the appropriation of it's lands in severality, it will be
taken by the first occupants. These will generally be the wife

and children of the decedent. If they have formed rules of appropriation, those rules may give it to the wife and children, or to some one of them, or to the legatee of the deceased. So they may give it to his creditor. But the child, the legatee, or creditor takes it, not by any natural right, but by a law of the society of which they are members, and to which they are subject. Then no man can, by *natural right*, oblige the lands he occupied, or the persons who succeed him in that occupation, to the paiment of debts contracted by him. For if he could, he might, during his own life, eat up the usufruct of the lands for several generations to come, and then the lands would belong to the dead, and not to the living, which would be the reverse of our principle.

What is true of every member of the society individually, is true of them all collectively, since the rights of the whole can be no more than the sum of the rights of the individuals.—To keep our ideas clear when applying them to a multitude, let us suppose a whole generation of men to be born on the same day, to attain mature age on the same day, and to die on the same day, leaving a succeeding generation in the moment of attaining their mature age all together. Let the ripe age be supposed of 21. years, and their period of life 34. years more, that being the average term given by the bills of mortality to persons who have already attained 21. years of age. Each successive generation would, in this way, come on, and go off the stage at a fixed moment, as individuals do now. Then I say the earth belongs to each of these generations, during its course, fully, and in their own right. The 2d. generation receives it clear of the debts and incumberances of the 1st. the 3d of the 2d. and so on. For if the 1st. could charge it with a debt, then the earth would belong to the dead and not the living generation. Then no generation can contract debts greater than may be paid during the course of its own existence. At 21. years of age they may bind themselves and their lands for 34. years to come: at 22. for 33: at 23. for 32. and at 54. for one year only; because these are the terms of life which remain to them at those respective epochs.—But a material difference must be noted between the succession of an individual, and that of a whole generation. Individuals are parts only of a society, subject to the laws of the whole. These laws may appropriate the portion of land occupied by a decedent to his creditor rather than to any other, or to his child on condition he satisfies the creditor. But when a whole generation, that is, the whole society dies, as in the case we have supposed, and another generation or society succeeds, this forms a whole, and there is no superior who can give their territory to a third society, who may have lent money to their predecessors beyond their faculties of paying.

What is true of a generation all arriving to self-government on the same day, and dying all on the same day, is true of those in a constant course of decay and renewal, with this only difference. A generation coming in and going out entire, as in the first case, would have a right in the 1st. year of their self-dominion to contract a debt for 33. years, in the 10th. for 24. in the 20th. for 14. in the 30th. for 4. whereas generations, changing daily by daily deaths and births, have one constant term, beginning at the date of their contract, and ending when a majority of those of full age at that date shall be dead. The length of that term may be estimated from the tables of mortality, corrected by the circumstances of climate, occupation &c. peculiar to the country of the contractors. Take, for instance, the table of M. de Buffon wherein he states 23,994 deaths, and the ages at which they happened. Suppose a society in which 23,994 persons are born every year, and live to the ages stated in this table. The conditions of that society will be as follows. 1st. It will consist constantly of 617,703. persons of all ages. 2ly. Of those living at any one instant of time, one half will be dead in 24. years 8. months. 3dly. 10,675 will arrive every year at the age of 21. years complete. 4ly. It will constantly have 348,417 persons of all ages above 21. years. 5ly. And the half of those of 21. years and upwards living at any one instant of time will be dead in 18. years 8. months, or say 19. years as the nearest integral number. Then 19. years is the term beyond which neither the representatives of a nation, nor even the whole nation itself assembled, can validly extend a debt. . . .

. . . suppose Louis XV and his cotemporary generation had said to the money-lenders of Genoa, give us money that we may eat, drink, and be merry in our day; and on condition you will demand no interest till the end of 19. years you shall then for ever after recieve an annual interest of *12 5/8 per cent. The money is lent on these conditions, is divided among the living, eaten, drank, and squandered. Would the present generation be obliged to apply the produce of the earth and of their labour to replace their dissipations? Not at all.

I suppose that the recieved opinion, that the public debts of one generation devolve on the next, has been suggested by our seeing habitually in private life that he who succeeds to lands is required to pay the debts of his ancestor or testator: without considering that this requisition is municipal only, not moral; flowing from the will of the society, which has found it convenient to appropriate lands, become vacant by the death of their occupant, on the condition of a paiment of his debts: but that between society and society, or generation and generation, there is no municipal obligation, no umpire but the law of nature. We seem not to have percieved that, by the law of nature, one generation is to another as one independant nation to another.

The interest of the national debt of France being in fact but a two thousandth part of it's rent roll, the paiment of it is practicable enough: and so becomes a question merely of honor, or of expediency. But with respect to future debts, would it not be wise and just for that nation to declare, in the constitution they are forming, that neither the legislature, nor the nation itself, can validly contract more debt than they may pay within their own age, or within the term of 19. years? And that all future contracts will be deemed void as to what shall remain unpaid at the end of 19. years from their date? This would put the lenders, and the borrowers also, on their guard. By reducing too the faculty of borrowing within it's natural limits, it would bridle the spirit of war, to which too free a course has been procured by the inattention of money-lenders to this law of nature, that succeeding generations are not responsible for the preceding.

On similar ground it may be proved that no society can make a perpetual constitution, or even a perpetual law. The earth belongs always to the living generation. They may manage it then, and what proceeds from it, as they please, during their usufruct. They are masters too of their own persons, and consequently may govern them as they please. But persons and property make the sum of the objects of government. The constitution and the laws of their predecessors extinguished then in their natural course with those who gave them being. This could preserve that being till it ceased to be itself, and no longer. Every constitution then, and every law, naturally expires at the end of 19 years. If it be enforced longer, it is an act of force, and not of right. —It may be said that the succeeding generation exercising in fact the power of repeal, this leaves them as free as if the constitution or law had been expressly limited to 19 years only. In the first place, this objection admits the right, in proposing an equivalent. But the power of repeal is not an equivalent. It might be indeed if every form of government were so perfectly contrived that the will of the majority could always be obtained fairly and without impediment. But this is true of no form. The people cannot assemble themselves. Their representation is unequal and vicious. Various checks are opposed to every legislative proposition. Factions get possession of the public councils. Bribery corrupts them. Personal interests lead them astray from the general interests of their constituents: and other impediments arise so as to prove to every practical man that a law of limited duration is much more manageable than one which needs a repeal. . . .

Turn this subject in your mind, my dear Sir, and particularly as to the power of contracting debts; and develope it with that perspicuity and cogent logic so peculiarly yours. Your station in the councils of our country gives you an opportunity of producing it to public consideration, of forcing it into discussion. At first blush it may be rallied, as a theoretical speculation: but examination will prove it to be solid and salutary. It would furnish matter for a fine preamble to our first law for appropriating the public revenue; and it will exclude at the threshold of our new government the contagious and ruinous errors of this quarter of the globe, which have armed despots with means, not sanctioned by nature, for binding in chains their fellow men. We have already given in example one effectual check to the Dog of war by transferring the power of letting him loose from the Executive to the Legislative body, from those who are to spend to those who are to pay. I should be pleased to see this second obstacle held out by us also in the first instance. No nation can make a declaration against the validity of long-contracted debts so disinterestedly as we, since we do not owe a shilling which may not be paid with ease, principal and interest, within the time of our own lives.—

The Anas. *Writings of Jefferson,* I, 270-78.

I returned . . . in the first year of the new government, having landed in Virginia in December, 1789, and proceeded to New York in March, 1790, to enter on the office of Secretary of State. . . . Hamilton's financial system had then passed. It had two objects; 1st, as a puzzle, to exclude popular understanding and inquiry; 2d, as a machine for the corruption of the legislature; for he avowed the opinion, that man could be governed by one of two motives only, force or interest; force, he observed, in this country was out of the question, and the interests, therefore, of the members must be laid hold of, to keep the legislative in unison with the executive. And with grief and shame it must be acknowledged that his machine was not without effect; that even in this, the birth of our government, some members were found sordid enough to bend their duty to their interests, and to look after personal rather than public good.

It is well known that during the war the greatest difficulty we encountered was the want of money or means to pay our soldiers who fought, or our farmers, manufacturers and merchants, who furnished the necessary supplies of food and clothing for them. After the expedient of paper money had exhausted itself, certificates of debt were given to the individual creditors, with assurance of payment so soon as the United States should be able. But the distresses of these people often obliged them to part with these for the half, the fifth, and even a tenth of their value; and speculators had made a trade of cozening them from the holders by the most fraudulent practices, and persuasions that they would never be paid. In the bill for funding and paying these, Hamilton made no difference between the original holders and the fraudulent purchasers of this paper. Great and just repugnance arose at putting these two classes of creditors on the same footing, and great exertions were used to pay the former the full value, and to the latter, the price only which they had paid, with interest. But this would have prevented the game which was to be played, and for which the minds of greedy members were already tutored and prepared. When the trial of strength on these several efforts had indicated the form in which the bill would finally pass, this being known within doors sooner than without, and especially, than to those who were in distant parts of the Union, the base scramble began. Couriers and relay horses by land, and swift sailing pilot boats by sea, were flying in all directions. Active partners and agents were associated and employed in every State, town, and country neighborhood, and this paper was bought up at five shillings, and even as low as two shillings in the pound, before the holder knew that Congress had already provided for its redemption at par. Immense sums were thus filched from the poor and ignorant, and fortunes accumulated by those who had themselves been poor enough before. Men thus enriched by the dexterity of a leader, would follow of course the chief who was leading them to fortune, and become the zealous instruments of all his enterprises.

This game was over, and another was on the carpet at the moment of my arrival; and to this I was most ignorantly and innocently made to hold the candle. This fiscal manoeuvre is well known by the name of the Assumption. Independently of the debts of Congress, the States had during the war contracted separate and heavy debts; . . . and the more debt Hamilton could rake up, the more plunder for his mercenaries. This money, whether wisely or foolishly spent, was pretended to have been spent for general purposes, and ought, therefore, to be paid from the general purse. But it was objected, that nobody knew what these debts were, what their amount, or what their proofs. No matter; we will guess them to be twenty millions. But of these twenty millions, we do not known how much should be reimbursed to one State, or how much to another. No matter; we will guess. And so another scramble was set on foot among the several States, and some got much, some little, some nothing. But the main object was obtained, the phalanx of the Treasury was reinforced by additional recruits. This measure produced the most bitter and angry contest ever known in Congress, before or since the Union of the States. I arrived in the midst of it. But a stranger to the ground, a stranger to the actors on it, so long absent as to have lost all familiarity with the subject, and as yet unaware of its object, I took no concern in it.

The great and trying question, however, was lost in the House of Representatives. So high were the feuds excited by this subject, that on its rejection business was suspended. Congress met and adjourned from day to day without doing anything, the parties being too much out of temper to do business together. The eastern members particularly, who, with Smith from South Carolina, were the principal gamblers in these scenes, threatened a secession and dissolution. Hamilton was in despair. As I was going to the President's one day, I met him in the street. He walked me backwards and forwards before the President's door for half an hour. He painted pathetically the temper into which the legislature had been wrought; the disgust of those who were called the creditor States; the danger of the *secession* of their members, and the separation of the States. He observed that the members of the administration ought to act in concert; that though this question was not of my department, yet a common duty should make it a common concern; that the President was the centre on which all administrative questions ultimately rested, and that all of us should rally around him, and support, with joint efforts, measures approved by him; and that the question having been lost by a small majority only, it was probable that an appeal from me to the judgment and discretion of some of my friends, might effect a change in the vote, and the machine of government, now suspended, might be again set into motion. I told him that I was really a stranger to the whole subject; that not having yet informed myself of the system of finances adopted, I knew not how far this was a necessary sequence; that undoubtedly, if its rejection endangered a dissolution of our Union at this incipient stage, I should deem that the most unfortunate of all consequences, to avert which all partial and temporary evils should be yielded. I proposed to him, however, to dine with me the next day, and I would invite another friend or two, bring them into conference together, and I thought it impossible that reasonable men, consulting together coolly, could fail, by some mutual sacrifices of opinion, to form a compromise which was to save the Union.

The discussion took place. I could take no part in it but an exhortatory one, because I was a stranger to the circumstances which should govern it. But it was finally agreed, that whatever importance had been attached to the rejection of this proposition, the preservation of the Union and of concord among the States was more important, and that therefore it would be better that the vote of rejection should be rescinded, to effect which, some members should change their votes. But it was observed that this pill would be peculiarly bitter to the southern States, and that some concomitant measure should be adopted, to sweeten it a little to them. There had before been propositions to fix the seat of government either at Philadelphia, or at Georgetown on the Potomac; and it was thought that by giving it to Philadelphia for ten years, and to Georgetown permanently afterwards, this might, as an anodyne, calm in some degree the ferment which might be excited by the other measure alone. So two of the Potomac members (White and Lee, but White with a revulsion of stomach almost convulsive,) agreed to change their votes, and Hamilton undertook to carry the other point. In doing this, the influence he had established over the eastern members, with the agency of Robert Morris with those of the middle States, effected his side of the engagement; and so the Assumption was passed, and twenty millions of stock divided among favored States, and thrown in as a pabulum to the stock-jobbing herd. This added to the number of votaries to the Treasury, and made its chief the master of every vote in the legislature, which might give to the government the direction suited to his political views. . . .

. . . Still the machine was not complete. The effect of the funding system, and of the Assumption, would be temporary; it would be lost with the loss of the individual members whom it has enriched, and some engine of influence more permanent must be contrived, while these myrmidons were yet in place to carry it through all opposition. This engine was the Bank of the United States. . . .

Here then was the real ground of the opposition which was made to the course of administration. Its object was to preserve the legislature pure and independent of the executive, to restrain the administration to republican forms and principles, and not permit the constitution to be construed into a monarchy, and to be warped, in practice, into all the principles and pollutions of their favorite English model. Nor was this an opposition to General Washington. He was true to the republican charge confided to him; and has solemnly and repeatedly protested to me, in our conversations, that he would lose the last drop of his blood in support of it; and he did this the oftener and with the more earnestness, because he knew my suspicions of Hamilton's designs against it, and wished to quiet them. For he was not aware of the drift, or of the effect of Hamilton's schemes. Unversed in financial projects and calculations and budgets, his approbation of them was bottomed on his confidence in the man.

Letter to Thomas Leiper, January 21, 1809. *Writings of Jefferson*, XII, 207 08.

. . . You know that every syllable uttered in my name becomes a text for the federalists to torment the public mind on by their paraphrases and perversions. I have lately inculcated the encouragement of manufactures to the extent of our own consumption at least, in all articles of which we raise the raw material. On this the federal papers and meetings have sounded the alarm of Chinese policy, destruction of commerce, etc.; that is to say, the iron which we make must not be wrought here into ploughs, axes, hoes, etc., in order that the ship-owner may have the profit of carrying it to Europe, and bringing it back in a manufactured form, as if after manufacturing our own raw materials for our own use, there would not be a surplus produce sufficient to employ a due proportion of navigation in carrying it to market and exchanging it for those articles of which we have not the raw material. Yet this absurd hue and cry has contributed much to federalize New England, their doctrine goes to the sacrificing agriculture and manufactures to commerce; to the calling all our people from the interior country to the sea-shore to turn merchants, and to convert this great agricultural country into a city of Amsterdam. But I trust the good sense of our country will see that its greatest prosperity depends on a due balance between agriculture, manufactures and commerce, and not in this protuberant navigation which has kept us in hot water from the commencement of our government, and is now engaging us in war. . . .

Letter to John Melish, January 13, 1813. *Writings of Jefferson,*
XIII, 207-8. Melish, a Scot, had written favorably on his visit
to the United States.

. . . As to the Western States, particularly, it has greatly
edified me; for of the actual condition of that interesting portion
of our country, I had not an adequate idea. I feel myself now as
familiar with it as with the condition of the maritime States. I
had no conception that manufactures had made such progress
there, and particularly of the number of carding and spinning
machines dispersed through the whole country. We are but beginning here to have them in our private families. Small spinning
jennies of from half a dozen to twenty spindles, will soon, however,
make their way into the humblest cottages, as well as the richest
houses; and nothing is more certain, than that the coarse and
middling clothing for our families, will forever hereafter continue to be made within ourselves. I have hitherto myself
depended entirely on foreign manufactures; but I have now thirty-
five spindles agoing, a hand carding machine, and looms with the
flying shuttle, for the supply of my own farms, which will never
be relinquished in my time. The continuance of the war will fix
the habit generally, and out of the evils of impressment and of
the orders of council a great blessing for us will grow. I have
not formerly been an advocate for great manufactories. I doubted
whether our labor, employed in agriculture, and aided by the
spontaneous energies of the earth, would not procure us more than
we could make ourselves of other necessaries. But other considerations entering into the question, have settled my doubts.

Letter to Dr. Thomas Cooper, September 10, 1814. *Writings
of Jefferson,* XIV, 182-83.

And, first, we have no paupers, the old and crippled among
us, who possess nothing and have no families to take care of
them, being too few to merit notice as a separate section of society,
or to affect a general estimate. The great mass of our population
is of laborers; our rich, who can live without labor, either
manual or professional, being few, and of moderate wealth. Most
of the laboring class possess property, cultivate their own lands,
have families, and from the demand for their labor are enabled
to exact from the rich and the competent such prices as enable
them to be fed abundantly, clothed above mere decency, to labor
moderately and raise their families. They are not driven to the

ultimate resources of dexterity and skill, because their wares will sell although not quite so nice as those of England. The wealthy, on the other hand, and those at their ease, know nothing of what the Europeans call luxury. They have only somewhat more of the comforts and decencies of life than those who furnish them. Can any condition of society be more desirable than this? Nor in the class of laborers do I mean to withhold from the comparison that portion whose color has condemned them, in certain parts of our Union, to a subjection to the will of others. Even these are better fed in these States, warmer clothed, and labor less than the journeymen or day-laborers of England. They have the comfort, too, of numerous families, in the midst of whom they live without want, or fear of it; a solace which few of the laborers of England possess. They are subject, it is true, to bodily coercion; but are not the hundreds of thousands of British soldiers and seamen subject to the same, without seeing, at the end of their career, when age and accident shall have rendered them unequal to labor, the certainty, which the other has, that he will never want? And has not the British seaman, as much as the African, been reduced to this bondage by force, in flagrant violation of his own consent, and of his natural right in his own person? and with the laborers of England generally, does not the moral coercion of want subject their will as despotically to that of their employer, as the physical constraint does the soldier, the seaman, or the slave?

Letter to Benjamin Austin, January 9, 1816. *Writings of Jefferson,* XIV, 389-93.

You tell me I am quoted by those who wish to continue our dependence on England for manufactures. There was a time when I might have been so quoted with more candor, but within the thirty years which have since elapsed, how are circumstances changed! We were then in peace. Our independent place among nations was acknowledged. A commerce which offered the raw material in exchange for the same material after receiving the last touch of industry, was worthy of welcome to all nations. It was expected that those especially to whom manufacturing industry was important, would cherish the friendship of such customers by every favor, by every inducement, and particularly cultivate their peace by every act of justice and friendship. Under this prospect the question seemed legitimate, whether, with such an immensity of unimproved land, courting the hand of husbandry, the industry of agriculture or that of manufactures, would add most to the national wealth? And the doubt was entertained on this consideration chiefly, that to the labor of the husbandman a vast addition is made by the spontaneous energies of the earth on which it is employed: for one grain of wheat committed to the earth, she renders twenty, thirty, and even fifty fold, whereas to the labor of the manufacturer nothing is added.

. . . This was the state of things in 1785, when the "Notes on Virginia" were first printed; when, the ocean being open to all nations, and their common right in it acknowledged and exercised under regulations sanctioned by the assent and usage of all, it was thought that the doubt might claim some consideration. But who in 1785 could foresee the rapid depravity which was to render the close of that century the disgrace of the history of man? Who could have imagined that the two most distinguished in the rank of nations, for science and civilization, would have suddenly descended from that honorable eminence, and setting at defiance all those moral laws established by the Author of nature between nation and nation, as between man and man, would cover earth and sea with robberies and piracies, merely because strong enough to do it with temporal impunity; and that under this disbandment of nations from social order, we should have been despoiled of a thousand ships, and have thousands of our citizens reduced to Algerine slavery. Yet all this has taken place. One of these nations interdicted to our vessels all harbors of the globe without having first proceeded to some one of hers, there paid a tribute proportioned to the cargo, and obtained her license to proceed to the port of destination. The other declared them to be lawful prize if they had touched at the port, or been visited by a ship of the enemy nation. Thus were we completely excluded from the ocean. Compare this state of things with that of '85, and say whether an opinion founded in the circumstances of that day can be fairly applied to those of the present. We have experienced what we did not then believe, that there exist both profligacy and power enough to exclude us from the field of interchange with other nations: that to be independent for the comforts of life we must fabricate them ourselves. We must now place the manufacturer by the side of the agriculturist. The former question is suppressed, or rather assumes a new form. Shall we make our own comforts, or go without them, at the will of a foreign nation? He, therefore, who is now against domestic manufacture, must be for reducing us either to dependence on that foreign nation, or to be clothed in skins, and to live like wild beasts in dens and caverns. I am not one of these; experience has taught me that manufactures are now as necessary to our independence as to our comfort; and if those who quote me as of a different opinion, will keep pace with me in purchasing nothing foreign where an equivalent of domestic fabric can be obtained, without regard to difference of price, it will not be our fault if we do not soon have a supply at home equal to our demand, and wrest that weapon of distress from the hand which has wielded it. If it shall be proposed to go beyond our own supply, the question of '85 will then recur, will our *surplus* labor be then most beneficially employed in the culture of the earth, or in the fabrications of art? We have time yet for consideration, before that question will press upon us; and the maxim to be applied will depend on the circumstances which shall then exist; for in so complicated a science as political economy, no one axiom can be laid down as wise and expedient for all times and circumstances, and for their contraries. Inattention to this is what has called for this explanation, which reflection would have rendered unnecessary with the candid, while nothing will do it with those who use the former opinion only as a stalking horse, to cover their disloyal propensities to keep us in eternal vassalage to a foreign and unfriendly people.

The Jefferson Administrations

THOMAS JEFFERSON

Letter to Wilson Cary Nicholas, September 7, 1803. Nicholas, a senator from Virginia, had been a firm supporter of Jeffersonian construction of the Constitution, but he had second thoughts when the Senate was faced with the opportunity to purchase the immense Louisiana Territory. *Writings of Jefferson*, X, 418-20.

. . . Whatever Congress shall think it necessary to do, should be done with as little debate as possible, and particularly so far as respects the constitutional difficulty. I am aware of the force of the observations you make on the power given by the Constitution to Congress, to admit new States into the Union, without restraining the subject to the territory then constituting the United States. But when I consider that the limits of the United States are precisely fixed by the treaty of 1783, that the Constitution expressly declares itself to be made for the United States, I cannot help believing the intention was not to permit Congress to admit into the Union new States, which should be formed out of the territory for which, and under whose authority alone, they were then acting. I do not believe it was meant that they might receive England, Ireland, Holland, etc. into it, which would be the case on your construction. When an instrument admits two constructions, the one safe, the other dangerous, the one precise, the other indefinite, I prefer that which is safe and precise. I had rather ask an enlargement of power from the nation, where it is found necessary, than to assume it by a construction which would make our powers boundless. Our peculiar security is in the possession of a written Constitution. Let us not make it a blank paper by construction. I say the same as to the opinion of those who consider the grant of the treaty making power as boundless. If it is, then we have no Constitution. If it has bounds, they can be no others than the definitions of the powers which that instrument gives. It specifies and delineates the operations permitted to the federal government, and gives all the powers necessary to carry these into execution. Whatever of these enumerated objects is proper for a law, Congress may make the law; whatever is proper to be executed by way of a treaty, the President and Senate may enter into the treaty; whatever is to be done by a judicial sentence, the judges may pass the sentence. Nothing is more likely than that their enumeration of powers is defective. This is the ordinary case of all human works. Let us go on then perfecting it, by adding, by way of amendment to the Constitution, those powers which time and trial show are still wanting. . . . I confess, then, I think it important, in the present case, to set an example against broad construction, by appealing for new power to the people. If, however, our friends shall think differently, certainly I shall acquiesce with satisfaction; confiding, that the good sense of our country will correct the evil of construction when it shall produce ill effects.

Rules of Etiquette in Washington, November 7, 1803. *Writings of Jefferson*, XVII, 365-66. These rules were in striking constrast to the formalities which prevailed during the administrations of Washington and Adams.

i. In order to bring the members of society together in the first instance, the custom of the country has established that residents shall pay the first visit to strangers, and, among strangers, first comers to later comers. . . .

ii. When brought together in society, all are perfectly equal, whether foreign or domestic, titled or untitled, in or out of office.

All other observances are but exemplifications of these two principles. . . .

II. 1st. No title being admitted here, those of foreigners give no precedence.

2d. Differences of grade among diplomatic members, give no precedence.

3d. At public ceremonies, to which the government invites the presence of foreign ministers and their families, a convenient seat or station will be provided for them, with any other strangers invited and the families of the national ministers, each taking place as they arrive, and without any precedence.

Letter to Postmaster-General Gideon Granger, April 16, 1804. *Writings of Jefferson,* XI, 24. As a result of the successes of Jefferson's first administration the Federalists rapidly declined in influence. The remnant of the party retreated to a state rights position.

. . . The federalists know, that, *eo nomine* [by that name], they are gone forever. Their object, therefore, is, how to return into power under some other form. Undoubtedly they have but one means, which is to divide the republicans, join the minority, and barter with them for the cloak of their name. I say, *join the minority;* because the majority of the republicans not needing them, will not buy them. The minority, having no other means of ruling the majority, will give a price for auxiliaries, and that price must be principle. It is true that the federalists, needing their numbers also, must also give a price, and principle is the coin they must pay in. Thus a bastard system of federo-republicanism will rise on the ruins of the true principles of our revolution. And when this party is formed, who will constitute the majority of it, which majority is then to dictate? Certainly the federalists. . . .

Letter to Philip Mazzei, July 18, 1804. *Writings of Jefferson,* XI, 40.

. . . we pay seven or eight millions of dollars annually of our public debt, and shall completely discharge it in twelve years more. That done, our annual revenue, now thirteen millions of dollars, which by that time will be twenty-five, will pay the expenses of any war we may be forced into, without new taxes or loans. The spirit of republicanism is now in almost all its ancient vigor, five-sixths of the people being with us. Fourteen of the seventeen States are completely with us, and two of the other three will be in one year. . . .

Second Inaugural Address, March 4, 1805. *Writings of Jefferson,* III, 375-81.

On taking this station on a former occasion, I declared the principles on which I believed it my duty to administer the affairs of our commonwealth. My conscience tells me that I have, on every occasion, acted up to that declaration, according to its obvious import, and to the understanding of every candid mind.

In the transaction of your foreign affairs, we have endeavored to cultivate the friendship of all nations, and especially of those with which we have the most important relations. . . .

At home, fellow citizens, you best know whether we have done well or ill. The suppression of unnecessary offices, of useless establishments and expenses, enabled us to discontinue our internal taxes. These covering our land with officers, and opening our doors to their intrusions, had already begun that process of domiciliary vexation which, once entered, is scarcely to be restrained from reaching successively every article of produce and property. . . .

The remaining revenue on the consumption of foreign articles, is paid cheerfully by those who can afford to add foreign luxuries to domestic comforts, being collected on our seaboards and frontiers only, and incorporated with the transactions of our mercantile citizens, it may be the pleasure and pride of an American to ask, what farmer, what mechanic, what laborer, ever sees a tax-gatherer of the United States? These contributions enable us to support the current expenses of the government, to fulfil contracts with foreign nations, to extinguish the native right of soil within our limits, to extend those limits, and to apply such a surplus to our public debts, as places at a short day their final redemption, and that redemption once effected, the revenue thereby liberated may, by a just repartition among the states, and a corresponding amendment of the constitution, be applied, *in time of peace*, to rivers, canals, roads, arts, manufactures, education, and other great objects within each state. . . .

I have said, fellow citizens, that the income reserved had enabled us to extend our limits; but that extension may possibly pay for itself before we are called on, and in the meantime, may keep down the accruing interest; in all events, it will repay the advances we have made. I know that the acquisition of Louisiana has been disapproved by some, from a candid apprehension that the enlargement of our territory would endanger its union. But who can limit the extent to which the federative principle may operate effectively? The larger our association, the less will it be shaken by local passions; and in any view, is it not better that the opposite bank of the Mississippi should be settled by our own brethren and children, than by strangers of another family? With which shall we be most likely to live in harmony and friendly intercourse?

In matters of religion, I have considered that its free exercise is placed by the constitution independent of the powers of the general government. I have therefore undertaken, on no occasion, to prescribe the religious exercises suited to it; but have left them, as the constitution found them, under the direction and discipline of State or Church authorities acknowledged by the several religious societies. . . .

In giving these outlines, I do not mean, fellow citizens, to arrogate to myself the merit of the measures; that is due, in the first place, to the reflecting character of our citizens at large, who, by the weight of public opinion, influence and strengthen the public measures; it is due to the sound discretion with which they select from among themselves those to whom they confide the legislative duties; it is due to the zeal and wisdom of the characters thus selected, who lay the foundations of public happiness in wholesome laws, the execution of which alone remains for others; and it is due to the able and faithful auxiliaries, whose patriotism has associated with me in the executive functions.

During this course of administration, and in order to disturb it, the artillery of the press has been levelled against us, charged with whatsoever its licentiousness could devise or dare. These abuses of an institution so important to freedom and science, are deeply to be regretted, inasmuch as they tend to lessen its usefulness, and to sap its safety; they might, indeed, have been corrected by the wholesome punishments reserved and provided by the laws of the several States against falsehood and defamation; but public duties more urgent press on the time of public servants, and the offenders have therefore been left to find their punishment in the public indignation.

Nor was it uninteresting to the world, that an experiment should be fairly and fully made, whether freedom of discussion, unaided by power, is not sufficient for the propagation and protection of truth. . . .

Sixth Annual Message, December 2, 1806. *Writings of Jefferson*, III, 422-23.

. . . The question, therefore, now comes forward,—to what other objects shall these surpluses be appropriated, and the whole surplus of impost, after the entire discharge of the public debt, and during those intervals when the purposes of war shall not call for them? Shall we suppress the impost and give that advantage to foreign over domestic manufactures? On a few articles of more general and necessary use, the suppression in due season will doubtless be right, but the great mass of the articles on which impost is paid is foreign luxuries, purchased by those only who are rich enough to afford themselves the use of them. Their patriotism would certainly prefer its continuance and application to the great purposes of the public education, roads, rivers, canals, and such other objects of public improvement as it may be thought proper to add to the constitutional enumeration of federal powers. By these operations new channels of communication will be opened between the States; the lines of separation will disappear, their interests will be identified, and their union cemented by new and indissoluble ties. Education is here placed among the articles of public care, not that it would be proposed to take its ordinary branches out of the hands of private enterprise, which manages so much better all the concerns to which it is equal; but a public institution can alone supply those sciences which, though rarely called for, are yet necessary to complete the circle, all the parts of which contribute to the improvement of the country, and some of them to its preservation. . . .

Letter to the Representatives of the New Jersey Legislature, December 10, 1807. *Writings of Jefferson*, XVI, 296.

I perceive with sincere pleasure that my conduct in the chief magistracy has so far met your approbation, that my continuance in that office, after its present term, would be acceptable to you. But that I should lay down my charge at a proper period is as much a duty as to have borne it faithfully. If some termination to the services of the chief magistrate be not fixed by the Constitution, or supplied by practice, his office, nominally for years, will, in fact, become for life, and history shows how easily that degenerates into an inheritance. Believing that a representative government, responsible at short periods of election, is that which produces the greatest sum of happiness to mankind, I feel it a duty to do no act which shall essentially impair that principle; and I should unwillingly be the person who, disregarding the sound precedent set by an illustrious predecessor, should furnish the first example of prolongation beyond the second term of office.

Letter to Pierre Samuel Du Pont de Nemours, March 2,
1809. *Writings of Jefferson*, XII, 259-60.

. . . Within a few days I retire to my family, my books and
farms; and having gained the harbor myself, I shall look on my
friends still buffeting the storm with anxiety indeed, but not with
envy.   Never did a prisoner, released from his chains, feel such
relief as I shall on shaking off the shackles of power. Nature
intended me for the tranquil pursuits of science, by rendering
them my supreme delight.   But the enormities of the times in
which I have lived, have forced me to take a part in resisting
them, and to commit myself on the boisterous ocean of political
passions.   I thank God for the opportunity of retiring from them
without censure, and carrying with me the most consoling proofs
of public approbation. . . .

ALEXANDER HAMILTON

Letter to Oliver Wolcott, December 17, 1800. *Works of
Hamilton*, X, 393-97.

There is no circumstance which has occurred in the course
of our political affairs that has given me so much pain as the idea
that Mr. Burr might be elevated to the Presidency by the means
of the Federalists.   I am of opinion that this party has hitherto
solid claims of merit with the public, and so long as it does
nothing to forfeit its title to confidence, I shall continue to hope
that our misfortunes are temporary, and that the party will
erelong emerge from its depression.   But if it shall act a foolish
or unworthy part in any capital instance, I shall then despair.

Such, without doubt, will be the part it will act, if it shall
seriously attempt to support Mr. Burr, in opposition to Mr.
Jefferson. . . .

Trust me, my dear friend, you cannot render a greater
service to your country than to resist this project.   Far better
will it be to endeavor to obtain from Jefferson assurances on
some cardinal points:

1st. The preservation of the actual fiscal system.

2d. Adherence to the neutral plan.

3d. The preservation and gradual increase of the navy.

4th. The continuance of our friends in the offices they fill,
except in the great departments, in which he ought to be left
free.

Letter to James A. Bayard, January 16, 1801. *Works of Hamilton*, X, 412-13.

I admit that [Jefferson's] politics are tinctured with fanaticism; that he is too much in earnest in his democracy; that he has been a mischievous enemy to the principal measures of our past administration; that he is crafty and persevering in his objects; that he is not scrupulous about the means of success, nor very mindful of truth, and that he is a contemptible hypocrite. But it is not true, as is alleged, that he is an enemy to the power of the Executive, or that he is for confounding all the powers in the House of Representatives. It is a fact which I have frequently mentioned, that, while we were in the administration together, he was generally for a large construction of the Executive authority and not backward to act upon it in cases which coincided with his views. . . . Nor is it true that Jefferson is zealot enough to do any thing in pursuance of his principles which will contravene his popularity or his interest. He is as likely as any man I know to temporize—to calculate what will be likely to promote his own reputation and advantage; and the probable result of such a temper is the preservation of systems, though originally opposed, which, being once established, could not be overturned without danger to the person who did it. To my mind a true estimate of Mr. Jefferson's character warrants the expectation of a temporizing rather than a violent system. . . .

Letter to Gouverneur Morris, February 27, 1802. *Works of Hamilton*, X, 425-26.

Mine is an odd destiny. Perhaps no man in the United States has sacrificed or done more for the present Constitution than myself; and contrary to all my anticipations of its fate, as you know from the very beginning, I am still laboring to prop the frail and worthless fabric. Yet I have the murmurs of its friends no less than the curses of its foes for my reward. What can I do better than withdraw from the scene? Every day proves to me more and more, that this American world was not made for me.

Letter to Gouverneur Morris, March 4, 1802. *Works of Hamilton*, X, 427.

You have seen certain resolutions unanimously pass our Legislature for amending the Constitution; 1st, by designating separately the candidates for President and Vice-President; 2d, by having electors chosen by the people in districts under the direction of the national Legislature.

After mature reflection, I was thoroughly confirmed in my full impression, that it is true federal policy to promote the adoption of these amendments. . . .

Of the second, because it removes thus far the intervention of the State governments, and strengthens the connection between the Federal head and the people, and because it diminishes the means of party combination, in which also, the burning zeal of our opponents will be generally an overmatch for our temperate flame.

I shall be very happy that our friends may think with me, and that no temporary motive may induce them to let slip the precious occasion in which personal motives induce the other party to forget their true policy.

Letter to James A. Bayard, April, 1802. *Works of Hamilton*, X, 433-35.

. . . Men are rather reasoning than reasonable animals, for the most part governed by the impulse of passion. This is a truth well understood by our adversaries, who have practised upon it with no small benefit to their cause; for at the very moment they are eulogizing the reason of men, and professing to appeal only to that faculty, they are courting the strongest and most active passion of the human heart, *vanity!* It is no less true, that the Federalists seem not to have attended to the fact sufficiently; and that they erred in relying so much on the rectitude and utility of their measures as to have neglected the cultivation of popular favor, by fair and justifiable expedients. The observation has been repeatedly made by me to individuals with whom I particularly conversed, and expedients suggested for gaining good will, which were never adopted. Unluckily, however, for us, in the competition for the passions of the people, our opponents have great advantages over us; for the plain reason that the vicious are far more active than the good passions; and that, to win the former to our side, we must renounce our principles and our objects, and unite in corrupting public opinion till it becomes fit for nothing but mischief. Yet, unless we can contrive to take hold of, and carry along with us some strong feelings of the mind, we shall in vain calculate upon any substantial or durable results. . . . In my opinion, the present Constitution is the standard to which we are to cling. Under its banners, *bona fide*, must we combat our political foes, rejecting all changes but through the channel itself provides for amendments. By these general views of the subject have my reflections been guided. I now offer you the outline of the plan which they have suggested. Let an association be formed to be denominated "The Christian Constitutional Society." Its objects to be:

1st. The support of the Christian religion.

2d. The support of the Constitution of the United States. . . .

Letter to Rufus King, June 3, 1802. *Works of Hamilton*, X, 440.

Truly, my dear sir, the prospects of our country are not brilliant. The mass is far from sound. At headquarters a most visionary theory presides. Depend upon it, this is the fact to a great extreme. No army, no navy, no *active* commerce; national defence, not by arms, but by embargoes, prohibitions of trade, etc.; as little government as possible within;—these are the pernicious dreams which, as far and as fast as possible, will be attempted to be realized. Mr. Jefferson is distressed at the codfish having latterly emigrated to the southern coast, lest the people there should be tempted to catch them, and commerce, of which we have already too much, receive an accession. Be assured this is no pleasantry, but a very sober anecdote.

Letter to Charles Cotesworth Pinckney, December 29, 1802. *Works of Hamilton*, X, 445-46.

. . . Amidst the triumphant reign of democracy, do you retain sufficient interest in public affairs to fool any curiosity about what is going on? In my opinion, the follies and vices of the administration have as yet made no material impression to their disadvantage. On the contrary, I think the malady is rather progressive than upon the decline in our Northern quarter. The last *lullaby* message, instead of inspiring contempt, attracts praise. Mankind are forever destined to be the dupes of bold and cunning imposture. But a difficult knot has been twisted by the incidents of the cession of Louisiana, and the interruption of the deposit of New Orleans. You have seen the soft turn given to this in the message. Yet we are told that the President, in conversation, is very stout. The great embarrassment must be how to carry on the war without taxes. The pretty scheme of substituting economy to taxation will not do here. And a war would be a terrible comment upon the abandonment of the internal revenue. Yet how is popularity to be preserved with the Western partisans if their interests are tamely sacrificed? Will the artifice be for the chief to hold a bold language, and the subalterns to act a feeble part? Time must explain. You know my general theory as to our Western affairs. I have always held that the *unity of our empire* and the best interests of our nation require that we shall annex to the United States all the territory east of the Mississippi, New Orleans included. Of course I infer that, in an emergency like the present, energy is wisdom.

Article in New York *Evening Post*, July 5, 1803.

Purchase of Louisiana.—At length the business of New Orleans has terminated favorably to this country. . . . This, it will be allowed, is an important acquisition; not, indeed, as territory, but as being essential to the peace and prosperity of our Western country, and as opening a free and valuable market to our commercial states. This purchase has been made during the period of Mr. Jefferson's presidency, and will, doubtless, give éclat to his administration. Every man, however, possessed of the least candor and reflection will readily acknowledge that the acquisition has been solely owing to a fortuitous concurrence of unforeseen and unexpected circumstances, and not to any wise or vigorous measures on the part of the American government. . . .

. . . it may be said, and this probably is the most favorable point of view in which it can be placed, that although not valuable to the United States for settlement, it is so to Spain, and will become more so, and therefore at some distant period will form an object which we may barter with her for the Floridas, obviously of far greater value to us than all the immense, undefined region west of the river. . . .

. . . And when we consider the present extent of the United States, and that not one sixteenth part of its territory is yet under occupation, the advantage of the acquisition, as it relates to actual settlement, appears too distant and remote to strike the mind of a sober politician with much force. This, therefore, can only rest in speculation for many years, if not centuries to come, and consequently will not perhaps be allowed very great weight in the account by the majority of readers. But it may be added, that should our own citizens, more enterprising than wise, become desirous of settling this country, and emigrate thither, it must not only be attended with all the injuries of a too widely dispersed population, but by adding to the great weight of the western part of our territory, must hasten the dismemberment of a large portion of our country, or a dissolution of the government. On the whole, we think it may with candor be said, that whether the possession at this time of any territory west of the river Mississippi will be advantageous, is at best extremely problematical. . . .

Letter to Philip J. Schuyler, April 20, 1804. *Works of Hamilton*, X, 457.

I say nothing on politics, with the course of which I am too disgusted to give myself any future concern about them.

Letter to Theodore Sedgwick, July 10, 1804, the day before his fatal duel with Aaron Burr. *Works of Hamilton*, X, 458.

I will here express but one sentiment, which is, that dismemberment of our empire will be a clear sacrifice of great positive advantages without any counterbalancing good, administering no relief to our real disease, which is *democracy*, the poison of which, by a subdivision, will only be the more concentrated in each part, and consequently the more virulent. . . . God bless you.

Chapter II

THE AMERICAN SYSTEM
AND JACKSONIAN DEMOCRACY

HENRY CLAY

and

ANDREW JACKSON

Introduction

Conflicting ideas on the destiny of the United States in the second generation of its independence were illustrated by the attitudes and actions of Henry Clay and Andrew Jackson. Was the United States to be a powerful nation whose economic and physical needs would be met and conquered by the central government, or was it to be a federal system in which the basic domestic functions of government would be exercised by the states? Would the government have the authority to assist private enterprise in the development of industries important to the American people? Should the central government, in its quest for its proper role, seek the maximum power permissible, or the minimum power possible? Another basic issue was the role which the common man should play in his government.

One of the leading statesmen of the so-called "Silver Age" was Henry Clay. He was a man of strong opinions who labored ceaselessly to make his views prevail. He was also blessed with one of the most charming personalities ever to grace American politics. Even John C. Calhoun, who came to hate Clay's American System, could not hate Clay himself. "He is a bad man, an impostor, a creature of wicked schemes," Calhoun said; "I won't speak to him, but, by God, I love him."

Henry Clay was born in Virginia in 1777. His mother was widowed soon after his birth, and the boy knew considerable poverty. He had only three years of formal schooling, but his pleasing personality brought him the help and encouragement he needed to study and master law. He was admitted to the bar in 1797, and he then moved to Lexington, Kentucky, the area where he lived for the remainder of his life. He became an outstanding criminal lawyer whose clients were seldom convicted, thanks to his legal and oratorical mastery. He served for three years in the state legislature and for two brief tenures in the United States Senate (1806-1807, 1810-1811), but his national prominence came in 1811, when he moved to the House of Representatives because of his desire to be an "immediate representative of the people." He sat in that House from 1811 to 1814, 1815 to 1821, and 1823 to 1825, and he was Speaker of the House throughout his tenure, except for the year 1821. As Speaker and as leader of the War Hawks, those Western and Southern members of Congress who

115

demanded war with England, Clay was the leading figure in taking the United States into the War of 1812. He was also a member of the peace commission which negotiated an end to that war.

Angered at James Monroe for offering him only the appointment of Secretary of War rather than the more politically promising office of Secretary of State — then the stepping stone to the White House — Clay led the opposition to Monroe. He remained the leader of the opposition to one President or another for most of the rest of his life. He was stricken with Presidential ambitions and was an active candidate for the office in 1824, 1832, 1840, 1844, and 1848. In 1824 he settled for appointment as Secretary of State under John Quincy Adams. Most of the rest of his political life was spent in the Senate. He served there from 1831 to 1842 and from 1849 to 1852, the year of his death.

In 1824 he won the highest tariff yet imposed by the United States, but he was destined to see the bulk of his "American System" systematically upset by vetoes during the 1830's. Anticipating final victory in 1841, when a Whig became President, Clay was horrified once more to find himself in the opposition. William Henry Harrison died after only a month in office and was succeeded by the former Democrat John Tyler, a state-rights Virginian, who demolished Clay's program just as Jackson had.

Clay won lasting fame as "the Great Compromiser" for his leadership in three of the compromises which postponed sectional conflict: the Missouri Compromise of 1820, which set bounds for slavery in the Louisiana Purchase; the Compromise of 1833, which resulted in a tariff reduction which soothed South Carolina and caused it to rescind its nullification of the tariff of 1832; and the Compromise of 1850, which brought in California as a free state and temporarily assuaged sectional confict. Clay's winning ways made him especially well suited for the role of compromiser.

Andrew Jackson did not share Clay's view of the powers of the central government. Furthermore, he hated Henry Clay! He blamed Clay for slanders on his wife — and even, in part, for her death on the eve of Jackson's assumption of the Presidency in 1829—and for depriving him of the Presidency in 1824. Probably this hatred of Clay was as responsible as Jackson's view of the proper functions of government for his unceasing opposition to the Clay program, for Jackson was a man of passion and emotion.

He was born in 1767 in a backwoods area of South Carolina. Despite his moderate means, he practiced law in the 1790's and soon amassed sufficient property to become a Tennessee planter and gentleman lawyer. He was that state's first representative in Congress (1796) and was twice a United States Senator

(1797-1798 and 1823-1825), but he resigned all of these legislative positions after a very brief service. He was also a judge of the Tennessee Supreme Court from 1798 to 1804. Yet he remained basically a Tennessee planter and part-time militia leader until the War of 1812 made him a future President. His startling victory at New Orleans was one of the few victories about which Americans could boast, and the reputation of Andrew Jackson was established.

In 1824 Jackson became the "people's" candidate for President. As a war hero who had risen from the masses, he seemed the perfect candidate to win the support of the many new voters who were profiting at this time from the broad extension of the suffrage. During the decade after the War of 1812, new Western states entered the Union with democratic institutions, and several of the older states steadily democratized their own institutions, sometimes surpassing the Western states in the advancement of the principles of political democracy. The 1824 campaign was cynically managed for the sake of votes rather than for the asserted democratic ideals. Jackson gained a plurality of votes but was deprived of the Presidency by the House of Representatives, when the states supporting Henry Clay swung to John Quincy Adams, who had been second to Jackson both in popular and electoral votes. Speaker Clay was made Secretary of State after aiding in the election of Adams, and the Jackson men had the issue which they needed; the "Corrupt Bargain" issue swept them to victory in 1828. Although Jackson may at first have been an artificial democrat, in the course of his administrations he took up the cry of the people. Thus it is fitting that by the time he was elected his followers had dropped the "Jackson Men" label and become "Democrats." The common men remained faithful to Jackson to the end. In time he came to justify the sentiment of an admirer, exulting on his inauguration day, that "It was a proud day for the *people*—General Jackson is *their own* president!," and of Justice Joseph Story, who remarked gloweringly on the same day: "The reign of *King Mob* seemed triumphant."

Because Jackson had been elected for his personality rather than his program, it was not known where he would stand on the issues of the day. As a Senator in the 1820's he had supported the tariff and internal improvements, so Clay's followers had hopes; and as late as 1830, Calhoun hoped that Jackson would side with him on the issue of nullification. Both were disillusioned. As might be expected of a Southern slaveowner, Jackson was a consistent expansionist and was eager to extend the territorial bounds of the United States in whatever direction he could. And as might be expected of an old Indian fighter, he detested the Indians and did all in his power to remove them from the states, even going so far as to ignore—or nullify!—a ruling of the Supreme Court. Jackson was no theorist, but he did epitomize the arrival of the American common man as a political being. And he introduced a vast new authority into the executive branch of the United States government. Through judicious—though often passionate—use of the executive veto, his vast personal popularity, patronage in offices, and browbeating of Congress, he made the Presidency a much more powerful office than it was when he assumed it eight years before. The Jackson period also saw the re-establishment of a two-party system and the establishment of new political institutions to meet the needs of a changing electorate, the most notable being the nominating convention and the proliferation of "professional" politicians.

Recommended Readings
(Titles followed by an asterisk are available in paperback editions)

A book contrasting the ideas of Clay and Jackson is David Lindsey, *Clay/Jackson: Democracy and Enterprise.** Clay's papers are available in two editions edited by one of his contemporaries, Calvin Colton, but a new and "definitive" edition, *The Papers of Henry Clay,* has begun publication under the editorial guidance of James F. Hopkins. The *Correspondence of Andrew Jackson* has been edited in seven volumes by John Spencer Bassett. Many of Jackson's ideas are available in more convenient form in Harold C. Syrett, *Andrew Jackson: His Contribution to the American Tradition,* and in Joseph L. Blau, *Social Theories of Jacksonian Democracy: Representative Writings of the Period, 1825-1850.** Jackson is more a figurehead than a prominent figure in the latter, however. George R. Taylor, *Jackson versus Biddle—The Struggle over the Second Bank of the United States,** gives contrasting views on one important issue.

Clay has received scant attention from modern historians. The best recent studies are Glyndon G. Van Deusen, *The Life of Henry Clay,** and Clement Eaton, *Henry Clay and the Art of American Politics.** Jackson, on the other hand, has received much attention, and there are wide variances in the view taken of him and his associates. Notable works are Marquis James, *The Life of Andrew Jackson** (a splendidly readable biography which is sympathetic to Jackson); Arthur M. Schlesinger, Jr., *The Age* *of Jackson** (espies class conflict and roots of the New Deal in the Jackson era); Thomas Perkins Abernethy, *From Frontier to Plantation in Tennessee* (sees "arrant opportunism" rather than democracy as the key to understanding the West); Marvin Meyers, *The Jacksonian Persuasion: Politics and Belief,** and John W. Ward, *Andrew Jackson: Symbol for an Age** (both see Jackson's symbolic value in the attempt to regain a long-lost, and mythical, way of life); and Glyndon G. Van Deusen, *The Jacksonian Era, 1828-1848** (a mildly critical summary of the period). Good surveys of Jackson historiography are James L. Bugg, Jr., ed., *Jacksonian Democracy: Myth or Reality?** and Charles G. Sellers, "Andrew Jackson vs. the Historians," *Mississippi Valley Historical Review*, XLIV, 615-34.

Worthy studies of some of the significant issues of the day include Ralph C. H. Catterall, *The Second Bank of the United States;* Bray Hammond, "Jackson, Biddle, and the Bank of the United States," *Journal of Economic History*, VII, 1-23, and his *Banks and Politics in America, from the Revolution to the Civil War;* E. Malcolm Carroll, *Origins of the Whig Party;* Wilfred E. Binkley, *The Powers of the President: Problems of American Democracy;* Leonard D. White, *The Jacksonians: A Study of Administrative History, 1829-1861;* Chilton Williamson, *American Suffrage: From Property to Democracy, 1760-1860;* George R. Taylor, *The Transportation Revolution, 1815-1860;* Frederick Jackson Turner, *The Frontier in American History*;* Frank W. Taussig, *The Tariff History of the United States*;* and, of course, the classic on the Jacksonian era, Alexis de Tocqueville's *Democracy in America.**

Americanization of Industry

HENRY CLAY

Speech on Domestic Manufactures, U.S. Senate, March 26, 1810. James F. Hopkins, ed., *The Papers of Henry Clay* (Lexington, Ky., 1959—), I, 459-62.

In inculcating the advantages of domestic manufactures, it never entered the head, I presume, of any one to change the habits of the nation from an agricultural to a manufacturing society. No one I am persuaded ever thought of converting the plough share and the sickle into the spindle and shuttle. And yet this is the delusive view too often taken of the subject. The opponents of the manufacturing system transport themselves to the establishments of Manchester and Birmingham, and perceiving the indigence, vice and wretchedness prevailing there, by pushing it to an *extreme*, argue that its introduction into this country will be attended by the same mischievous consequences . . . . But if we *limit* our efforts by our own wants, the evils apprehended would be found to be chimerical.—The invention and improvement of machinery, for which the present age is so remarkable, dispensing in a great degree with manual labour; & the employment of those persons, who, if we are engaged in the pursuits of agriculture alone, would be either unproductive, or exposed to indolence and immorality, will enable us to supply our wants without withdrawing our attention from agriculture, that first and greatest source of our wealth and happiness. A judicious American farmer, in the household way, manufactures whatever is requisite for his family. He squanders but little in the gewgaws of Europe. He presents in epitome what the nation ought to do. Their manufactories ought to bear the same proportion, and effect the same object in relation to the whole community that the part of his household employed in domestic manufacturing does to the whole family. It is certainly desirable that the exports of the country should continue to be the surplus production of tillage, and not become those of manufacturing establishments. But it is important to diminish our imports—to furnish ourselves with clothing made by our own industry—and to cease to be dependent for the very coat we wear upon a foreign and perhaps inimical country. The nation that imports its cloathing from abroad is but little less dependent than if it imported its bread . . . .

Aid may be given to native institutions in the form of bounties and of protecting duties. But against bounties it is urged that you tax the *whole*, for the benefit of a *part* only, of the community; and in opposition to duties it is alledged that you make the interest of one part, the consumer, bend to that of another part, the manufacturer. The sufficiency of the answer is not always admitted, that the sacrifice is merely temporary, being ultimately compensated by the greater abundance and superiority of the article produced by the stimulus. . . .

Speech on the American System, U.S. House of Representatives, March 30-31, 1824.   Calvin Colton, *The Life, Correspondence, and Speeches of Henry Clay. In Six Volumes* (New York, 1857), V, 256-94.

Two classes of politicans divide the people of the United States. According to the system of one, the produce of foreign industry should be subjected to no other impost than such as may be necessary to provide a public revenue; and the produce of American industry should be left to sustain itself, if it can, with no other than that incidental protection, in its competition, at home as well as abroad, with rival foreign articles. According to the system of the other class, while they agree that the imposts should be mainly, and may under any modification be safely, relied on as a fit and convenient source of public revenue, they would so adjust and arrange the duties on foreign fabrics as to afford a gradual but adequate protection to American industry, and lessen our dependence on foreign nations, by securing a certain and ultimately a cheaper and better supply of our own wants from our own abundant resources.   Both classes are equally sincere in their respective opinions, equally honest, equally patriotic, and desirous of advancing the prosperity of the country. In the discussion and consideration of these opposite opinions, for the purpose of ascertaining which has the support of truth and reason, we should, therefore, exercise every indulgence, and the greatest spirit of mutual moderation and forbearance. And, in our deliberations on this great question, we should look fearlessly and truly at the actual condition of the country, retrace the causes which have brought us into it, and snatch, if possible, a view of the future. We should, above all, consult experience—the experience of other nations, as well as our own—as our truest and most unerring guide. . . .

What, again I would ask, is the CAUSE of the unhappy condition of our country, which I have faintly depicted? It is to be found in the fact, that during almost the whole existence of this government, we have shaped our industry, our navigation, and our commerce, in reference to an extraordinary war in Europe, and to foreign markets, which no longer exist; in the fact, that we have depended too much upon foreign sources of supply, and excited too little the native; in the fact that, while we have cultivated, with assiduous care, our foreign resources, we have suffered those at home to wither, in a state of neglect and abandonment. . . . It is most desirable that there should be both a home and a foreign market. But, with respect to their relative superiority, I can not entertain a doubt. The home market is first in order, and paramount in importance. The object of the bill under consideration, is, to create this home market, and to lay the foundations of a genuine American policy. It is opposed; and it is incumbent upon the partisans of the foreign policy (terms which I shall use without any invidious intent), to demonstrate that the foreign market is an adequate vent for the surplus produce of our labor. . . .

Our agriculture is our greatest interest. It ought ever to be predominant. All others should bend to it. And, in considering what is for its advantage, we should contemplate it in all its varieties, of planting, farming and grazing. Can we do nothing to invigorate it; nothing to correct the errors of the past, and to brighten the still more unpromising prospects which lie before us? We have seen, I think, the causes of the distresses of the country. We have seen, that an exclusive dependence upon the foreign market must lead to still severer distress, to impoverishment, to ruin. We must then change somewhat our course. We must give a new direction to some portion of our industry. We must speedily adopt a genuine American policy. Still cherishing the foreign market, let us create also a home market, to give further scope to the consumption of the produce of American industry. Let us counteract the policy of foreigners, and withdraw the support which we now give to their industry, and stimulate that of our own country. It should be a prominent object with wise legislators, to multiply the vocations and extend the business of society, as far as it can be done, by the protection of our interests at home, against the injurious effects of foreign legislation. . . .

The creation of a home market is not only necessary to procure for our agriculture a just reward for its labors, but it is indispensable to obtain a supply for our necessary wants. If we can not sell, we can not buy. That portion of our population (and we have seen that it is not less than four fifths), which makes comparatively nothing that foreigners will buy, has nothing to make purchases with from foreigners. It is in vain that we are told of the amount of our exports supplied by the planting interest. They may enable the planting interest to supply all its wants; but they bring no ability to the interests not planting; unless, which can not be pretended, the planting interest was an adequate vent for the surplus produce of the labor of all other interests. It is in vain to tantalize us with the greater cheapness of foreign fabrics. There must be an ability to purchase, if an article be obtained, whatever may be the price, high or low, at which it is sold. And a cheap article is as much beyond the grasp of him who has no means to buy, as a high one. Even if it were true that the American manufacturer would supply consumption at dearer rates, it is better to have his fabrics than the unattainable foreign fabrics; because it is better to be ill supplied than not supplied at all. A coarse coat, which will communicate warmth and cover nakedness, is better than no coat. The superiority of the home market results, first, from its steadiness and comparative certainty at all times; secondly, from the creation of reciprocal interest; thirdly, from its greater security; and, lastly, from an ultimate and not distant augmentation of consumption (and consequently of comfort), from increased quantity and reduced prices. But this home market, highly desirable as it is, can only be created and cherished by the PROTECTION of our own legislation against the inevitable prostration of our industry, which must ensue from the action of FOREIGN policy and legislation. . . . For, under all the modifications of social industry, if you will secure to it a just reward, the greater attractions of agriculture will give to it that proud superiority which it has always maintained. If we suppose no actual abandonment of farming, but, what is most likely, a gradual and imperceptible employment of population in the business of manufacturing, instead of being compelled to resort to agriculture, the salutary effect would be nearly the same. . . .

. . . Is there no remedy within the reach of the government? Are we doomed to behold our industry languish and decay yet more and more? But there is a remedy, and that remedy consists in modifiying our foreign policy, and in adopting a genuine American System. We must naturalize the arts in our country; and we must naturalize them by the only means which the wisdom of nations has yet discovered to be effectual; by adequate protection against the otherwise overwhelming influence of foreigners. This is only to be accomplished by the establishment of a tariff, to the consideration of which I am now brought.

And what is this tariff? It seems to have been regarded as a sort of monster, huge and deformed—a wild beast, endowed with tremendous powers of destruction, about to be let loose among our people, if not to devour them at least to consume their substance. But let us calm our passions, and deliberately survey this alarming, this terrific being. The sole object of the tariff is to tax the produce of foreign industry, with the view of promoting American industry. The tax is exclusively leveled at foreign industry. That is the avowed and the direct purpose of the tariff. If it subjects any part of American industry to burdens, that is an effect not intended, but is altogether incidental, and perfectly voluntary.

It has been treated as an imposition of burdens upon one part of the community by design, for the benefit of another; as if, in fact, money were taken from the pockets of one portion of the people and put into the pockets of another. But is that a fair representation of it? No man pays the duty assessed on the foreign article by compulsion, but voluntarily; and this voluntary duty, if paid, goes into the common exchequer, for the common benefit of all. Consumption has four objects of choice. First, it may abstain from the use of the foreign article, and thus avoid the payment of the tax. Second, it may employ the rival American fabric. Third, it may engage in the business of manufacturing, which this bill is designed to foster. Fourth, or it may supply itself from the household manufactures. . . .

The third objection to the tariff is, that it will diminish our navigation. This great interest deserves every encouragement, consistent with the paramount interest of agriculture. In the order of nature it is secondary to both agriculture and manufactures. Its business is the transportation of the productions of those two superior branches of industry. It can not therefore be expected, that they shall be molded or sacrificed to suit its purposes; but on the contrary, navigation must accommodate itself to the actual state of agriculture and manufactures. . . .

. . . I have very little doubt, with my colleague (Mr. Trimble), that the revenue will be increased considerably, for some years at least, under the operation of this bill. The diminution in the quantity imported will be compensated by the augmentation of the duty. . . . And then there are some other articles which will continue to be introduced in as large quantities as ever, notwithstanding the increase of duty, the object in reference to them being revenue, and not the encouragement of domestic manufactures. . . . Thus, by a postponement of the payment of the principal of the public debt, in which the public creditors would gladly acquiesce, and confiding, for the means of redeeming it, in the necessary increase of our revenue from the natural augmentation of our population and consumption, we may safely adopt the proposed measure, even if it should be attended (which is confidently denied) with the supposed diminution of revenue. We shall not, then, have occasion to vary the existing system of taxation; we shall be under no necessity to resort either to direct taxes or to an excise. . . . National wealth is the source of all taxation. And, my word for it, the people are too intelligent to be deceived by mere names, and not to give a decided preference to that system which is based upon their wealth and prosperity, rather than to that which is founded upon their impoverishment and ruin.

. . . In considering the fitness of a nation for the establishment of manufactures, we must no longer limit our views to the state of its population, and the price of wages. All circumstances must be regarded, of which that is, perhaps, the least important. Capital, ingenuity in the construction, and adroitness in the use of machinery, and the possession of the raw materials, are those which deserve the greatest consideration. All these circumstances (except that of capital, of which there is no deficiency) exist in our country in an eminent degree, and more than counterbalance the disadvantage, if it really existed, of the lower wages of labor in Great Britain. . . . Why should we fail? Nations, like men, fail in nothing which they boldly attempt, when sustained by virtuous purpose and firm resolution. I am not willing to admit this depreciation of American skill and enterprise. I am not willing to strike before an effort is made. All our past history exhorts us to proceed, and inspires us with animating hopes of success. Past predictions of our incapacity have failed, and present predictions will not be realized. . . . We are now, and ever will be, essentially an agricultural people. Without a material change in the fixed habits of the country, the friends of the measure desire to draw to it, as a powerful auxiliary to its industry, the manufacturing arts. The difference between a nation with and without the arts, may be conceived by the difference between a keel-boat and a steamboat, combating the rapid torrent of the Mississippi. . . . If I were to attempt to particularize the causes which prevent the success of the manufacturing arts, without protection, I should say that they are, first, the obduracy of fixed habits. No nation, no individual, will easily change an established course of business, even if it be unprofitable; and least of all is an agricultural people prone to innovation. With what reluctance do they adopt improvements in the instruments of husbandry, or in modes of cultivation!. . . Secondly, the uncertainty, fluctuation, and un-steadiness, of the home market, when liable to an unrestricted influx of fabrics from all foreign nations; and, thirdly, the superior advance of skill, and amount of capital, which foreign nations have obtained, by the protection of their own industry. From the latter or from other causes, the unprotected manufactures of a country are exposed to the danger of being crushed in their infancy, either by the design or from the necessities of foreign manufacturers. . . . From this view of the subject, it follows, that, if we would place the industry of our country upon a solid and unshakable foundation, we must adopt the protecting policy, which has everywhere succeeded, and reject that which would abandon it, which has everywhere failed.

. . . The best security against the demoralization of society is the constant and profitable employment of its members. The greatest danger to public liberty is from idleness and vice. If manufactures form cities, so does commerce. And the disorders and violence which proceed from the contagion of the passions, are as frequent in one description of those communities as in the other. There is no doubt but that the yeomanry of a country is the safest depository of public liberty. In all time to come, and under any probable direction of the labor of our population, the agri-cultural class must be much the most numerous and powerful, and will ever retain, as it ought to retain, a preponderating in-fluence in our councils. The extent and the fertility of our lands constitute an adequate security against an excess in manufactures, and also against oppression, on the part of capitalists, toward the laboring portions of the community.

. . . If we attempt to provide for the internal improvement of the country, the Constitution, according to some gentlemen, stands in our way. If we attempt to protect American industry against foreign policy and the rivalry of foreign industry, the Constitution presents an insuperable obstacle. This Constitution must be a most singular instrument! It seems to be made for any other people than our own. Its action is altogether foreign. Congress has power to lay duties and imposts, under no other limitation whatever than that of their being uniform throughout the United States. But they can only be imposed, according to the honorable gentleman, for the sole purpose of revenue. This is a restriction which we do not find in the Constitution. No doubt revenue was a principal object with the framers of the Constitution in investing Congress with the power. But, in executing it, may not the duties and imposts be so laid as to secure domestic interests? Or is Congress denied all discretion as to the amount or the distribution of the duties and imposts?

The gentleman from Virginia has, however, entirely mistaken the clause of the Constitution on which we rely. It is that which gives to Congress the power to regulate commerce with foreign nations. The grant is plenary, without any limitation whatever, and includes the whole power of regulation, of which the subject to be regulated is susceptible. It is as full and complete a grant of the power as that is to declare war. What is a regulation of commerce? It implies the admission or exclusion of the object of it, and the terms. Under this power some articles, by the existing laws, are admitted freely; others are subjected to duties so high as to amount to their prohibition, and various rates of duties are applied to others. Under this power, laws of total non-intercourse with some nations, embargoes, producing an entire cessation of commerce with all foreign countries have been, from time to time, passed. . . .

Mr. Chairman, our confederacy comprehends, with its vast limits, great diversity of interests: agricultural, planting, farming, commerical, navigating, fishing, manufacturing. No one of these interests is felt in the same degree, and cherished with the same solicitude, throughout all parts of the Union. Some of them are peculiar to particular sections of our common country. But all these great interests are confided to the protection of one government—to the fate of one ship—and a most gallant ship it is, with a noble crew. If we prosper, and are happy, protection must be extended to all; it is due to all. It is the great principle on which obedience is demanded from all. If our essential interests can not find protection from our own government against the policy of foreign powers, where are they to get it? We did not unite for sacrifice, but for preservation. The inquiry should be, in reference to the great interests of every section of the Union (I speak not of minute subdivisions), what would be done for those interests if that section stood alone and separated from the residue of the republic? If the promotion of those interests would not injuriously affect any other section, then every thing should be done for them, which would be done if it formed a distinct government. . . . The South entertains one opinion, and imagines that a modification of the existing policy of the country, for the protection of American industry, involves the ruin of the South. The North, the East, the West, hold the opposite opinion, and feel and contemplate, in a longer adherence to the foreign policy, as it now exists, their utter destruction. Is it true that the interests of these great sections of our country are irreconcilable with each other? Are we reduced to the sad and afflicting dilemma of determining which shall fall a victim to the prosperity of the other? Happily, I think, there is no such distressing alternative. If the North, the West, and the East, formed an independent State, unassociated with the South, can there be a doubt that the restrictive system would be carried to the point of prohibition of every foreign fabric of which they produce the raw material, and which they could manufacture? Such would be their policy, if they stood alone; but they are fortunately connected with the South, which believes its interests to require a free admission of foreign manufactures. Here then is a case for mutual concession, for fair compromise. The bill under consideration presents this compromise. It is a medium between the absolute exclusion and the unrestricted admission of the produce of foreign industry. It sacrifices the interest of neither section to that of the other; neither, it is true, gets all that it wants, nor is subject to all that it fears. . . .

Even if the benefits of the policy were limited to certain sections of our country, would it not be satisfactory to behold American industry, wherever situated, active, animated, and thrifty, rather than persevere in a course which renders us subservient to foreign industry? But these benefits are twofold, direct, and collateral, and, in the one shape or the other, they will diffuse themselves throughout the Union. All parts of the Union will participate, more or less, in both. As to the direct benefit, it is probable that the North and the East will enjoy the largest share. But the West and the South will also participate in them. Philadelphia, Baltimore, and Richmond, will divide with the northern capitals the business of manufacturing. The latter city unites more advantages for its successful prosecution than any other place I know, Zanesville, in Ohio, only excepted. And where the direct benefit does not accrue, that will be enjoyed of supplying the raw material and provisions for the consumption of artisans. Is it not most desirable to put at rest and prevent the annual recurrence of this unpleasant subject, so well fitted, by the various interests to which it appeals, to excite irritation and to produce discontent? Can that be effected by its rejection? . . . You think the measure injurious to you; we believe our preservation depends upon its adoption. Our convictions, mutually honest, are equally strong. What is to be done? I invoke that saving spirit of mutual concession under which our blessed Constitution was formed, and under which alone it can be happily administered. I appeal to the South—to the high-minded, generous, and patriotic South—with which I have so often co-operated, in attempting to sustain the honor and to vindicate the rights of our country. Should it not offer, upon the alter of the public good, some sacrifice of its peculiar opinions? Of what does it complain? A possible temporary enhancement in the objects of consumption. Of what do we complain? A total incapacity, produced by the foreign policy, to purchase, at any price, necessary foreign objects of consumption. In such an alternative, inconvenient only to it, ruinous to us, can we expect too much from southern magnanimity? The just and confident expectation of the passage of this bill has flooded the country with recent importations of foreign fabrics. If it should not pass, they will complete the work of destruction of our domestic industry. If it should pass, they will prevent any considerable rise in the price of foreign commodities, until our own industry shall be able to supply competent substitutes.

To the friends of the tariff I would also anxiously appeal. Every arrangement of its provisions does not suit each of you; you desire some further alterations; you would make it perfect. You want what you will never get. Nothing human is perfect. . . . I call, therefore, upon the friends of the American policy, to yield somewhat of their own peculiar wishes, and not to reject the practicable in the idle pursuit after the unattainable. Let us imitate the illustrious example of the framers of the Constitution, and always remembering that whatever springs from man partakes of his imperfections, depend upon experience to suggest, in future, the necessary amendments.

We have had great difficulties to encounter. First, the splendid talents which are arrayed in this House against us. Second, we are opposed by the rich and powerful in the land. Third, the executive government, if any, affords us but a cold and equivocal support. Fourth, the importing and navigating interest, I verily believe from misconception, are adverse to us. Fifth, the British factors and the British influence are inimical to our success. Sixth, long-established habits and prejudices oppose us. Seventh, the reviewers and literary speculators, foreign and domestic. And, lastly, the leading presses of the country, including the influence of that which is established in this city, and sustained by the public purse.

From some of these, or other causes, the bill may be postponed, thwarted, defeated. But the cause is the cause of the country, and it must and will prevail. It is founded in the interests and affections of the people. It is as native as the granite deeply imbosomed in our mountains. And, in conclusion, I would pray God, in his infinite mercy, to avert from our country the evils which are impending over it, and, by enlightening our councils, to conduct us into that path which leads to riches, to greatness, to glory.

Speech on the American System, U.S. Senate, February 2, 3, and 6, 1832. *Life, Correspondence, Speeches of Clay,* V, 440-86.

. . . If I were to select any term of seven years since the adoption of the present Constitution which exhibited a scene of the most wide-spread dismay and desolation, it would be exactly that term of seven years which immediately preceded the establishment of the tariff of 1824.

. . . If the term of seven years were to be selected, of the greatest prosperity which this people have enjoyed since the establishment of their present Constitution, it would be exactly that period of seven years which immediately followed the passage of the tariff of 1824.

. . . Under the operation of the American system, the objects which it protects and fosters are brought to the consumer at cheaper prices than they commanded prior to its introduction, or, than they would command if it did not exist. If that be true, ought not the country to be contented and satisfied with the system, unless the second proposition, which I mean presently also to consider is unfounded? And that is, that the tendency of the system is to sustain, and that it has upheld, the prices of all our agricultural and other produce, including cotton. . . .

I plant myself upon this fact, of cheapness and superiority, as upon impregnable ground. Gentlemen may tax their ingenuity, and produce a thousand speculative solutions of the fact, but the fact itself will remain undisturbed. . . .

Gentlemen have allowed to the manufacturing portions of the community no peace; they have been constantly threatened with the overthrow of the American system. From the year 1820, if not from 1816, down to this time, they have been held in a condition of constant alarm and insecurity. Nothing is more prejudicial to the great interests of a nation than unsettled and varying policy. . . . Let the country breathe, let its vast resources be developed, let its energies be fully put forth, let it have tranquillity, and my word for it, the degree of perfection in the arts which it will exhibit, will be greater than that which has been presented, astonishing as our progress has been. Although some branches of our manufactures might, and in foreign markets now do, fearlessly contend with similar foreign fabrics, there are many others yet in their infancy, struggling with the difficulties which encompass them. We should look at the whole system, and recollect that time, when we contemplate the great movements of a nation, is very different from the short period which is allotted for the duration of individual life. . . .

. . . the revenue ought to be reduced, so as to accommodate it to the fact of the payment of the public debt. And the alternative is, or may be, to preserve the protecting system, and repeal the duties on the unprotected articles, or to preserve the duties on unprotected articles, and endanger, if not destroy, the system. . . .

. . . It is quite probable that beneficial modifications of the system may be made without impairing its efficacy. But to make it fulfill the purposes of its institution, the measure of protection ought to be adequate. If it be not, all interests will be injuriously affected. . . .

ANDREW JACKSON

Letter to James Hamilton, Jr., June 29, 1828. John Spencer Bassett, ed., *Correspondence of Andrew Jackson* (Washington, D.C., 1927-35), III, 411.

I regretted to see the subject of a Tariff discussed under the strong feelings of political excitement that pervaded the whole nation, and congress. To regulate a Judicious tariff is a subject of great difficulty at all times, and ought to be discussed, with great calmness and due deliberation, with an eye to the prosperity of the whole Union, and not of any particular part[,] viewing the whole as one great family, and extending impartial Justice to every branch with feelings of mutual concession, extending to all equal benefits, and each bearing a Just portion of the burdens the Tariff may impose. Whether the late act will operate equally upon every section of the union, can only be tested by experience.

First Inaugural Address, March 4, 1829. James D. Richardson, ed., *A Compilation of the Messages and Papers of the Presidents* . . . (New York, 1897-1917), III, 1000.

With regard to a proper selection of the subjects of impost with a view to revenue, it would seem to me that the spirit of equity, caution, and compromise in which the Constitution was formed requires that the great interests of agriculture, commerce, and manufactures should be equally favored, and that perhaps the only exception to this rule should consist in the peculiar encouragement of any products of either of them that may be found essential to our national independence.

First Annual Message, December 8, 1829. *Messages of the Presidents*, III, 1012-13.

. . . I invite your attention to the existing tariff, believing that some of its provisions require modification.

The general rule to be applied in graduating the duties upon articles of foreign growth or manufacture is that which will place our own in fair competition with those of other countries; and the inducements to advance even a step beyond this point are controlling in regard to those articles which are of primary necessity in time of war. When we reflect upon the difficulty and delicacy of this operation, it is important that it should never be attempted but with the utmost caution. Frequent legislation in regard to any branch of industry, affecting its value, and by which its capital may be transferred to new channels, must always be productive of hazardous speculation and loss. . . .

The agricultural interest of our country is so essentially connected with every other and so superior in importance to them all that it is scarcely necessary to invite to it your particular attention. It is principally as manufactures and commerce tend to increase the value of agricultural productions and to extend their application to the wants and comforts of society that they deserve the fostering care of Government.

Second Annual Message, December 6, 1830. *Messages of the Presidents*, III, 1086-88.

The power to impose duties on imports originally belonged to the several States. The right to adjust those duties with a view to the encouragement of domestic branches of industry is so completely incidental to that power that it is difficult to suppose the existence of the one without the other. The States have delegated their whole authority over imports to the General Government without limitation or restriction, saving the very inconsiderable reservation relating to their inspection laws. This authority having thus entirely passed from the States, the right to exercise it for the purpose of protection does not exist in them, and consequently if it be not possessed by the General Government it must be extinct. Our political system would thus present the anomaly of a people stripped of the right to foster their own industry and to counteract the most selfish and destructive policy which might be adopted by foreign nations. This surely can not be the case. This indispensable power thus surrendered by the

States must be within the scope of the authority on the subject expressly delegated to Congress. . . .

It is an infirmity of our nature to mingle our interests and prejudices with the operation of our reasoning powers, and attribute to the objects of our likes and dislikes qualities they do not possess and effects they can not produce. The effects of the present tariff are doubtless overrated, both in its evils and in its advantages. By one class of reasoners the reduced price of cotton and other agricultural products is ascribed wholly to its influence, and by another the reduced price of manufactured articles. The probability is that neither opinion approaches the truth, and that both are induced by that influence of interests and prejudices to which I have referred. . . .

While the chief object of duties should be revenue, they may be so adjusted as to encourage manufactures. In this adjustment, however, it is the duty of the Government to be guided by the general good. Objects of national importance alone ought to be protected. Of these the productions of our soil, our mines, and our workshops, essential to national defense, occupy the first rank. Whatever other species of domestic industry, having the importance to which I have referred, may be expected, after temporary protection, to compete with foreign labor on equal terms merit the same attention in a subordinate degree.

The present tariff taxes some of the comforts of life unnecessarily high; it undertakes to protect interests too local and minute to justify a general exaction, and it also attempts to force some kinds of manufactures for which the country is not ripe. Much relief will be derived in some of these respects from the measures of your last session.

The best as well as fairest mode of determining whether from any just considerations a particular interest ought to receive protection would be to submit the question singly for deliberation. If after due examination of its merits, unconnected with extraneous considerations—such as a desire to sustain a general system or to purchase support for a different interest—it should enlist in its favor a majority of the representatives of the people, there can be little danger of wrong or injury in adjusting the tariff with reference to its protective effect. If this obviously just principle were honestly adhered to, the branches of industry which deserve protection would be saved from the prejudice excited against them when that protection forms part of a system by which portions of the country feel or conceive themselves to be oppressed. What is incalculably more important, the vital principle of our system—that principle which requires acquiescence in the will of the majority—would be secure from the discredit and danger to which it is exposed by the acts of majorities founded not on identity of conviction, but on combinations of small minorities entered into for the purpose of mutual assistance in measures which, resting solely on their own merits, could never be carried.

Fourth Annual Message, December 4, 1832. *Messages of the Presidents*, III, 1160-61.

I cannot too cordially congratulate Congress and my fellow-citizens on the near approach of that memorable and happy event— the extinction of the public debt of this great and free nation. . . .
. . . it is due, in justice to the interests of the different States, and even to the preservation of the Union itself, that the protection afforded by existing laws to any branches of the national industry should not exceed what may be necessary to counteract the regulations of foreign nations and to secure a supply of those articles of manufacture essential to the national independence and safety in time of war. If upon investigation it shall be found, as it is believed it will be, that the legislative protection granted to any particular interest is greater than is indispensably requisite for these objects, I recommend that it be gradually diminished, and that as far as may be consistent with these objects the whole scheme of duties be reduced to the revenue standard as soon as a just regard to the faith of the Government and to the preservation of the large capital invested in establishments of domestic industry will permit.
    That manufactures adequate to the supply of our domestic consumption would in the abstract be beneficial to our country there is no reason to doubt, and to effect their establishment there is perhaps no American citizen who would not for awhile be willing to pay a higher price for them. . . . Experience, however, our best guide on this as on other subjects, makes it doubtful whether the advantages of this system are not counterbalanced by many evils, and whether it does not tend to beget in the minds of a large portion of our countrymen a spirit of discontent and jealousy dangerous to the stability of the Union.

Paper read to the Cabinet, September 18, 1833. *Correspondence of Jackson*, V, 194.

. . . The misnamed American system is this British system of corrupt influence in Embryo. A Bank, with power over currency and commerce, over the people and their Representatives—a High Tariff to favor particular classes of capitalists and to accumulate revenue to be disbursed in jobs for the benefit of Politicians who shall have obtained controlling stations in the Government—may well be considered as forming a sure lodgement for a dangerous aristocratic influence in this country.

The President has felt it his duty to exert the power with which the confidence of his countrymen has clothed him in attempting to purge the Government of all sinister influences which have been incorporated with its administration. The system of favoritism in behalf of the monied classes masked under an unequal Tariff, in the name of protection; and the system of bargaining which appertained to the distribution of immense public revenues in jobs disguised under the name of internal improvements, have lost their hold on the Government. . . .

Internal Improvements

HENRY CLAY

Speech on internal improvements, U. S. House of Representatives, March 7, 1818. *Papers of Clay*, II, 449-63.

. . . On looking at the political condition of this country, we discover twenty local sovereignties, having charge of their interior concerns, and of whatever regards the rights of property and municipal regulation, and one great sovereignty, for the purpose of general defence, for the preservation of the public peace, and for the regulation of commerce, internal and external. These objects, for which the general government was established, ought to be constantly kept in view; and he would act contrary to the interest of his country who should deny to the constitution, the sheet-anchor of the national safety, that vigor which is necessary, in the exercise of its powers, to fulfil the purposes of its institution, and to carry this country to the high destiny which it is one day to reach.

In expounding the instrument, he said, constructions unfavorable to personal freedom, or those which might lead to great abuse, ought to be carefully avoided. But if, on the contrary, the construction insisted upon, was, in all its effects and consequences, beneficent; if it were free from the danger of abuse; if it promoted and advanced all the great objects which led to the confederacy; if it materially tended to effect that greatest of all those objects, the cementing of the Union, the construction was recommended by the most favorable considerations. . . . We were to look at the whole constitution; at the history of the times when it was adopted; at contemporaneous expositions; and, above all, at the great aim and object of its framers. And, he would say, he hoped, without giving just cause for alarm, that he would give to the constitution, in all that relates essentially to the preservation of this Union, a liberal construction. In cases, where the power is admitted to reside somewhere in the general government, but it was doubtful in which branch, he would contend, that it belonged to Congress, as the safest repository. He would not yield his assent to what, he feared, was the too fashionable and prevailing sentiment, that of aggrandizing the Executive branch, and disparaging the Legislative. . . .

Union, then, Mr. C. repeated, peace external and internal, and commerce, but most particularly union and peace were the great objects of the framers of this constitution, and should be kept steadily in view in the interpretation of any clause of it. . . .

. . . We, said he, are not legislating for this moment only, or for the present generation, or for the present populated limits of these states; but our acts must embrace a wider scope; reaching northwestwardly to the Pacific, and more southwardly to the river Del Norte. Imagine this extent of territory covered with sixty, or seventy, or an hundred millions of people. The powers which exist in this government now, will exist then, and those which will exist then exist now. . . .

But the gentleman had asked, would we make a road for ordinary purposes, under the power to make a military road? Yes, said Mr. C. I would. It is no objection to constructing a post road or military road, that it may also be used for the purpose of circulating the commodities of the country, for the purpose of travelling, or, in short, for any of the general purposes of commerce and of society

. . . He rested the power for which he contended on the provisions of the constitution, construed with a due and necessary regard to the objects with a view to which it was formed. We are not to look at that instrument, said he, with the eye of an ingenious advocate, who is seeking to screen from merited punishment a convicted felon. You are, said he, to take into view the great destinies of our country; to reflect, that the powers granted by the constitution are the same at all times; that they apply with precisely the same extent to a population of five as of fifty millions. You are to look to the great purposes for which the constitution was made. That of Union was the first and dearest object, to which the attention of the country was turned in all its deliberations; &, although I should be the last to deny that you are to find your power to do a particular act in the specific grants in the constitution, when you apply to them rules of construction, you are not to forget the purposes of the constitution, and the duties you are called on to fulfil, that of preserving union being one of the greatest magnitude. The facilitation of commerce among the several states being greatly promotive of that object, ought to receive our attention. The transportation of military force and means, for the preservation of internal tranquillity, or for repelling foreign aggression, being important to the execution of either of these duties, it ought to be provided for with a due forecast, by the construction of roads and of canals. To these purposes, and to the circulation of intelligence necessary to the existence of our government, it is indispensable that we should have them;

whilst, by so doing, no legitimate power of the state governments is intrenched upon, no attribute usurped—for to them is still left every municipal power, and every power essential to their sovereign characters as federative states.

Speech on internal improvements, U. S. House of Representatives, March 13, 1818. *Papers of Clay*, II, 473-87.

. . . I am a friend, said Mr. C. a true friend to state rights; but not in all cases as they are asserted. The states have their appointed orbit; so has the union; and each should be confined within its fair, legitimate and constitutional sphere. We should equally avoid that subtle process of argument which dissipates into air the powers of this government, and that spirit of encroachment which would snatch from the states powers not delegated to the general government. . . . No man deprecates more than I do, the idea of consolidation; yet, between separation and consolidation, painful as would be the alternative, he should greatly prefer the latter.

. . . in a new country the condition of society may be ripe for public works long before there is, in the hands of individuals, the necessary accumulation of capital to effect them; and, besides, there is generally, in such a country, not only a scarcity of capital, but such a multiplicity of profitable objects presenting themselves as to distract the judgment. Further, the aggregate benefit resulting to the whole society, from a public improvement may be such as to amply justify the investment of capital in its execution, and yet that benefit may be so distributed among different and distant persons as that they can never be got to act in concert. The Turnpike roads wanted to pass the Allegany mountains, and the Delaware and Chesapeake Canal are objects of this description. Those who would be most benefited by these improvements reside at a considerable distance from the scites [*sic*] of them; many of those persons never have seen and never will, see them. . . .

. . . Of all the modes in which a government can employ its surplus revenue, none is more permanently beneficial than that of internal improvement. Fixed to the soil, it becomes a durable part of the land itself, diffusing comfort and activity and animation on all sides. The first direct effect was on the agricultural community, into whose pockets came the difference in the expence of transportation between good and bad ways. . . .

Remarks on Maysville veto, Cincinnati, August 3, 1830. *Life, Correspondence, Speeches of Clay,* V, 409-13. Martin Van Buren, the "American Talleyrand," was a major foe of internal improvements at national expense.

I can not, therefore, consider the message as conveying the sentiments and views of the president. It is impossible. It is the work of his cabinet; and if, unfortunately, they were not practically irresponsible to the people of the United States, they would deserve severe animadversion for having prevailed upon the president, in the precipitation of business, and perhaps without his spectacles, to put his name to such a paper. . . . I never can peruse it without thinking of diplomacy, and the name of Talleyrand, Talleyrand, Talleyrand, perpetually recurring. It seems to have been written in the spirit of an accommodating soul, who, being determined to have fair weather in any contingency, was equally ready to cry out, good Lord, good devil. Are you for internal improvements? You may extract from the message texts enough to support your opinion. Are you against them? The message supplies you with abundant authority to countenance your views. . . .

. . . What is or is not a national road, the message supposes may admit of controversy, and is not susceptible of precise definition. The difficulty which its authors imagine, grows out of their attempt to substitute a rule founded upon the extent and locality of the road, instead of the use and purposes to which it is applicable. If the road facilitates, in a considerable degree, the transportation of the mail to a considerable portion of the Union, and at the same time promotes internal commerce among several States, and may tend to accelerate the movement of armies, and the distribution of the munitions of war, it is of national consideration. Tested by this, the true rule, the Maysville road was undoubtedly national. . . .

ANDREW JACKSON

First Annual Message, December 8, 1829. *Messages of the Presidents,* III, 1014-15.

After the extinction of the public debt it is not probable that any adjustment of the tariff upon principles satisfactory to the people of the Union will until a remote period, if ever, leave the Government without a considerable surplus in the Treasury beyond what may be required for its current service. . . . Considered in connection with the difficulties which have heretofore attended appropriations for purposes of internal improvement, and with those which this experience tells us will certainly arise whenever power over such subjects may be exercised by the General Government, it is hoped that [the surplus] may lead to the adoption of some plan which will reconcile the diversified interests of the States and strengthen the bonds which unite them. Every member of the Union, in peace and in war, will be benefited by the improvement of inland navigation and the construction of highways in the several States. Let us, then, endeavor to attain this benefit in a mode which will be satisfactory to all. That hitherto adopted has by many of our fellow-citizens been deprecated as an infraction of the Constitution, while by others it has been viewed as inexpedient. All feel that it has been employed at the expense of harmony in the legislative councils.

To avoid these evils it appears to me that the most safe, just, and federal disposition which could be made of the surplus revenue would be its apportionment among the several States according to their ratio of representation, and should this measure not be found warranted by the Constitution that it would be expedient to propose to the States an amendment authorizing it. I regard an appeal to the source of power in cases of real doubt, and where its exercise is deemed indispensable to the general welfare, as among the most sacred of all our obligations. Upon this country more than any other has, in the providence of God, been cast the special guardianship of the great principle of adherence to written constitutions. If it fail here, all hope in regard to it will be extinguished. That this was intended to be a government of limited and specific, and not general, powers must be admitted by all, and it is our duty to preserve for it the character intended by its framers. If experience points out the necessity for an enlargement of these powers, let us apply for it to those for whose benefit it is to be exercised, and not undermine the whole system by a resort to overstrained constructions. The scheme has worked well. It has exceeded the hopes of those who devised it, and became an object of admiration to the world. We are responsible to our country and to the glorious cause of self-government for the preservation of so great a good. The great mass of legislation relating to our internal affairs was intended to be left where the Federal Convention found it—in the State governments. Nothing is clearer, in my view, than that we are chiefly indebted for the success of the Constitution under which we are now acting to the watchful and auxiliary operation of the State authorities. This is not the reflection of a day, but belongs to the most deeply rooted convictions of my mind. I can not, therefore, too strongly or too earnestly, for my own sense of its importance, warn you against all encroachments upon the legitimate sphere of State sovereignty. Sustained by its healthful and invigorating influence the federal system can never fall.

Maysville Road veto, May 27, 1830. *Messages of the Presidents*, III, 1046-56.

GENTLEMEN: I have maturely considered the bill proposing to authorize "a subscription of stock in the Maysville, Washington, Paris, and Lexington Turnpike Road Company," and now return the same to the House of Representatives, in which it originated, with my objections to its passage. . . .

The constitutional power of the Federal Government to construct or promote works of internal improvement presents itself in two points of view—the first as bearing upon the sovereignty of the States within whose limits their execution is contemplated, if jurisdiction of the territory which they may occupy be claimed as necessary to their preservation and use; the second as asserting the simple right to appropriate money from the National Treasury in aid of such works when undertaken by State authority, surrendering the claim of jurisdiction. In the first view the question of power is an open one, and can be decided without the embarrassments attending the other, arising from the practice of the Government. Although frequently and strenuously attempted, the power to this extent has never been exercised by the Government in a single instance. It does not, in my opinion, possess it; and no bill, therefore, which admits it can receive my official sanction.

. . . although it is the duty of all to look to that sacred instrument [the Constitution] instead of the statute book, to repudiate at all times encroachments upon its spirit, which are too apt to be effected by the conjuncture of peculiar and facilitating circumstances, it is not less true that the public good and the nature of our political institutions require that individual differences should yield to a well-settled acquiescence of the people and confederated authorities in particular constructions of the Constitution on doubtful points. Not to concede this much to the spirit of our institutions would impair their stability and defeat the objects of the Constitution itself.

. . . such grants have always been professedly under the control of the general principle that the works which might be thus aided should be "of a general, not local, national, not State," character. A disregard of this distinction would of necessity lead to the subversion of the federal system. That even this is an unsafe one, arbitrary in its nature, and liable, consequently, to great abuses, is too obvious to require the confirmation of experience. It is, however, sufficiently definite and imperative to my mind to forbid my approbation of any bill having the character of the one under consideration. ... I am not able to view it in any other light than as a measure of purely local character; or, if it can be considered national, that no further distinction between the appropriate duties of the General and State Governments need be attempted, for there can be no local interest that may not with equal propriety be denominated national. It has no connection with any established system of improvements; is exclusively within the limits of a State, starting at a point on the Ohio River and running out 60 miles to an interior town, and even as far as the State is interested conferring partial instead of general advantages. ...

But although I might not feel it to be my official duty to interpose the Executive veto to the passage of a bill appropriating money for the construction of such works as are authorized by the States and are national in their character, I do not wish to be understood as expressing an opinion that it is expedient at this time for the General Government to embark in a system of this kind. . . .

. . . Without a well-regulated system of internal improvement this exhausting mode of appropriation is not likely to be avoided, and the plain consequence must be either a continuance of the national debt or a resort to additional taxes.

. . . The preservation and success of the republican principle rest with us. To elevate its character and extend its influence rank among our most important duties, and the best means to accomplish this desirable end are those which will rivet the attachment of our citizens to the Government of their choice by the comparative lightness of their public burthens and by the attraction which the superior success of its operations will present to the admiration and respect of the world. Through the favor of an overruling and indulgent Providence our country is blessed with general prosperity and our citizens exempted from the pressure of taxation, which other less favored portions of the human family are obliged to bear; yet it is true that many of the taxes collected from our citizens through the medium of imposts have for a considerable period been onerous. In many particulars these taxes have borne severely upon the laboring and less prosperous classes of the community, being imposed on the necessaries of life, and this, too, in cases where the burthen was not relieved by the consciousness that it would ultimately contribute to make us independent of foreign nations for articles of prime necessity by the encouragement of their growth and manufacture at home. They have been cheerfully borne because they were thought to be necessary to the support of Government and the payment of the debts unavoidably incurred in the acquisition and maintenance of our national rights and liberties. But have we a right to calculate on the same cheerful acquiescence when it is known that the necessity for their continuance would cease were it not for irregular, improvident, and unequal appropriations of the public funds? Will not the people demand, as they have a right to do, such a prudent system of expenditure as will pay the debts of the Union and authorize the reduction of every tax to as low a point as the wise observance of the necessity to protect that portion of our manufactures and labor whose prosperity is essential to our national safety and independence will allow? When the national debt is paid, the duties upon those articles which we do not raise may be repealed with safety, and still leave, I trust, without oppression to any section of the country, an accumulating surplus fund, which may be beneficially applied to some well-digested system of improvement.

Under this view the question as to the manner in which the Federal Government can or ought to embark in the construction of roads and canals, and the extent to which it may impose burthens on the people for these purposes, may be presented on its own merits, free of all disguise and of every embarrassment, except such as may arise from the Constitution itself. . . . In the best view of these appropriations, the abuses to which they lead far exceed the good which they are capable of promoting. They may be resorted to as artful expedients to shift upon the Government the losses of unsuccessful private speculation, and thus, by ministering to personal ambition and self-aggrandizement, tend to sap the foundations of public virtue and taint the administration of the Government with a demoralizing influence.

. . . if it is expected that the people of this country, reckless of their constitutional obligations, will prefer their local interest to the principles of the Union, such expectations will in the end be disappointed; or if it be not so, then indeed has the world but little to hope from the example of free government. When an honest observance of constitutional compacts can not be obtained from communities like ours, it need not be anticipated elsewhere, and the cause in which there has been so much martyrdom, and from which so much was expected by the friends of liberty, may be abandoned, and the degrading truth that man is unfit for self-government admitted. And this will be the case if *expediency* be made a rule of construction in interpreting the Constitution. Power in no government could desire a better shield for the insidious advances which it is ever ready to make upon the checks that are designed to restrain its action.

But I do not entertain such gloomy apprehensions. If it be the wish of the people that the construction of roads and canals should be conducted by the Federal Government, it is not only highly expedient, but indispensably necessary, that a previous amendment of the Constitution, delegating the necessary power and defining and restricting its exercise with reference to the sovereignty of the States, should be made. Without it nothing extensively useful can be effected. . . .

If it be the desire of the people that the agency of the Federal Government should be confined to the appropriation of money in aid of such undertakings, in virtue of State authorities, then the occasion, the manner, and the extent of the appropriations should be made the subject of constitutional regulation. This is the more necessary in order that they may be equitable among the several States, promote harmony between different sections of the Union and their representatives, preserve other parts of the Constitution from being undermined by the exercise of doubtful powers or the too great extension of those which are not so, and protect the whole subject against the deleterious influence of combinations to carry by concert measures which, considered by themselves, might meet but little countenance. . . .

A supposed connection between appropriations for internal improvements and the system of protecting duties, growing out of the anxieties of those more immediately interested in their success, has given rise to suggestions which it is proper I should notice on this occasion. My opinions on these subjects have never been concealed from those who had a right to know them. . . .

As long as the encouragment of domestic manufactures is directed to national ends it shall receive from me a temperate but steady support. There is no necessary connection between it and the system of appropriations.

Second Annual Message, December 6, 1830. *Messages of the Presidents*, III, 1072-73.

In speaking of direct appropriations I mean not to include a practice which has obtained to some extent, and to which I have in one instance, in a different capacity, given my assent—

that of subscribing to the stock of private associations. Positive experience and a more thorough consideration of the subject have convinced me of the impropriety as well as inexpediency of such investments. All improvements effected by the funds of the nation for general use should be open to the enjoyment of all our fellow-citizens, exempt from the payment of tolls or any imposition of that character. The practice of thus mingling the concerns of the Government with those of the States or of individuals is inconsistent with the object of its institution and highly impolitic. The successful operation of the federal system can only be preserved by confining it to the few and simple, but yet important, objects for which it was designed.

. . . The interests of the nation would doubtless be better served by avoiding all such indirect modes of aiding particular objects. In a government like ours more especially should all public acts be, as far as practicable, simple, undisguised, and intelligible, that they may become fit subjects for the approbation or animadversion of the people.

Letter to Amos Kendall, Washington, D.C., July 23, 1832. *Correspondence of Jackson*, IV, 465.

My Dear Sir: I am off this morning; the *veto works well*. I wish you to look at the Harbor Bill, and compare it with my veto message on the Maysville Road Bill, and my message to Congress in 1830. I have left a report on the items in the bill, from which you will find that many are local and useless; few that are National. I am determined in my message if I live to make one to Congress, to put an end to this waste of public money, and to appropriations for internal improvements, until a system be adopted by Congress, and an amendment of the Constitution; in short to stop this corrupt, log-rolling system of legislation. . . .

Fourth Annual Message, December 4, 1832. *Messages of the Presidents*, III, 1165-66.

Being solemnly impressed with the conviction that the extension of the power to make internal improvements beyond the limit I have suggested, even if it be deemed constitutional, is subversive of the best interest of our country, I earnestly recommend to Congress to refrain from its exercise in doubtful cases, except in relation to improvements already begun, unless they shall first procure from the States such an amendment of the Constitution as will define its character and prescribe its bounds. If the States feel themselves competent to these objects, why should this government wish to assume the power? If they do not, then they will not hesitate to make the grant. Both Governments are the Governments of the people; improvements must be made with the money of the people, and if the money can be collected and applied by those more simple and economical political machines, the State governments, it will unquestionably be safer and better for the people than to add to the splendor, the patronage, and the power of the General Government. But if the people of the several States think otherwise they will amend the Constitution, and in their decision all ought cheerfully to acquiesce.

Sixth Annual Message, December 1, 1834. *Messages of the Presidents*, III, 1337-42.

. . . against the dangers of unconstitutional acts which, instead of menacing the vengeance of offended authority, proffer local advantages and bring in their train the patronage of the Government, we are, I fear, not so safe. To suppose that because our Government has been instituted for the benefit of the people it must therefore have the power to do whatever may seem to conduce to the public good is an error into which even honest minds are too apt to fall. . . .

I am not hostile to internal improvements, and wish to see them extended to every part of the country. But I am fully persuaded, if they are not commenced in a proper manner, confined to proper objects, and conducted under an authority generally conceded to be rightful, that a successful prosecution of them can not be reasonably expected. The attempt will meet with resistance where it might otherwise receive support, and instead of strengthening the bonds of our Confederacy it will only multiply and aggravate the causes of disunion.

The National Bank

HENRY CLAY

Speech on bill to recharter the Bank of the United States, U. S. Senate, February 15, 1811. *Papers of Clay,* I, 530-38.

I contend that the states have the exclusive power to regulate contracts, to declare the capacities and incapacities to contract, and to provide as to the extent of responsibility of debtors to their creditors. If Congress have the power to erect an artificial body and say it shall be endowed with the attributes of an individual—if you can bestow on this object of your creation the ability to contract, may you not, in contravention of state rights, confer upon slaves, infants and femes covert, the ability to contract? And if you have the power to say that an association of individuals shall be responsible for their debts only in a certain limited degree, what is to prevent an extension of a similar exemption to individuals? Where is the limitation upon this power to set up corporations? . . .

It is urged by the gentleman from Massachusetts (Mr. Lloyd) that as this nation progresses in commerce, wealth, and population, new energies will be unfolded, new wants and exigencies will arise, and hence he infers that powers must be implied from the constitution. But, sir, the question is shall we stretch the instrument to embrace cases not fairly within its scope, or shall we resort to that remedy, by amendment, which the constitution prescribes? . . .

This doctrine of precedents, applied to the legislature, appears to me to be fraught with the most mischievous consequences. The great advantage of our system of government over all others, is, that we have a *written* constitution defining its limits, and prescribing its authorities; and that, however, for a time, faction may convulse the nation, and passion and party prejudice sway its functionaries, the season of reflection will recur, when calmly retracing their deeds, all aberrations from fundamental principle will be corrected. But once substitute *practice* for principle— the expositions of the constitution for the text of the constitution, and in vain shall we look for the instrument in the instrument itself! . . .

I conceive then, sir, that we are not empowered by the constitution, nor bound by any practice under it, to renew the charter of this bank. . . .

Speech on the Bank of the United States, Lexington, Kentucky, June 3, 1816. *Papers of Clay*, II, 201-4.

The constructive powers being auxiliary to the specifically granted powers, and depending for their sanction and existence, upon a necessity to give effect to the latter, which necessity is to be sought for and ascertained by a sound and honest discretion, it is manifest that this necessity may not be perceived, at one time, under one state of things, when it is perceived at another time, under a different state of things. The constitution, it is true, never changes; it is always the same; but the force of circumstances and the lights of experience, may evolve to the fallible persons, charged with its administration, the fitness and necessity of a particular exercise of constructive power to day, which they did not see at a former period. . . .

Considering then, that the state of the currency was such that no thinking man could contemplate it without the most serious alarm, that it threatened general distress, if it did not ultimately lead to convulsion and subversion of the government, it appeared to him to be the duty of Congress to apply a remedy, if a remedy could be devised. A National Bank, with other auxiliary measures was proposed as that remedy. [And] looking at the subject with the light shed upon it by events happening since the commencement of the war he could no longer doubt. A Bank appeared to him not only necessary, but indispensibly necessary, in connexion with another measure, to remedy the evils of which all were but too sensible. He preferred to the suggestions of the pride of consistency, the evident interests of the community, and determined to throw himself upon their candor and justice. That which appeared to him in 1811, under the state of things then existing, not to be necessary to the general government, seemed now to be necessary, under the present state of things. Had he then foreseen what now exists, and no objection had laid against the renewal of the charter other than that derived from the constitution, he should have voted for the renewal. . . .

If the constitution then warranted the establishment of a bank, other considerations besides those already mentioned strongly urged it. The want of a general medium is every where felt. Exchange varies continually not only between different parts of the Union, but between different parts of the same state, and even different parts of the same city. If the paper of a National Bank were not redeemed in specie, it would be much better than the current paper, since although its value in comparison with specie might fluctuate, it would afford an uniform standard. . . .

Campaign Speech at Sandersville, Kentucky, July 25, 1816. *Papers of Clay*, II, 218-19.

. . . a national bank is necessary to enable the government to transact its business without loss, to restore confidence to the country and keep within the bounds of duty & propriety the multitudes of little monied institutions. It has been said, that I considered the constitution a pliant thing, which may be made to conform itself to the necessity of the times or the conveniance of those in power. I spurn the idea. The Constitution is *immutable;* but we may really and honestly change our opinion about its constructive powers. It is I who have changed and not the Constitution. The bank was just as constitutional in 1811 as at the present moment; but I did not then think so. The reasons for my change of opinion I have several times laid before my constituents and if you are not satisfied that I have acted correctly, then turn me out. . . .

In McCulloch *v.* Maryland, decided in 1819, the Supreme Court of the United States unanimously upheld the constitutionality of the Second Bank of the United States and declared unconstitutional a Maryland law taxing the Baltimore branch of the bank. Chief Justice John Marshall delivered the opinion of the court. McCulloch *v.* Maryland, 4 *Wheaton* 401-21.

The first question made in this cause is, has Congress power to incorporate a bank?

It has been truly said, that this can scarcely be considered as an open question, entirely unprejudiced by the former proceedings of the nation respecting it. The principle now contested was introduced at a very early period of our history, has been recognized by many successive legislatures, and has been acted upon by the judicial department, in cases of peculiar delicacy, as a law of undoubted obligation. . . .

In discussing this question, the counsel for the State of Maryland have deemed it of some importance, in the construction of the constitution, to consider that instrument not as emanating from the people, but as the act of sovereign and independent States. The powers of the general government, it has been said, are delegated by the States, who alone are truly sovereign; and must be exercised in subordination to the States, who alone possess supreme dominion.

It would be difficult to sustain this proposition. The convention which framed the constitution was, indeed, elected by the State legislatures. But the instrument, when it came from their hands, was a mere proposal, without obligation, or pretensions to it. It was reported to the then existing Congress of the United States, with a request that it might "be submitted to a convention of Delegates, chosen in each State, by the people thereof, under the recommendation of its legislature, for their assent and ratification." This mode of proceeding was adopted; and by the Convention, by Congress, and by the State Legislatures, the instrument was submitted to the people. They acted upon it, in the only manner in which they can act safely, effectively, and wisely, on such a subject, by assembling in Convention. It is true, they assembled in their several States—and where else should they have assembled? No political dreamer was ever wild enough to think of breaking down the lines which separate the States, and of compounding the American people into one common mass. Of consequence, when they act, they act in their States. But the measures they adopt do not, on that account, cease to be the measures of the people themselves, or become the measures of the state governments. . . .

The government of the Union, then (whatever may be the influence of this fact on the case), is emphatically and truly a government of the people. In form and in substance it emanates from them, its powers are granted by them, and are to be exercised directly on them, and for their benefit.

This government is acknowledged by all to be one of enumerated powers. The principle, that it can exercise only the powers granted to it, would seem too apparent to have required to be enforced by all those arguments which its enlightened friends, while it was depending before the people, found it necessary to urge. That principle is now universally admitted. But the question respecting the extent of the powers actually granted, is perpetually arising, and will probably continue to arise, as long as our system shall exist. In discussing these questions, the conflicting powers of the State and general governments must be brought into view, and the supremacy of their respective laws, when they are in opposition, must be settled. . . .

The government of the United States, then, though limited in its powers, is supreme; and its laws, when made in pursuance of the constitution, form the supreme law of the land, "anything in the constitution or laws of any State, to the contrary, notwithstanding."

Among the enumerated powers, we do not find that of establishing a bank or creating a corporation. But there is no phrase in the instrument which, like the articles of confederation, excludes incidental or implied powers; and which requires that everything granted shall be expressly and minutely described. Even the 10th amendment, which was framed for the purpose of quieting the excessive jealousies which had been excited, omits the word "expressly," and declares only that the powers "not delegated to the United States, nor prohibited to the States, are reserved to the States or to the people;" thus leaving the question, whether the particular power which may become the subject of contest has been delegated to the one government, or prohibited to the other, to depend on a fair construction of the whole instrument. The men who drew and adopted this amendment had experienced the embarrassments resulting from the insertion of this word in the articles of confederation, and probably omitted it to avoid those embarrassments. A constitution, to contain an accurate detail of all the subdivisions of which its great powers will admit, and of all the means by which they may be carried into execution, would partake of the prolixity of a legal code, and could scarcely be embraced by the human mind. It would probably never be understood by the public. Its nature, therefore, requires that only its great outlines should be marked, its important objects designated, and the minor ingredients which compose those objects be deduced from the nature of the objects themselves. That this idea was entertained by the framers of the American constitution, is not only to be inferred from the nature of the instrument, but from the language. Why else were some of the limitations, found in the 9th section of the first article, introduced? It is also, in some degree, warranted by their having omitted to use any restrictive term which might prevent its receiving a fair and just interpretation. In considering this question, then, we must never forget, that it is a constitution we are expanding. . . .

. . . It is not denied that the powers given to the government imply the ordinary means of execution. That, for example, of raising revenue and applying it to national purposes, is admitted to imply the power of conveying money from place to place, as the exigencies of the nation may require, and of employing the usual means of conveyance. But it is denied that the government has its choice of means, or that it may employ the most convenient means, if to employ them it be necessary to erect a corporation. . . .

The government which has a right to do an act, and has imposed on it the duty of performing that act, must, according to the dictates of reason, be allowed to select the means; and those who contend that it may not select any appropriate means, that one particular mode of effecting the object is excepted, take upon themselves the burden of establishing that exception.

. . . the constitution of the United States has not left the right of Congress to employ the necessary means, for the execution of the powers conferred on the government to general reasoning. To its enumeration of powers is added that of making "all laws which shall be necessary and proper, for carrying into execution the foregoing powers, and all other powers vested by this constitution, in the government of the United States, or in any department thereof."

The counsel for the State of Maryland have urged various arguments, to prove that this clause, though in terms a grant of power, is not so in effect; but is really restrictive of the general right, which might otherwise be implied, of selecting means for executing the enumerated powers. . . .

But the argument on which most reliance is placed, is drawn from the peculiar language of this clause. Congress is not empowered by it to make all laws, which may have relation to the powers conferred on the government, but such only as may be "necessary and proper" for carrying them into execution. The word "necessary" is considered as controlling the whole sentence, and as limiting the right to pass laws for the execution of the granted powers, to such as are indispensable, and without which the power would be nugatory. That it excludes the choice of means, and leaves to Congress, in each case, that only which is most direct and simple.

It is true that this is the sense in which the word "necessary" is always used? Does it always import an absolute physical necessity, so strong that one thing, to which another may be termed necessary, cannot exist without that other? We think it does not. If reference be had to its use, in the common affairs of the world, or in approved authors, we find that it frequently imports no more than that one thing is convenient, or useful, or essential to another. To employ the means necessary to an end, is generally understood as employing any means calculated to produce the end, and not as being confined to those single means, without which the end would be entirely unattainable. Such is the character of human language, that no word conveys to the mind, in all situations, one single definite idea; and nothing is more common than to use words in a figurative sense. Almost all compositions contain words, which, taken in their rigorous sense, would convey a meaning different from that which is obviously intended. It is essential to just construction, that many words which import something excessive should be understood in a more mitigated sense—in that sense which common usage justifies. The word ''necessary'' is of this description. It has not a fixed character peculiar to itself. It admits of all degrees of comparison; and is often connected with other words, which increase or diminish the impression the mind receives of the urgency it imports. A thing may be necessary, very necessary, absolutely or indispensably necessary. To no mind would the same idea be conveyed by these several phrases. . . . This word, then, like others, is used in various senses; and, in its construction, the subject, the context, the intention of the person using them, are all to be taken into view. . . .

We admit, as all must admit, that the powers of the government are limited, and that its limits are not to be transcended. But we think the sound construction of the constitution must allow to the national legislature that discretion, with respect to the means by which the powers it confers are to be carried into execution, which will enable that body to perform the high duties assigned to it, in the manner most beneficial to the people. Let the end be legitimate, let it be within the scope of the constitution, and all means which are appropriate, which are plainly adapted to that end, which are not prohibited, but consist with the letter and spirit of the constitution, are constitutional.

Henry Clay, Speech on nullification and other topics, Cincinnati, August 3, 1830. *Life, Correspondence, Speeches of Clay*, V, 395-96.

. . . As to the existing bank, I think it has been generally administered, and particularly of late years, with great ability and integrity; that it has fulfilled all the reasonable expectations of those who constituted it; and, with the same committees, I think it has made an approximation toward the equalization of the currency, as great as is practicable. Whether the charter ought to be renewed or not, near six years hence, in my judgment, is a question of expediency to be decided by the then existing state of the country. . . . The question is premature. I may not be alive to form any opinion upon it. It belongs to posterity, and if they would have the goodness to decide for us some of the perplexing and practical questions of the present day, we might be disposed to decide that remote question for them. As it is, it ought to be indefinitely postponed.

Speech on the veto of the Bank Act, U.S. Senate, July 10, 1832. *Life, Correspondence, Speeches of Clay*, V, 525-35.

No question has been more generally discussed, within the last two years, by the people at large, and in State Legislatures, than that of the bank. And this consideration of it has been prompted by the president himself. . . . And yet his friends now declare the agitation of the question to be premature! It was not premature, in 1829, to present the question, but it is premature in 1832 to consider and decide it!
. . . I believe it may be truly affirmed, that from the commencement of the government to this day, there has not been a Congress opposed to the bank of the United States, upon the distinct ground of a want of power to establish it.
And here, Mr. President, I must request the indulgence of the Senate, while I express a few words in relation to myself.
I voted, in 1811, against the old bank of the United States, and I delivered, on that occasion, a speech, in which, among other reasons, I assigned that of its being unconstitutional. My speech has been read to the Senate, during the progress of this bill, but the reading of it excited no other regret than that it was read in such a wretched, bungling, mangling manner. During a long public life (I mention the fact not as claiming any merit for it), the only great question on which I have ever changed my opinion, is that of the bank of the United States. . . .
The interest which foreigners hold in the existing bank of the United States, is dwelt upon in the message as a serious objection to the recharter. But this interest is the result of the assignable nature of the stock; and if the objection be well founded, it applies to government stock, to the stock in local banks, in canal and other companies, created for internal improvements, and

every species of money or movables in which foreigners may acquire an interest. The assignable character of the stock is a quality conferred not for the benefit of foreigners, but for that of our own citizens. And the fact of its being transferred to them is the effect of the balance of trade being against us—an evil, if it be one, which the American system will correct. . . .

The president assigns in his message a conspicuous place to the alleged injurious operation of the bank on the interests of the western people. They ought to be much indebted to him for his kindness manifested toward them; although I think they have much reason to deprecate it. The people of all the West owe to this bank about thirty millions, which have been borrowed from it; and the president thinks that the payments for the interest, and other facilities which they derive from the operation of the bank, are so onerous as to produce "a drain of their currency, which no country can bear without inconvenience and occasional distress." His remedy is to compel them to pay the whole of the debt which they have contracted in a period short of four years. Now, Mr. President, if they can not pay the interest without distress, how are they to pay the principal? If they can not pay a part, how are they to pay the whole?. . .

. . . It is to confound cause and effect, to attribute to the bank the transfer of money from the West to the East. Annihilate the bank to-morrow, and similar transfers of capital, the same description of pecuniary operations, must be continued; not so well, it is true, but performed they must be, ill or well, under any state of circumstances.

The true questions are, how are they now performed, how were they conducted prior to the existence of the bank? how would they be after it ceased? I can tell you what was our condition before the bank was established; and, as I reason from the past to future experience, under analogous circumstances, I can venture to predict what it will probably be without the bank.

. . . Why, Mr. President, all things—governments, republics, empires, laws, human life—doubtless are to have an end; but shall we therefore accelerate their termination? The West is now young, wants capital, and its vast resources, needing nourishment, are daily developing. By-and-by, it will accumulate wealth from its industry and enterprise, and possess its surplus capital. The charter is not made perpetual, because it is wrong to bind posterity perpetually. At the end of the term limited for its renewal, posterity will have the power of determining for itself, whether the bank shall then be wound up, or prolonged another term. And that question may be decided, as it now ought to be, by a consideration of the interests of all parts of the Union, the West among the rest. Sufficient for the day is the evil thereof.

The president tells, that if the executive had been called upon to furnish the project of a bank, the duty would have been cheerfully performed; and he states that a bank, competent to all the duties which may be required by the government, might be so organized as not to infringe on our own delegated powers, or the reserved rights of the States. The president is a co-ordinate branch of the legislative department. As such, bills which have passed both Houses of Congress are presented to him for his approval or rejection. The idea of going to the president for the project of a law, is totally new in the practice, and utterly contrary to the theory of the government. What would we think of the Senate calling upon the House, or the House upon the Senate, for the project of a law?

. . . Must all legislation, in its commencement and in its termination concentrate in the president? When we shall have reached that state of things, the election and annual session of Congress will be a useless charge upon the people, and the whole business of government may be economically conducted by ukases and decrees. . . .

Mr. President, I protest against the right of any chief magistrate to come into either House of Congress, and scrutinize the motives of its members; to examine whether a measure has been passed with promptitude or repugnance; and to pronounce upon the willingness or unwillingness with which it has been adopted or rejected. It is an interference in concerns which partake of a domestic nature. The official and constitutional relations between the president and the two Houses of Congress subsist with them as organized bodies. His action is confined to their consummated proceedings, and does not extend to measures in their incipient stages, during their progress through the Houses, nor to the motives by which they are actuated. There are some parts of this message that ought to excite deep alarm; and that especially in which the president announces, that each public officer may interpret the Constitution as he pleases. . . . Now, Mr. President, I conceive, with great deference, that the president has mistaken the purport of the oath to support the Constitution of the United States. No one swears to support it as he understands it, but to support it simply as it is in truth. All men are bound to obey the laws, of which the Constitution is the supreme; but must they obey them as they are, or as they understand them? If the obligation of obedience is limited and controlled by the measure of information;

in other words, if the party is bound to obey the Constitution only *as he understands it;* what would be the consequence?. . . We should have nothing settled, nothing stable, nothing fixed. There would be general disorder and confusion throughout every branch of administration, from the highest to the lowest officers—universal nullification. For what is the doctrine of the president but that of South Carolina applied throughout the Union? The president independent both of Congress and the Supreme Court! only bound to execute the laws of the one and decisions of the other, as far as they conform to the Constitution of the United States, *as far as he understands it!* Then it should be the duty of every president, on his installation into office, to carefully examine all the acts in the statute book, approved by his predecessors, and mark out those which he was resolved not to execute, and to which he meant to apply this new species of veto, because they were repugnant to the Constitution *as he understands it.* And, after the expiration of every term of the Supreme Court, he should send for the record of its decisions, and discriminate between those which he would, and those which he would not, execute, because they were or were not agreeable to the Constitution, *as he understands it.*

ANDREW JACKSON

First Annual Message, December 8, 1829. *Messages of the Presidents,* III, 1025.

The charter of the Bank of the United States expires in 1836, and its stockholders will most probably apply for a renewal of their privileges. In order to avoid the evils resulting from precipitancy in a measure involving such important principles and such deep pecuniary interests, I feel that I can not, in justice to the parties interested, too soon present it to the deliberate consideration of the Legislature and the people. Both the constitutionality and the expediency of the law creating this bank are well questioned by a large portion of our fellow-citizens, and it must be admitted by all that it has failed in the great end of establishing a uniform and sound currency.

Under these circumstances, if such an institution is deemed essential to the fiscal operations of the Government, I submit to the wisdom of the Legislature whether a national one, founded upon the credit of the Government and its revenues, might not be devised which would avoid all constitutional difficulties and at the same time secure all the advantages to the Government and country that were expected to result from the present bank.

Second Annual Message, December 6, 1830. *Messages of the Presidents*, III, 1091-92.

The importance of the principles involved in the inquiry whether it will be proper to recharter the Bank of the United States requires that I should again call the attention of Congress to the subject. Nothing has occurred to lessen in any degree the dangers which many of our citizens apprehend from that institution as at present organized. . . .

It is thought practicable to organize such a bank with the necessary officers as a branch of the Treasury Department, based on the public and individual deposits, without power to make loans or purchase property, which shall remit the funds of the Government, and the expense of which may be paid, if thought advisable, by allowing its officers to sell bills of exchange to private individuals at a moderate premium. Not being a corporate body, having no stockholders, debtors, or property, and but few officers, it would not be obnoxious to the constitutional objections which are urged against the present bank; and having no means to operate on the hopes, fears, or interests of large masses of the community, it would be short of the influence which makes that bank formidable. The States would be strengthened by having in their hands the means of furnishing the local paper currency through their own banks, while the Bank of the United States, though issuing no paper, would check the issues of the State banks by taking their notes in deposit and for exchange only so long as they continue to be redeemed with specie. In times of public emergency the capacities of such an institution might be enlarged by legislative provisions.

Veto of Bank Act, July 10, 1832. *Messages of the Presidents*, III, 1139-54.

. . . deeply impressed with the belief that some of the powers and privileges possessed by the existing bank are unauthorized by the Constitution, subversive of the rights of the States, and dangerous to the liberties of the people, I felt it my duty at an early period of my Administration to call the attention of Congress to the practicability of organizing an institution combining all its advantages and obviating these objections. I sincerely regret that in the act before me I can perceive none of those modifications of the bank charter which are necessary, in my opinion, to make it compatible with justice, with sound policy, or with the Constitution of our country.

. . . It enjoys an exclusive privilege of banking under the authority of the General Government, a monopoly of its favor and support, and, as a necessary consequence, almost a monopoly of the foreign and domestic exchange. . . .

. . . More than eight millions of the stock of this bank are held by foreigners. By this act the American Republic proposes virtually to make them a present of some millions of dollars. For these gratuities to foreigners and to some of our own opulent citizens the act secures no equivalent whatever. They are the certain gains of the present stockholders under the operation of this act, after making full allowance for the payment of the bonus.

Every monopoly and all exclusive privileges are granted at the expense of the public, which ought to receive a fair equivalent. The many millions which this act proposes to bestow on the stockholders of the existing bank must come directly or indirectly out of the earnings of the American people. . . .

. . . If we must have such a corporation, why should not the Government sell out the whole stock and thus secure to the people the full market value of the privileges granted?. . .

But this act does not permit competition in the purchase of this monopoly. It seems to be predicated on the erroneous idea that the present stockholders have a prescriptive right not only to the favor but to the bounty of Government. It appears that more than a fourth part of the stock is held by foreigners and the residue is held by a few hundred of our own citizens, chiefly of the richest class. For their benefit does this act exclude the whole American people from competition in the purchase of this monopoly and dispose of it for many millions less than it is worth. . . .

. . . If a State bank in Philadelphia owe the Bank of the United States and have notes issued by the St. Louis branch, it can pay the debt with those notes, but if a merchant, mechanic, or other private citizen be in like circumstances he can not by law pay his debt with those notes, but must sell them at a discount or send them to St. Louis to be cashed. This boon conceded to the State banks, though not unjust in itself, is most odious because it does not measure out equal justice to the high and the low, the rich and the poor. To the extent of its practical effect it is a bond of union among the banking establishments of the nation, erecting them into an interest separate from that of the people, and its necessary tendency is to unite the Bank of the United States and the State banks in any measure which may be thought conducive to their common interest.

. . . The amount of stock held in the nine Western and Southwestern States is \$150,200, and in the four Southern States is \$5,623,100, and in the Middle and Eastern States is about \$13,522,000. . . . As little stock is held in the West, it is obvious that the debt of the people in that section to the bank is principally a debt to the Eastern and foreign stockholders; that the interest they pay upon it is carried into the Eastern States and into Europe, and that it is a burden upon their industry and a drain of their currency, which no country can bear without inconvenience and occasional distress. . . .

. . . It will make the American people debtors to aliens in nearly the whole amount due to this bank, and send across the Atlantic from two to five millions of specie every year to pay the bank dividends.

In another of its bearings this provision is fraught with danger. Of the twenty-five directors of this bank five are chosen by the Government and twenty by the citizen stockholders. From all voice in these elections the foreign stockholders are excluded by the charter. In proportion, therefore, as the stock is transferred to foreign holders the extent of suffrage in the choice of directors is curtailed. Already is almost a third of the stock in foreign hands and not represented in elections. It is constantly passing out of the country, and this act will accelerate its departure. The entire control of the institution would necessarily fall into the hands of a few citizen stockholders, and the ease with which the object would be accomplished would be a temptation to designing men to secure that control in their own hands by monopolizing the remaining stock. There is danger that a president and directors would then be able to elect themselves from year to year, and without responsibility or control manage the whole concerns of the bank during the existence of its charter. It is easy to conceive that great evils to our country and its institutions might flow from such a concentration of power in the hands of a few men irresponsible to the people.

Is there no danger to our liberty and independence in a bank that in its nature has so little to bind it to our country? The president of the bank has told us that most of the State banks exist by its forbearance. Should its influence become concentered, as it may under the operation of such an act as this, in the hands of a self-elected directory whose interests are identified with those of the foreign stockholders, will there not be cause to tremble for the purity of our elections in peace and for the independence of our country in war? . . .

Should the stock of the bank principally pass into the hands of the subjects of a foreign country, and we should unfortunately become involved in a war with that country, what would be our condition?. . . Controlling our currency, receiving our public moneys, and holding thousands of our citizens in dependence, it would be more formidable and dangerous than the naval and military power of the enemy.

If we must have a bank with private stockholders, every consideration of sound policy and every impulse of American feeling admonishes that it should be *purely American*. Its stockholders should be composed exclusively of our own citizens, who at least ought to be friendly to our Government and willing to support it in times of difficulty and danger. . . .

It is maintained by the advocates of the bank that its constitutionality in all its features ought to be considered as settled by precedent and by the decision of the Supreme Court. To this conclusion I can not assent. Mere precedent is a dangerous source of authority, and should not be regarded as deciding questions of constitutional power except where the acquiescence of the people and the States can be considered as well settled. . . .

If the opinion of the Supreme Court covered the whole ground of this act, it ought not to control the coordinate authorities of this Government. The Congress, the Executive, and the Court must each for itself be guided by its own opinion of the Constitution. Each public officer who takes an oath to support the Constitution swears that he will support it as he understands it, and not as it is understood by others. It is as much the duty of the House of Representatives, of the Senate, and of the President to decide upon the constitutionality of any bill or resolution which may be presented to them for passage or approval as it is of the supreme judges when it may be brought before them for judicial decision. The opinion of the judges has no more authority over Congress than the opinion of Congress has over the judges, and on that point the President is independent of both. The authority of the Supreme Court must not, therefore, be permitted to control the Congress or the Executive when acting in their legislative capacities, but to have only such influence as the force of their reasoning may deserve. . . .

The principle here affirmed [in McCulloch *v.* Maryland] is that the "degree of its necessity," involving all the details of a banking institution, is a question exclusively for legislative consideration. A bank is constitutional, but it is the province of the Legislature to determine whether this or that particular power, privilege, or exemption is "necessary and proper" to enable the bank to discharge its duties to the Government, and from their decision there is no appeal to the courts of justice. Under the decision of the Supreme Court, therefore, it is the exclusive province of Congress and the President to decide whether the particular features of this act are *necessary* and *proper* in order to enable the bank to perform conveniently and efficiently the public duties assigned to it as a fiscal agent, and therefore constitutional, or *unnecessary* and *improper,* and therefore unconstitutional.

. . . It will be found that many of the powers and privileges conferred on it can not be supposed necessary for the purpose for which it is proposed to be created, and are not, therefore, means necessary to attain the end in view, and consequently not justified by the Constitution. . . .

If Congress possessed the power to establish one bank, they had power to establish more than one if in their opinion two or more banks had been "necessary" to facilitate the execution of the powers delegated to them in the Constitution. . . . [The power]! was possessed by one Congress as well as another, and by all Congresses alike, and alike at every session. But the Congress of 1816 have taken it away from their successors for twenty years, and the Congress of 1832 proposes to abolish it for fifteen years more. It can not be *"necessary"* or *"proper"* for Congress to barter away or divest themselves of any of the powers vested in them by the Constitution to be exercised for the public good. It is not *"necessary"* to the efficiency of the bank, nor is it *"proper"* in relation to themselves and their successors. They may *properly* use the discretion vested in them, but they may not limit the discretion of their successors. This restriction on themselves and grant of a monopoly to the bank is therefore unconstitutional. . . .

On two subjects only does the Constitution recognize in Congress the power to grant exclusive privileges or monopolies. . . . On every other subject which comes within the scope of Congressional power there is an ever-living discretion in the use of proper means, which can not be restricted or abolished without an amendment of the Constitution. Every act of Congress, therefore, which attempts by grants of monopolies or sale of exclusive privileges for a limited time or a time without limit, to restrict or extinguish its own discretion in the choice of means to execute its delegated powers is equivalent to a legislative amendment of the Constitution, and palpably unconstitutional. . . .

The bonus which is exacted from the bank is a confession upon the face of the act that the powers granted by it are greater than are *"necessary"* to its character of a fiscal agent. . . . It is therefore for "exclusive privileges and benefits" conferred for their own use and emolument, and not for the advantage of the Government, that a bonus is exacted. These surplus powers for which the bank is required to pay can not surely be *"necessary"* to make it the fiscal agent of the Treasury. If they were, the exaction of a bonus for them would not be *"proper."*

It is maintained by some that the bank is a means of executing the constitutional power "to coin money and regulate the value thereof." Congress have established a mint to coin money and passed laws to regulate the value thereof. The money so coined, with its value so regulated, and such foreign coins as Congress may adopt are the only currency known to the Constitution. But if they have other power to regulate the currency, it was conferred to be exercised by themselves, and not to be transferred to a corporation. If the bank be established for that purpose, with a charter unalterable without its consent, Congress have parted with their power for a term of years, during which the Constitution is a dead letter. It is neither necessary nor proper to transfer its legislative power to such a bank, and therefore unconstitutional.

By its silence, considered in connection with the decision of the Supreme Court in the case of McCulloch against the State of Maryland, this act takes from the States the power to tax a portion of the banking business carried on within their limits, in subversion of one of the strongest barriers which secured them against Federal encroachments. Banking, like farming, manufacturing, or any other occupation or profession, is a *business*, the right to follow which is not originally derived from the laws. . . .

. . . Every private business, whether carried on by an officer of the General Government or not, whether it be mixed with public concerns or not, even if it be carried on by the Government of the United States itself, separately or in partnership, falls within the scope of the taxing power of the State. Nothing comes more fully within it than banks and the business of banking, by whomsoever instituted and carried on. . . .

. . . It may be safely assumed that none of those sages who had an agency in forming or adopting our Constitution ever imagined that any portion of the taxing power of the States not prohibited to them nor delegated to Congress was to be swept away and annihilated as a means of executing certain powers delegated to Congress.

. . . That a bank of the United States, competent to all the duties which may be required by the Government, might be so organized as not to infringe on our own delegated powers or the reserved rights of the States I do not entertain a doubt. Had the Executive been called upon to furnish the project of such an institution, the duty would have been cheerfully performed. In the absence of such a call it was obviously proper that he should confine himself to pointing out those prominent features in the act presented which in his opinion make it incompatible with the Constitution and sound policy. A general discussion will now take place, eliciting new light and settling important principles; and a new Congress, elected in the midst of such discussion, and furnishing an equal representation of the people according to the last census, will bear to the Capitol the verdict of public opinion, and, I doubt not, bring this important question to a satisfactory result. . . .

The bank is professedly established as an agent of the executive branch of the Government, and its constitutionality is maintained on that ground. Neither upon the propriety of present action nor upon the provisions of this act was the Executive consulted. It has had no opportunity to say that it neither needs nor wants an agent clothed with such powers and favored by such exemptions. There is nothing in its legitimate functions which makes it necessary or proper. Whatever interest or influence, whether public or private, has given birth to this act, it can not be found either in the wishes or necessities of the executive department, by which present action is deemed premature, and the powers conferred upon its agent not only unnecessary, but dangerous to the Government and country.

It is to be regretted that the rich and powerful too often bend the acts of government to their selfish purposes. Distinctions in society will always exist under every just government. Equality of talents, of education, or of wealth can not be produced by human institutions. In the full enjoyment of the gifts of Heaven and the fruits of superior industry, economy, and virtue, every man is equally entitled to protection by law; but when the laws undertake to add to these natural and just advantages artificial distinctions, to grant titles, gratuities, and exclusive privileges, to make the rich richer and the potent more powerful, the humble members of society—the farmers, mechanics, and laborers—who have neither the time nor the means of securing like favors to themselves, have a right to complain of the injustice of their Government. There are no necessary evils in government. Its evils exist only in its abuses. If it would confine itself to equal protection, and, as Heaven does its rains, shower its favors alike on the high and the low, the rich and the poor, it would be an unqualified blessing. In the act before me there seems to be a wide and unnecessary departure from these just principles.

Nor is our Government to be maintained or our Union preserved by invasions of the rights and powers of the several States. In thus attempting to make our General Government strong we make it weak. Its true strength consists in leaving individuals and States as much as possible to themselves—in making itself felt, not in its power, but in its beneficence; not in its control, but in its protection; not in binding the States more closely to the center, but leaving each to move unobstructed in its proper orbit.

. . . If we can not at once, in justice to interests vested under improvident legislation, make our Government what it ought to be, we can at least take a stand against all new grants of monopolies and exclusive privileges, against any prostitution of our Government to the advancement of the few at the expense of the many, and in favor of compromise and gradual reform in our code of laws and system of political economy.

. . . let us firmly rely on that kind Providence which I am sure watches with peculiar care over the destinies of our Republic, and on the intelligence and wisdom of our countrymen. Through *His* abundant goodness and *their* patriotic devotion our liberty and Union will be preserved.

Sixth Annual Message, December 1, 1834. *Messages of the Presidents*, III, 1327-28.

Circumstances make it my duty to call the attention of Congress to the Bank of the United States. Created for the convenience of the Government, that institution has become the scourge of the people. Its interference to postpone the payment of a portion of the national debt that it might retain the public money appropriated for that purpose to strengthen it in a political contest, the extraordinary extension and contraction of its accommodations to the community, its corrupt and partisan loans, its exclusion of the public directors from a knowledge of its most important proceedings, the unlimited authority conferred on the president to expend its funds in hiring writers and procuring the execution of printing, and the use made of that authority, the retention of the pension money and books after the selection of new agents, the groundless claim to heavy damages in consequence of the bill drawn on the French Government, have through various channels been laid before Congress. . . .

Events have satisfied my mind, and I think the minds of the American people, that the mischiefs and dangers which flow from a national bank far overbalance all its advantages. . . .

Eighth Annual Message, December 5, 1836. *Messages of the Presidents*, III, 1466-67.

Variableness must ever be the characteristic of a currency of which the precious metals are not the chief ingredient, or which can be expanded or contracted without regard to the principles that regulate the value of those metals as a standard in the general trade of the world. With us bank issues constitute such a currency. . . .

The progress of an expansion, or rather a depreciation, of the currency by excessive bank issues is always attended by a loss to the laboring classes. . . .

The Public Lands

HENRY CLAY

Speech on the public lands, U.S. Senate, June 20, 1832. *Life, Correspondence, Speeches of Clay*, V, 490-515.

No subject which had presented itself to the present, or perhaps any preceding Congress, was of greater magnitude than that of the public lands. There was another, indeed, which possessed a more exciting and absorbing interest; but the excitement was happily but temporary in its nature. Long after we shall cease to be agitated by the tariff, ages after our manufactures shall have acquired a stability and perfection which will enable them successfully to cope with the manufactures of any other country, the public lands will remain a subject of deep and enduring interest. In whatever view we contemplate them, there is no question of such vast importance. . . .

It has been only within a few years, that restless men have thrown before the public their visionary plans for squandering the public domain. . . .

Far from being discouraged by the fact of so much surveyed public land remaining unsold, we should rejoice that this bountiful resource, possessed by our country, remains in almost undiminished quantity, notwithstanding so many new and flourishing States have sprung up in the wilderness, and so many thousands of families have been accommodated. . . .

. . . The bill proposes a division of the net proceeds of the sales of the public lands, among the several States composing the Union, according to their federal representative population, as ascertained by the last census; and it provides for new States that may hereafter be admitted into the Union. . . .

The equity of the proposed distribution, as it respects the two classes of States, the old and the new, must be manifest to the Senate. It proposes to assign to the new States, besides the five per centum stipulated for in their several compacts with the general government, the further sum of ten per centum upon the net proceeds. . . .

If the power and the principle of the proposed distribution be satisfactory to the Senate, I think the objects can not fail to be equally so. They are education, internal improvements, and colonization, all great and beneficent objects, all national in their nature. . . .

The States, each judging for itself, will select among the objects enumerated in the bill, that which comports best with its own policy. There is no compulsion in the choice. . . .

Should a war break out during the term of five years, that the operation of the bill is limited to, the fund is to be withdrawn and applied to the vigorous prosecution of the war. If there be no war, Congress, at the end of the term, will be able to ascertain whether the money has been beneficially expended, and to judge of the propriety of continuing the distribution.

Three reports have been made on this great subject of the public lands. . . . All three of them agree, first, in the preservation of the control of the general government over the public lands; and, secondly, they concur in rejecting the plan of a cession of the public lands to the States in which they are situated, recommended by the secretary [of the Treasury].

. . . We are admonished by all our reflections, and by existing signs, of the duty of communicating strength and energy to the glorious Union which now encircles our favored country. Among the ties which bind us together, the public domain merits high consideration. And if we appropriate, for a limited time, the proceeds of that great resource, among the several States, for the important objects which have been enumerated, a new and powerful bond of affection and of interest will be added. The States will feel and recognize the operation of the general government, not merely in power and burdens, but in benefactions and blessings. And the general government in its turn will feel, from the expenditure of the money which it dispenses to the States, the benefits of moral and intellectual improvement of the people, of greater facility in social and commerical intercourse, and of the purification of the population of our country, themselves the best parental sources of national character, national union, and national greatness. . . .

Speech on the public lands, U.S. Senate, December 20, 1835. *Life, Correspondence, Speeches of Clay*, VI, 31.

Mr. President, I have ever regarded, with feelings of the profoundest regret, the decision which the President of the United States felt himself induced to make on the bill of 1833. If it had been his pleasure to approve it, the heads of departments would not now be taxing their ingenuity to find out useless objects of expenditure, or objects which may be well postponed to a more distant day. If the bill had passed, about twenty millions of dollars would have been, during the last three years, in the hands of the several States, applicable by them to the beneficent purposes of internal improvement, education, or colonization. What immense benefits might not have been diffused throughout the land by the active employment of that large sum? What new channels of commerce and communication might not have been opened? What industry stimulated, what labor rewarded? How many youthful minds might have received the blessings of education and knowledge, and been rescued from ignorance, vice, and ruin? How many descendants of Africa might have been transported from a country where they never can enjoy political or social equality, to the native land of their fathers, where no impediment exists to their attainment of the highest degree of elevation, intellectual, social, and political? Where they might have been successful instruments, in the hands of God, to spread the religion of his Son, and to lay the foundations of civil liberty!

. . . Instead of its being dedicated to the beneficent uses of the whole people, and our entire country, it has been an object of scrambling among local corporations, and locked up in the vaults, or loaned out by the directors of a few of them, who are not under the slightest responsibility to the government or people of the United States. Instead of liberal, enlightened, and national purposes, it has been partially applied to local, limited, and selfish uses. Applied to increase the semi-annual dividends of favorite stockholders in favorite banks! . . .

ANDREW JACKSON

Fourth Annual Message, December 4, 1832. *Messages of the Presidents*, III, 1163-64.

Among the interests which merit the consideration of Congress after the payment of the public debt, one of the most important, in my view, is that of the public lands. . . . In examining this question all local and sectional feelings should be discarded and the whole United States regarded as one people, interested alike in the prosperity of their common country.

It can not be doubted that the speedy settlement of these lands constitutes the true interest of the Republic. The wealth and strength of a country are its population, and the best part of that population are the cultivators of the soil. Independent farmers are everywhere the basis of society and true friends of liberty. . . .

It seems to me to be our true policy that the public lands shall cease as soon as practicable to be a source of revenue, and that they be sold to settlers in limited parcels at a price barely sufficient to reimburse to the United States the expense of the present system and the cost arising under our Indian compacts. The advantages of accurate surveys and undoubted titles now secured to purchasers seem to forbid the abolition of the present system, because none can be substituted which will more perfectly accomplish these important ends. It is desirable, however, that in convenient time this machinery be withdrawn from the States, and that the right of soil and the future disposition of it be surrendered to the States respectively in which it lies.

. . . it can not be expected that the new States will remain longer contented with the present policy after the payment of the public debt. To avert the consequences which may be apprehended from this cause, to put an end forever to all partial and interested legislation on the subject, and to afford to every American citizen of enterprise the opportunity of securing an independent freehold, it seems to me, therefore, best to abandon the idea of raising a future revenue out of the public lands.

Veto of Clay's Land Act, December 4, 1833. *Messages of the Presidents*, III, 1282-88.

The bill before me begins with an entire subversion of every one of the compacts by which the United States became possessed of their Western domain and treats the subject as if they never had existence and as if the United States were the original and unconditional owners of all the public lands. . . .

But this bill assumes a new principle. Its object is not to return to the people an unavoidable surplus of revenue paid in by them, but to create a surplus for distribution among the States. . . . It does not return to the people moneys accidentally or unavoidably paid by them to the Government, by which they are not wanted, but compels the people to pay moneys into the Treasury for the mere purpose of creating a surplus for distribution to their State governments. If this principle be once admitted, it is not difficult to perceive to what consequences it may lead. Already this bill, by throwing the land system on the revenues from imports for support, virtually distributes among the States a part of those revenues. . . .

It appears to me that a more direct road to consolidation can not be devised.   Money is power, and in that Government which pays all the public officers of the States will all political power be substantially concentrated.   The State governments, if governments they might be called, would lose all their independence and dignity; the economy which now distinguishes them would be converted into a profusion, limited only by the extent of the supply.   Being the dependents of the General Government, and looking to its Treasury as the source of all their emoluments, the State officers, under whatever names they might pass and by whatever forms their duties might be prescribed, would in effect be the mere stipendiaries and instruments of the central power. . . .

However willing I might be that any unavoidable surplus in the Treasury should be returned to the people through their State governments, I can not assent to the principle that a surplus may be created for the purpose of distribution. . . .

On the whole, I adhere to the opinion, expressed by me in my annual message of 1832, that it is our true policy that the public lands shall cease as soon as practicable to be a source of revenue, except for the payment of those general charges which grow out of the acquisition of the lands, their survey and sale.   Although these expenses have not been met by the proceeds of sales heretofore, it is quite certain they will be hereafter, even after a considerable reduction in the price.   By meeting in the Treasury so much of the general charge as arises from that source they will hereafter, as they have been heretofore, be disposed of for the common benefit of the United States, according to the compacts of cession.   I do not doubt that it is the real interest of each and all the States in the Union, and particularly of the new States, that the price of these lands shall be reduced and graduated, and that after they have been offered for a certain number of years the refuse remaining unsold shall be abandoned to the States and the machinery of our land system entirely withdrawn.   It can not be supposed the compacts intended that the United States should retain forever a title to lands within the States which are of no value, and no doubt is entertained that the general interest would be best promoted by surrendering such lands to the States.

The Presidency, Politics, and the People

HENRY CLAY

Toast at Frankfort, Kentucky, July 30, 1818. *Papers of Clay*, II, 588.

The only true and genuine cause of Legitimacy—the cause of the people.

Speech on Jackson Administration, Lexington, Kentucky, May 16, 1829. *Life, Correspondence, Speeches of Clay*, V, 373-76.

Government is a trust, and the officers of government are trustees; and both the trust and the trustees are created for the benefit of the people. Official incumbents are bound, therefore, to administer the trust, not for their own private or individual benefits, but so as to promote the prosperity of the people. This is the vital principle of a republic. If a different principle prevail, and a government be so adminstered as to gratify the passions or to promote the interests of a particular individual, the forms of free institutions may remain, but that government is essentially a monarchy. . . . If in one, nominally free, the chief magistrate, as soon as he is clothed with power, proceeds to exercise it, so as to minister to his passions, and to gratify his favorites, and systematically distributes his rewards and punishments, in the application of the power of patronage, with which he is invested for the good of the whole, upon the principle of devotion and attachment to him, and not according to the ability and fidelity with which the people are or may be served, that chief magistrate. . .is in fact, if not in form, a monarch. . . .

The president is invested with the tremendous power of dismission, to be exercised for the public good, and not to gratify any private passions or purposes. . . . it never was in the contemplation of Congress, that the power would or could be applied to the removal of competent, diligent, and faithful officers. Such an application of it is an act of arbitrary power, and a great abuse.

. . . now, persons are dismissed, not only without trial of any sort, but without charge. . . .

One of the worst consequences of the introduction of this tenure of public office will be, should it be permanently adopted, to substitute for a system of responsibility, founded upon the ability and integrity with which public officers discharge their duties to the community, a system of universal rapacity. Incumbents, feeling the instability of their situation and knowing their liability to periodical removals, at short terms, without any regard to the manner in which they have executed their trusts, will be disposed to make the most of their uncertain offices while they hold them.   And hence we may expect innumerable cases of fraud, peculation, and corruption.

Speech on veto of the Bank Act, U.S. Senate, July 10, 1832. *Life, Correspondence, Speeches of Clay,* V, 524-25.

The veto is hardly reconcilable with the genius of representative government.   It is totally irreconcilable with it, if it is to be frequently employed in respect to the expediency of measures, as well as their constitutionality. . . . If, after a respectful consideration of his objections urged against a bill, a majority of all the members elected to the Legislature, shall still pass it, notwithstanding his official influence, and the force of his reasons, ought it not to become a law?   Ought the opinion of one man to overrule that of a legislative body, twice deliberately expressed?

It can not be imagined that the Convention contemplated the application of the veto, to a question which has been so long, so often, and so thoroughly scrutinized, as that of the bank of the United States, by every department of the government, in almost every stage of its existence, and by the people, and by the State legislatures. . . .

Speech on the power of appointing and removing, U.S. Senate, February 11, 1835. *Life, Correspondence, Speeches of Clay,* VI, 15-23.

. . . The power of removal, as now exercised, is nowhere in the Constitution expressly recognized.   The only mode of displacing a public officer, for which it does provide, is by impeachment.   But it has been argued, on this occasion, that it is a sovereign power, an inherent power, and an executive power; and, therefore, that it belongs to the president. Neither the premises nor the conclusion can be sustained. . . .

. . . Inherent power! Whence is it derived? The Constitution created the office of president, and made it just what it is. It had no powers prior to its existence. It can have none but those which are conferred upon it by the instrument which created it, or laws passed in pursuance of that instrument. . . .

Motion to limit Presidency, U. S. Senate, January 24, 1842. *Life, Correspondence, Speeches of Clay*, VI, 303-4.

With this view, therefore, to the fundamental character of the government itself, and especially of the executive branch, it seems to me that, either by amendments of the Constitution, when they are necessary, or by remedial legislation, when the object falls within the scope of the powers of Congress, there should be,

First, a provision to render a person ineligible to the office of President of the United States after a service of one term. Much observation and deliberate reflection have satisfied me, that too much of the time, the thoughts, and the exertions of the incumbent, are occupied, during his first term, in securing his re-election. The public business, consequently, suffers; and measures are proposed or executed with less regard to the general prosperity than to their influence upon the approaching election. If the limitations to one term existed, the president would be exclusively devoted to the discharge of his public duties; and he would endeavor to signalize his administration by the beneficence and wisdom of its measures.

Secondly, that the veto power should be more precisely defined, and be subjected to further limitations and qualifications. . . .

ANDREW JACKSON

In December, 1824, Daniel Webster visited Thomas Jefferson. Later, he dictated his recollection of Jefferson's comments on Andrew Jackson. Fletcher Webster, ed., *The Writings and Speeches of Daniel Webster* (Boston, 1903), I, 371.

I feel much alarmed at the prospect of seeing General Jackson President. He is one of the most unfit men I know of for such a place. He has had very little respect for laws or constitutions, and

is, in fact, an able military chief. His passions are terrible. When
I was President of the Senate he was a Senator; and he could never
speak on account of the rashness of his feelings. I have seen him
attempt it repeatedly, and as often choke with rage. His passions
are no doubt cooler now; he has been much tried since I knew
him, but he is a dangerous man.

First Inaugural Address, March 4, 1829. *Messages of the
Presidents,* III, 1000-1001.

In administering the laws of Congress I shall keep steadily
in view the limitations as well as the extent of the Executive
power, trusting thereby to discharge the functions of my office
without transcending its authority. With foreign nations it will be
my study to preserve peace and to cultivate friendship on fair and
honorable terms, and in the adjustment of any differences that may
exist or arise to exhibit the forebearance becoming a powerful
nation rather than the sensibility belonging to a gallant people.

In such measures as I may be called on to pursue in regard
to the rights of the separate States I hope to be animated by a
proper respect for those sovereign members of our Union, taking
care not to confound the powers they have reserved to themselves
with those they have granted to the Confederacy. . . .

The recent demonstration of public sentiment inscribes on the
list of Executive duties, in characters too legible to be overlooked,
the task of *reform,* which will require particularly the correction
of those abuses that have brought the patronage of the Federal
Government into conflict with the freedom of elections, and the
counteraction of those causes which have disturbed the rightful
course of appointment and have placed or continued power in
unfaithful or incompetent hands.

First Annual Message, December 8, 1829. *Messages of the
Presidents,* III, 1010-12.

I consider it one of the most urgent of my duties to bring to
your attention the propriety of amending that part of our Constitution which relates to the election of President and Vice-
President. Our system of government was by its framers deemed
an experiment, and they therefore consistently provided a mode
of remedying its defects.

To the people belongs the right of electing their Chief Magistrate; it was never designed that their choice should in any case be defeated, either by the intervention of electoral colleges or by the agency confided, under certain contingencies, to the House of Representatives. Experience proves that in proportion as agents to execute the will of the people are multiplied there is danger of their wishes being frustrated. Some may be unfaithful; all are liable to err. So far, therefore, as the people can with convenience speak, it is safer for them to express their own will.

. . . although no evil of this character should result from such a perversion of the first principle of our system—*that the majority is to govern*—it must be very certain that a President elected by a minority can not enjoy the confidence necessary to the successful discharge of his duties. . . .

I would therefore recommend such an amendment of the Constitution as may remove all intermediate agency in the election of the President and Vice-President. The mode may be so regulated as to preserve to each State its present relative weight in the election, and a failure in the first attempt may be provided for by confining the second to a choice between the two highest candidates. In connection with such an amendment it would seem advisable to limit the service of the Chief Magistrate to a single term of either four or six years. If, however, it should not be adopted, it is worthy of consideration whether a provision disqualifying for office the Representatives in Congress on whom such an election may have devolved would not be proper. . . .

There are, perhaps, few men who can for any great length of time enjoy office and power without being more or less under the influence of feelings unfavorable to the faithful discharge of their public duties. Their integrity may be proof against improper considerations immediately addressed to themselves, but they are apt to acquire a habit of looking with indifference upon the public interests and of tolerating conduct from which an unpracticed man would revolt. Office is considered as a species of property, and government rather as a means of promoting individual interests than as an instrument created solely for the service of the people. Corruption in some and in others a perversion of correct feelings and principles divert government from its legitimate ends and make it an engine for the support of the few at the expense of the many. The duties of all public officers are, or at least admit of being made, so plain and simple that men of intelligence may readily qualify themselves for their performance; and I can not but believe that more is lost by the long continuance of men in office than is generally to be gained by their experience.   I submit, therefore, to your consideration whether the efficiency of the Government would not be promoted and official industry and integrity better secured by a general extension of the law which limits appointments to four years.

In a country where offices are created solely for the benefit of the people no one man has any more intrinsic right to official station than another.   Offices were not established to give support to particular men at the public expense.   No individual wrong is, therefore, done by removal, since neither appointment to nor continuance in office is matter of right.   The incumbent became an officer with a view to public benefits, and when these require his removal they are not to be sacrificed to private interests. It is the people, and they alone, who have a right to complain when a bad officer is substituted for a good one.   He who is removed has the same means of obtaining a living that are enjoyed by the millions who never held office.   The proposed limitation would destroy the idea of property now so generally connected with official station, and although individual distress may be sometimes produced, it would, by promoting that rotation which constitutes a leading principle in the republican creed, give healthful action to the system.

Second Annual Message, December 6, 1830. *Messages of the Presidents*, III, 1074-82.

. . . I know of no tribunal to which a public man in this country, in a case of doubt and difficulty, can appeal with greater advantage or more propriety than the judgment of the people; and although I must necessarily in the discharge of my official duties be governed by the dictates of my own judgment, I have no desire to conceal my anxious wish to conform as far as I can to the views of those for whom I act.

It is due to candor, as well as to my own feelings, that I should express the reluctance and anxiety which I must at all times experience in exercising the undoubted right of the Executive to withold his assent from bills on other grounds than their constitutionality.   That this right should not be exercised on slight occasions all will admit.   It is only in matters of deep interest, when the principle involved may be justly regarded as next in importance to infractions of the Constitution itself, that such a stop can be expected to meet with the approbation of the people. Such an occasion do I conscientiously believe the present to be.

In the discharge of this delicate and highly responsible duty I am sustained by the reflection that the exercise of this power has been deemed consistent with the obligation of official duty by several of my predecessors, and by the persuasion, too, that whatever liberal institutions may have to fear from the encroachments of Executive power, which has been everywhere the cause of so much strife and bloody contention, but little danger is to be apprehended from a precedent by which that authority denies to itself the exercise of powers that bring in their train influence and patronage of great extent, and thus excludes the operation of personal interests, everywhere the bane of official trust. I derive, too, no small degree of satisfaction from the reflection that if I have mistaken the interests and wishes of the people the Constitution affords the means of soon redressing the error by selecting for the place their favor has bestowed upon me a citizen whose opinions may accord with their own. . . .

A provision which does not secure to the people a direct choice of their Chief Magistrate, but has a tendency to defeat their will, presented to my mind such an inconsistency with the general spirit of our institutions that I was induced to suggest for your consideration the substitute which appeared to me at the same time the most likely to correct the evil and to meet the views of our constituents. The most mature reflection since has added strength to the belief that the best interests of our country require the speedy adoption of some plan calculated to effect this end. . . .

It was a leading object with the framers of the Constitution to keep as separate as possible the action of the legislative and executive branches of the Government. To secure this object nothing is more essential than to preserve the former from all temptations of private interest, and therefore so to direct the patronage of the latter as not to permit such temptations to be offered. Experience abundantly demonstrates that every precaution in this respect is a valuable safeguard of liberty, and one which my reflections upon the tendencies of our system incline me to think should be made still stronger. It was for this reason that, in connection with an amendment of the Constitution removing all intermediate agency in the choice of the President, I recommended some restrictions upon the reeligibility of that officer and upon the tenure of offices generally. The reason still exists, and I renew the recommendation with an increased confidence that its adoption will strengthen those checks by which the Constitution designed to secure the independence of each department of the Government and promote the healthful and equitable administration of all the trusts which it has created. The agent most likely

to contravene this design of the Constitution is the Chief Magistrate. In order, particularly, that his appointment may as far as
possible be placed beyond the reach of any improper influences;
in order that he may approach the solemn responsibilities of the
highest office in the gift of a free people uncommitted to any other
course than the strict line of constitutional duty, and that the
securities for this independence may be rendered as strong as
the nature of power and the weakness of its possessor will admit, I
can not too earnestly invite your attention to the propriety of
promoting such an amendment of the Constitution as will render
him ineligible after one term of service.

Protest against resolution of censure, April 15, 1834.
Messages of the Presidents, III, 1290-1312.

. . . But although for the special purposes which have been
mentioned there is an occasional intermixture of the powers of
the different departments, yet with these exceptions each of the
three great departments is independent of the others in its sphere
of action, and when it deviates from that sphere is not responsible
to the others further than it is expressly made so in the Constitution. In every other respect each of them is the coequal of the
other two, and all are the servants of the American people, without
power or right to control or censure each other in the service of
their common superior, save only in the manner and to the degree
which that superior has prescribed.

The whole executive power being vested in the President,
who is responsible for its exercise, it is a necessary consequence
that he should have a right to employ agents of his own choice
to aid him in the performance of his duties, and to discharge
them when he is no longer willing to be responsible for their acts.
In strict accordance with this principle, the power of removal,
which, like that of appointment, is an original executive power,
is left unchecked by the Constitution in relation to all executive
officers, for whose conduct the President is responsible, while
it is taken from him in relation to judicial officers, for whose acts
he is not responsible. . . .

. . . The President is the direct representative of the American
people, but the Secretaries are not. If the Secretary of the Treasury be independent of the President in the execution of the laws,
then is there no direct responsibility to the people in that important branch of this Government to which is committed the care
of the national finances. . . .

. . . If the censures of the Senate be submitted to by the President, the confidence of the people in his ability and virtue and the character and usefulness of his Administration will soon be at an end, and the real power of the Government will fall into the hands of a body holding their offices for long terms, not elected by the people and not to them directly responsible. . . .

. . . the ambition which leads me on is an anxious desire and a fixed determination to return to the people unimpaired the sacred trust they have confided to my charge; to heal the wounds of the Constitution and preserve it from further violation; to persuade my countrymen, so far as I may, that it is not in a splendid government supported by powerful monopolies and aristocratical establishments that they will find happiness or their liberties protection, but in a plain system, void of pomp, protecting all and granting favors to none, dispensing its blessings, like the dews of Heaven, unseen and unfelt save in the freshness and beauty they contribute to produce.

Jacksonian Democracy

Historians have debated for a century whether Andrew Jackson was truly a democratic leader or merely an outgrowth of a great democratic surge which would have gone on the same without him. In either event, however, Jackson is widely recognized as the symbol of the movement, in the decades after the War of 1812, which saw political rights extended to vastly greater numbers of Americans. Yet Jackson's own writings are singularly lacking in statements indicating a democratic philosophy. One must turn elsewhere to find writings reflective of the democratic impulse of the times.

Chancellor James Kent (1763-1847), speech in the New York constitutional convention of 1821. *Reports of the Proceedings and Debates of the Convention of 1821 Assembled for the Purpose of Amending the Constitution of the State of New York* (Albany, 1821), 220-22.

. . . By the report before us, we propose to annihilate, at one stroke, all those property distinctions and to bow before the idol of universal suffrage. That extreme democratic principle, when applied to the legislative and executive departments of government, has been regarded with terror by the wise men of every age because, in every European republic, ancient and modern, in which it has been tried, it has terminated disastrously and been productive of corruption, injustice, violence, and tyranny. And dare we flatter ourselves that we are a peculiar people who can run the career of history, exempted from the passions which have disturbed and corrupted the rest of mankind? If we are like other races of men, with similar follies and vices, then I greatly fear that our posterity will have reason to deplore, in sackcloth and ashes, the delusion of the day. . . .

Now, sir, I wish to preserve our senate as the representative of the landed interest. I wish those who have an interest in the soil to retain the exclusive possession of a branch in the legislature as a stronghold in which they may find safety through all the vicissitudes which the state may be destined, in the course of Providence, to experience. I wish them to be always enabled to say that their freeholds cannot be taxed without their consent. . . .

The apprehended danger from the experiment of universal suffrage applied to the whole legislative department is no dream of the imagination. It is too mighty an excitement for the moral constitution of men to endure. The tendency of universal suffrage is to jeopardize the rights of property and the principles of liberty. There is a constant tendency in human society, and the history of every age proves it; there is a tendency in the poor to covet and to share the plunder of the rich; in the debtor to relax or avoid the obligation of contracts; in the majority to tyrannize over the minority and trample down their rights; in the indolent and the profligate to cast the whole burthens of society upon the industrious and the virtuous; and *there is a tendency in ambitious and wicked men to inflame these combustible materials.* It requires a vigilant government, and a firm administration of justice, to counteract that tendency. Thou shall not covet; Thou shall not steal, are divine injunctions induced by this miserable depravity of our nature. . . . One-seventh of the population of the city of Paris at this day subsists on charity, and one-third of the inhabitants of that city die in the hospitals; what would become of such a city with universal suffrage? France has upward of four, and England upward of five millions of manufacturing and commercial laborers without property. Could these kingdoms sustain the weight of universal suffrage? The radicals in England, with the force of that mighty engine, would at once sweep away the property, the laws, and the liberties of that island like a deluge.

The growth of the city of New York is enough to startle and awaken those who are pursuing the *ignis fatuus* of universal suffrage.

. . . the individual who contributes only one cent to the common stock ought not to have the same power and influence in directing the property concerns of the partnership, as he who contributes his thousands. He will not have the same inducements to care, and diligence. . . .

Liberty, rightly understood, is an inestimable blessing, but liberty without wisdom, and without justice, is no better than wild and savage licentiousness. The danger which we have hereafter to apprehend is not the want, but the abuse, of liberty. We have to apprehend the oppression of minorities. . . .

. . . Universal suffrage once granted, is granted forever and never can be recalled. There is no retrograde step in the rear of democracy. However mischievous the precedent may be in its consequences, or however fatal in its effects, universal suffrage never can be recalled or checked but by the strength of the bayonet. We stand, therefore, this moment, on the brink of fate, on the very edge of the precipice. If we let go our present hold on the senate, we commit our proudest hopes and our most precious interests to the waves. . . .

Despite the efforts of James Kent, the following sections on suffrage were included in the New York Constitution of 1821. *The Constitution of the State of New York.* . . (Albany, 1826), 4-26.

ARTICLE FIRST. . .

Sec. VI. An enumeration of the inhabitants of the state, shall be taken, under the direction of the legislature, in the year one thousand eight hundred and twenty-five, and at the end of every ten years thereafer; and the said districts shall be so altered by the legislature, at the first session after the return of every enumeration, that each senate district shall contain, as nearly as may be, an equal number of inhabitants, excluding aliens, paupers, and persons of colour not taxed; and shall remain unaltered, until the return of another enumeration, and shall at all times, consist of contiguous territory; and no county shall be divided in the formation of a senate district.

Sec. VII. The members of the assembly shall be chosen by counties, and shall be apportioned among the several counties of the state, as nearly as may be, according to the number of their respective inhabitants, excluding aliens, paupers, and persons of colour not taxed. . . .

ARTICLE SECOND

Sec. I. Every male citizen, of the age of twenty-one years, who shall have been an inhabitant of this state one year preceding any election, and for the last six months a resident of the town or county where he may offer his vote; and shall have, within the year next preceding the election, paid a tax to the state or county, assessed upon his real or personal property; or shall by law be exempted from taxation; or being armed and equipped according to law, shall have performed within that year, military duty in the militia of this state; or who shall be exempted from performing militia duty in consequence of being a fireman in any city, town, or village, in this state: and also, every male citizen of the age of twenty-one years, who shall have been for three years next preceding such election, an inhabitant of this state; and for the last year, a resident in the town or county, where he may offer his vote; and shall have been, within the last year, assessed to labor on the public highways, and shall have performed the labor or paid an equivalent therefor, according to law; shall be entitled to vote in the town or ward where he actually resides, and not elsewhere, for all officers that now are, or hereafter may be, elective by the people: But no man of colour, unless he shall have been for three years a citizen of this state, and for one year next preceding any election, shall be seised and possessed of a freehold estate of the value of two hundred and fifty dollars, over and above all debts and incumbrances charged thereon; and shall have been actually rated, and paid a tax thereon, shall be entitled to vote at any such election. And no person of colour shall be subject to direct taxation, unless he shall be seised, and possessed, of such real estate as aforesaid. . . .

ARTICLE SEVENTH

Sec. I. No member of this state shall be disfranchised or deprived of any of the rights or privileges secured to any citizen thereof, unless by the law of the land, or the judgment of his peers. . . .

Sec. IV. *And whereas* the ministers of the gospel are, by their profession, dedicated to the service of God, and the cure of souls, and ought not to be diverted from the great duties of their functions; therefore, no minister of the gospel, or priest of any denomination whatsoever, shall at any time hereafter, under any pretence or description whatever, be eligible to, or capable of holding any civil or military office or place within this state.

[In 1826 the following amendment was added to the New York constitution.]

Second: That so much of the first section of the second article of the constitution as prescribes the qualification of voters, other than persons of colour, be and the same is hereby abolished, and that the following be substituted in the place thereof:

Every male citizen of the age of twenty-one years, who shall have been an inhabitant of this state one year next preceding any election, and for the last six months a resident of the county where he may offer his vote, shall be entitled to vote in the town or ward where he actually resides, and not elsewhere, for all officers that now are, or hereafter may be elective by the people.

The historian George Bancroft (1800-1891) was one of the most articulate philosophers of Jacksonian democracy. The following extracts are from his address at Williams College, in August, 1835. It is printed in his *Office of the People in Art, Government and Religion*, in *Literary and Historical Miscellanies* (New York, 1855), 408-19.

The best government rests on the people and not on the few, on persons and not on property, on the free development of public opinion and not on authority; because the munificent Author of our being has conferred the gifts of mind upon every member of the human race without distinction of outward circumstances. [Further,] mind eludes the power of appropriation; it exists only in its own individuality; it is a property which cannot be confiscated and cannot be torn away; it laughs at chains; it bursts from imprisonment; it defies monopoly. A government of equal rights must, therefore, rest upon mind; not wealth, not brute force, the sum of the moral intelligence of the community should rule the State. . . .

The public happiness is the true object of legislation, and can be secured only by the masses of mankind themselves awakening to the knowledge and the care of their own interests. Our free institutions have reversed the false and ignoble distinctions between men; and refusing to gratify the pride of caste, have acknowledged the common mind to be the true material for a Commonwealth. . . . The world can advance only through the culture of the moral and intellectual powers of the people. To accomplish this end by means of the people themselves is the highest purpose of government. If it be the duty of the individual to strive after a perfection like the perfection of God, how much more ought a nation to be the image of Deity. The common mind is the true Parian marble, fit to be wrought into likeness to a God. The duty of America is to secure the culture and the happiness of the masses by their reliance on themselves.

. . . Political action has never been so consistent and so unwavering, as when it results from a feeling or a principle, diffused through society. The people is firm and tranquil in its movements, and necessarily acts with moderation, because it becomes but slowly impregnated with new ideas; and effects no changes, except in harmony with the knowledge which it has acquired. Besides, where it is permanently possessed of power, there exists neither the occasion nor the desire for frequent change. It is not the parent of tumult; sedition is bred in the lap of luxury, and its chosen emissaries are the beggared spendthrift and the impoverished libertine. The government by the people is in very truth the strongest government in the world. Discarding the implements of terror, it dares to rule by moral force, and has its citadel in the heart.

Such is the political system which rests on reason, reflection, and the free expression of deliberate choice. There may be those who scoff at the suggestion, that the decision of the whole is to be preferred to the judgment of the enlightened few. They say in their hearts that the masses are ignorant; that farmers know nothing of legislation; that mechanics should not quit their workshops to join in forming public opinion. But true political science does indeed venerate the masses. It maintains, not as has been perversely asserted, that "the people can make right," but that the people can DISCERN right. Individuals are but shadows, too often engrossed by the pursuit of shadows; the race is immortal: individuals are of limited sagacity; the common mind is infinite in its experience: individuals are languid and blind; the many are ever wakeful: individuals are corrupt; the race has been redeemed: individuals are time-serving; the masses are ingenuous and sincere: individuals claim the divine sanction of truth for the deceitful conceptions of their own fancies; the Spirit of God breathes through the combined intelligence of the people. Truth is not to be ascertained by the impulses of an individual; it emerges from the contradictions of personal opinions; it raises itself in majestic serenity above the strifes of parties and the conflict of sects; it acknowledges neither the solitary mind, nor the separate faction as its oracle; but owns as its only faithful interpreter the dictates of pure reason itself, proclaimed by the general voice of mankind. The decrees of the universal conscience are the nearest approach to the presence of God in the soul of man.

Thus the opinion which we respect is, indeed, not the opinion of one or of a few, but the sagacity of the many. It is hard for the pride of cultivated philosophy to put its ear to the ground, and listen reverently to the voice of lowly humanity; yet the people collectively are wiser than the most gifted individual, for all his wisdom constitutes but a part of theirs. . . . It is when the multitude give counsel, that right purposes find safety; theirs is the fixedness that cannot be shaken; theirs is the understanding which exceeds in wisdom; theirs is the heart, of which the largeness is as the sand on the sea-shore.

It is not by vast armies, by immense natural resources, by accumulations of treasure, that the greatest results in modern civilization have been accomplished. . . . Not one benevolent institution, not one ameliorating principle in the Roman state, was a voluntary concession of the aristocracy; each useful element was borrowed from the Democracies of Greece, or was a reluctant concession to the demands of the people. The same is true in modern political life. It is the confession of an enemy to Democracy, that "ALL THE GREAT AND NOBLE INSTITUTIONS OF THE WORLD HAVE COME FROM POPULAR EFFORTS."

Reflective of Whig attempts to create a more democratic image for the party is this excerpt from a speech by Daniel Webster (1782-1852) in the Presidential campaign of 1840. A. B. Norton, *Reminiscences of the Log Cabin and Hard Cider Campaign* (Mount Vernon, Ohio, and Dallas, Tex., 1888), 238-39.

... There are two causes which keep back thousands of honest men from joining those who wish for a change.

The first of these is the fear of reproach from former associates, and the pain which party denunciation is capable of inflicting. ...

The other cause is the constant cry that the party of the administration is the true Democratic party, or the more popular party in the Government and in the country. The falsity of this claim has not been sufficiently exposed. It should have been met, and should be now met, not only by denial, but by proof. If they mean the new Democracy, the cry against credit, against industry, against labor, against a man's right to leave his own earnings to his own children—why, then, doubtless, they are right; all this sort of Democracy is theirs. But if by Democracy they mean a conscientious and stern adherence to the true popular principles of the Constitution and the Government, then I think they have very little claim to it. Is the augmentation of executive power a Democratic principle? Is the separation of the currency of Government from the currency of the people a Democratic principle? Is the embodying of a large military force, in time of peace, a Democratic principle?

Let us entreat honest men not to take names for things, nor pretences for proofs. If Democracy, in any constitutional sense belongs to our adversaries, let them show their title, and produce their evidence. Let the question be examined, and let not intelligent and well-meaning citizens be kept to the support of measures, which in their hearts and consciences they disapprove, because their authors put forth such loud claims to the sole profession of regard for the people.

Thomas Dorr (1805-1854), proposed constitution for Rhode Island, which was framed by the "people's convention" which assembled under his leadership in November, 1841. Jacob Frieze, *A Concise History of the Efforts to Obtain an Extension of Suffrage in Rhode Island* (Providence, 1842), 117-21.

Declaration of Principles and Rights. . .

3. All political power and sovereignty are originally vested in, and of right belong to the PEOPLE. All free governments are founded in their authority, and are established for the greatest good of the whole number. The PEOPLE have therefore an inalienable and indefeasible right, in their original, sovereign and unlimited capacity, to obtain and institute government, and, in the same capacity, to alter, reform, or totally change the same, whenever their safety or happiness requires.

4. No favor or disfavor ought to be shown in legislation toward any man, or party, or society, or religious denomination. The laws should be made not for the good of the few, but of the many; and the burdens of the State ought to be fairly distributed among its citizens. . . .

Of Electors and the Right of Suffrage

1. Every white male citizen of the United States, of the age of twenty-one years, who has resided in this State for one year, and in any town, city, or district of the same for six months, next preceding the election at which he offers to vote, shall be an elector of all officers, who are elected, or may hereafter be made eligible by the People.

Chapter III

THE HOUSE DIVIDING

JOHN C. CALHOUN and JEFFERSON DAVIS

and

ABRAHAM LINCOLN

Introduction

A seemingly interminable conflict over the real meaning of the Federal Union finally culminated in the Civil War. Slavery, combined with the related issues of sectionalism and westward expansion, seemed to make conflict between North and South irrepressible, and each section asserted that its course was the one laid out by the Constitution. Thus the state-rights position advanced by Jefferson's followers was twisted first into the state-sovereignty assertions of John C. Calhoun and finally into the state secessions attempted by Jefferson Davis and his constituents of the Confederate States of America. The most vital issue dividing North and South was the institution of slavery. Since the 1830's, Northerners had been increasingly critical of slavery; meanwhile, Southerners had ceased to defend slavery as a necessary evil and increasingly declared it a positive good.

John C. Calhoun, the philosopher of state sovereignty, nullification, and secession, was justly famed for his logic and for his undeviating attention to the interests of his section. He was so absorbed in his mission that he often appeared as an "abstract idea" rather than a man, even to those who knew him personally. Thus Harriet Martineau described him as "the cast-iron man, who looks as if he had never been born," and Henry Clay wittily characterized him as "tall, careworn, with fevered brow, haggard cheek and eye, intensely gazing, looking as if he were dissecting the last and newest abstraction which had sprung from some metaphysician's brain, and muttering to himself, in half-uttered words, 'This is indeed a crisis!' "

Calhoun was born into a slaveowning South Carolina family in 1782. He entered national politics as a "War Hawk" Congressman in 1811. As such, he played a key role in taking the country into the War of 1812 and was even more important for his efforts to provide the means to wage the war. Later he was the principal ally of Henry Clay in his attempt to enact a nationalist program of a national bank, internal improvements, and a protective tariff. He was James Monroe's Secretary of War (1817-1825) and was Vice-President under John Quincy Adams and Andrew Jackson (1825-1832). In 1844 and 1845 Calhoun again served in the executive branch, as the Secretary of State who carried through the acquisition of Texas. But his most memorable career was in the United States Senate. From 1832 to 1843, and 1845 to 1850, the senator from South Carolina was the South's greatest advocate.

His Presidential ambitions dashed by the unexpected longevity of Jackson and by Jackson's growing enmity for his Vice-President, and his dreams of an industrialized South Carolina wrecked by the state's inability to separate itself from a plantation economy, Calhoun resigned the Vice-Presidency so that he could defend his state's cause in the Senate, rather than merely preside over that body. Despite his contempt for sectional spirit and for "refined arguments on the constitution" during his nationalist period some sixteen years earlier, Calhoun became the leader of his section and of those professing to find strict constitutional limits upon the central government. He had disapproved of the protective tariff at least since 1827, and in 1828 he secretly wrote the "Exposition," which expressed his state's right to nullify unconstitutional federal legislation. Although he constantly sought some means of avoiding sectional conflict, as early as 1838 he began to contemplate separation from the Union. But still he hoped to avoid this "last resort." During the final years of his life (1845-1850), he labored on *A Disquisition on Government* and *A Discourse on the Constitution and Government of the United States*. The *Disquisition* sought to determine workable checks on government which would protect the minority from the majority, while the *Discourse* gave historical evidence in support of his denial of the supremacy of the central government and his assertion that sovereignty lay in the people of the individual states — that "We the people of the United States" meant "We the people of the several States of the Union."

Less philosophical and less fascinating than Calhoun, Jefferson Davis succeeded him as the principal spokesman of Southern sectionalism. Davis was born in Kentucky in 1808, near the birthplace of Abraham Lincoln and in economic circumstances similar to Lincoln's. The two, however, had little else in common. Davis went to Mississippi, where he rose to prominence as a planter, soldier, and statesman. He attended West Point and was commissioned in 1828. From 1833 to 1845 he tended his plantation in Mississippi. He was in Congress then for a year, but his political career was established in the Mexican War. His gallant action at Buena Vista, which may have converted defeat into glorious victory, made him a hero overnight.

He served in the United States Senate from 1847 to 1851 and 1857 to 1861 and was Secretary of War during the Franklin Pierce administration (1853-1857). A vigorous advocate of Southern interests, Davis often expressed a vision of Southern nationality. He heartily approved of President Polk's policies and supported Western expansion in the Senate, just as he was later to do in the Cabinet. He consistently defended the Southern institution of slavery and asserted the right to take slaves into the territories.

When the Southern secessions occurred in the winter of 1860-1861, Davis anticipated war and dreamed of military glory. Therefore he was grieved at news of his election as President of the Confederate States of America. He accepted, nevertheless, and was inaugurated on February 18, 1861. Unfortunately, his attempts to utilize his imagined "military genius" during the war darkened his record as President. Also, he was consistently hampered by the rabid state-rights advocates, who considered Davis a dictator for his efforts to bring efficiency into the central government.

He was a fugitive from Northern troops from April 3 to May 10, 1865, but was then captured and held as a political prisoner for two years, actually being kept in irons part of that time. He was never brought to trial, and was finally released on bond. He lived until 1889, largely unnoticed despite his attempts to justify the "Lost Cause." *The Rise and Fall of the Confederate Government* was his lengthy defense of the South, of secession, and of himself. Unsuccessful in several business ventures, he died a poor man. He could have partly recouped his political and financial fortunes by agreeing to his state's desire to return him to the United States Senate, but to do so he would have had to seek a Presidential pardon. This he refused to do.

Abraham Lincoln was the greatest spokesman of the Union in its time of crisis. Lincoln himself was the living proof of the democracy in which he so sincerely believed. Like Jackson before him, he rose from the lowliest of origins to become President of the United States. He was born in 1809 in what he described as "the most humble walks of life." Though he had little formal education, he thought deeply about what he did learn and made himself one of the leading lawyers in Illinois and a real force in state politics. In his initial venture into politics in 1834, Lincoln became floor leader of the Whig minority in the state legislature. He went to Congress in 1847, where his record was unmemorable except for his Whiggish assertions as to the injustice of the Mexican War and his consistent support of the Wilmot Proviso, a measure which would have disallowed the admission of slavery into the territories to be acquired from Mexico. His attacks on Polk offended his constituents, and he did not seek re-election. He returned to private practice until the renewal of the slavery question in 1854, when Stephen A. Douglas' Kansas-Nebraska Act expressly rescinded the restrictions on slavery expansion set up by the Missouri

Compromise of 1820 and in effect opened the unorganized territory remaining in the Louisiana Purchase to possible slave expansion. Although Lincoln attacked Douglas and the Democrats, he did not immediately enlist in the party formed to combat the Nebraska Act—the Republican Party; but his political leanings were sufficiently plain that by 1856 he received 110 votes in the balloting for a Republican nominee for Vice-President.

Lincoln opposed Douglas' candidacy for re-election in 1858 and challenged the Senator to a series of debates. As the competent oratorical foe of the leading Northern Democrat, Lincoln took long strides toward becoming a prominent spokesman of the Republican Party. Lincoln was not the leading candidate for the Presidential nomination in 1860, but he had very strong second-place support. When fears of William H. Seward as a "dangerous candidate" became manifest, it was quite natural for the convention to turn to Lincoln. The Democratic Party had split into a northern wing, which nominated Douglas, and a southern wing, which nominated John C. Breckinridge of Kentucky. Thus the Republicans were assured of victory in the populous northern states, provided they did not name a candidate who would cause the Democrats to reunite. Lincoln was elected without a single electoral vote from the South.

Preservation of the Union and democratic liberalism were the keys to Lincoln's political philosophy. As public sympathy and understanding of him increased, he came to a remarkable degree to personify the Union itself and to dramatize the war effort. Lincoln was influenced in his views of the Union by the speeches and messages of Daniel Webster and Andrew Jackson during the nullification crisis of the 1830's. He turned to them during the tense period between the first secessions and his own inauguration.

Lincoln's popularity rose and fell along with the successes and failures of the Union war effort. Although he was urged by some partisans to "postpone" the election of 1864 until the crisis was past, Lincoln insisted that the election be held on schedule. He used his shrewd political talents to the fullest extent, but still it seemed that he would surely be defeated by General George B. McClellan. Lincoln's victory was won by timely advances of the Union Army and judicious management of the soldier vote.

Lincoln was assassinated almost at the moment of victory. Like Franklin D. Roosevelt in 1945, Lincoln passed from the political scene while cloaked in the mantle of victory and was never confronted with the greater problems of making the peace. Therefore, succeeding generations could only wonder how Lincoln would have handled the problems of peace, and assume that he would have handled them better than his successor.

Recommended Readings

(Titles followed by an asterisk are available in paperback editions)

Books comparing the ideas of Lincoln and Davis are David Lindsey, *Lincoln/Davis: The House Divided,** and Irving Werstein, *Abraham Lincoln versus Jefferson Davis*. The best biography of Lincoln is James G. Randall's lengthy *Lincoln the President,* which casts aside many of the myths associated with the martyred President. Two excellent short studies are Randall, *Lincoln the Liberal Statesman,** and Benjamin Thomas, *Abraham Lincoln: A Biography*. Recent interpretations which are provocative include David Donald, *Lincoln Reconsidered,** and Richard Current, *The Lincoln Nobody Knows.** The outstanding biography of Calhoun is Charles M. Wiltse, *John Caldwell Calhoun*. A good, shorter presentation is Margaret Coit, *John C. Calhoun.** Probably the best biography of Davis is William E. Dodd, *Jefferson Davis*.

Multi-volume editions of the writings of Lincoln, Calhoun, and Davis are available—Lincoln's edited by Roy P. Basler; Calhoun's by Richard K. Crallé and a definitive edition is now in progress under the guidance of W. Edwin Hemphill as editor; and Davis' by Dunbar Rowland. Representative samples of their writings also appear in the following paperback editions: T. Harry Williams, ed., *Abraham Lincoln: Selected Speeches, Messages, and Letters,** C. Gordon Post, ed., *John C. Calhoun: Disquisition on Government and Selections from the Discourse;* and an abridgment of Jefferson Davis, *The Rise and Fall of the Confederate Government.**

Thomas J. Pressly, *Americans Interpret Their Civil War,** is an excellent account of the historiography of the Civil War. Kenneth M. Stampp, *The Causes of the Civil War,** contains a variety of views as to the causes of the war. When completed, Allan Nevins, *Ordeal of the Union*, will be a monument of Civil War historiography. An excellent one-volume history is J. G. Randall and David Donald, *Civil War and Reconstruction;* its long, analytical bibliography is splendid. More sympathetic to the South are Avery Craven, *The Coming of the Civil War* and *The Growth of Southern Nationalism*, *1848-1861*.

On the war itself, see T. Harry Williams, *Lincoln and His Generals;* Douglas S. Freeman, *Lee's Lieutenants;* Henry Steele Commager, *The Blue and the Gray,* a selection from letters and diaries of soldiers; and Bruce Catton's books, which are quite accurate and exceptionally well written. Important special studies are Clement Eaton, *A History of the Southern Confederacy,** and James C. Malin, *The Nebraska Question.*

John Hope Franklin, *From Slavery to Freedom: A History of American Negroes,* is standard in its field. Ulrich B. Phillips, *American Negro Slavery,* and *Life and Labor in the Old South,** views slavery as a benign institution; Kenneth M. Stampp, The *Peculiar Institution: Slavery in the Ante-Bellum South**; and Stanley M. Elkins, *Slavery; a Problem in American Institutional and Intellectual Life,** treat it as a malignant institution. Compare the traditional interpretation of Reconstruction, the most recent statement of which is E. Merton Coulter, *The South During Reconstruction, 1865-1877,* with the revisionist views of John Hope Franklin, *Reconstruction: After the Civil War**; and Kenneth M. Stampp, *The Era of Reconstruction, 1865-1877.* On a later period, see August Meier, *Negro Thought in America, 1880-1915;* and C. Vann Woodward, *The Strange Career of Jim Crow.** Gunnar Myrdal, *An American Dilemma,** is indispensable; the first edition of this study is abridged in Arnold Rose, *The Negro in America.**   Note, too, E. U. Essien-Udom, *Black Nationalism: A Search for an Identity in America.**

The Meaning of the Federal Union

FROM STATE RIGHTS TO STATE SECESSION

Thomas Jefferson's Kentucky Resolutions, November 16, 1798. Andrew Lipscomb and Albert Bergh, eds., *The Writings of Thomas Jefferson* (Washington, 1905), XVII, 380-90.

I. *Resolved*, that the several States composing the United States of America, are not united on the principle of unlimited submission to their general government; but that by compact under the style and title of a Constitution for the United States and of amendments thereto, they constituted a general government for special purposes, delegated to that government certain definite powers, reserving each State to itself, the residuary mass of right to their own self-government; and that whensoever the general government assumes undelegated powers, its acts are unauthoritative, void, and of no force: That to this compact each State acceded as a State, and is an integral party, its co-States forming, as to itself, the other party: That the government created by this compact was not made the exclusive or final judge of the extent of the powers delegated to itself; since that would have made its discretion, and not the Constitution, the measure of its powers; but that as in all other cases of compact among parties having no common Judge, each party has an equal right to judge for itself, as well of infractions as of the mode and measure of redress. ... That this Commonwealth does therefore call on its co-States for an expression of their sentiments on the acts concerning aliens, and for the punishment of certain crimes herein before specified, plainly declaring whether these acts are or are not authorized by the Federal Compact. And it doubts not that their sense will be so announced as to prove their attachment unaltered to limited government, whether general or particular, and that the rights and liberties of their co-States will be exposed to no dangers by remaining embarked on a common bottom with their own: That they will concur with this Commonwealth in considering the said acts as so palpably against the Constitution as to amount to an undisguised declaration, that the compact is not meant to be the measure of the powers of the general government, but that it will proceed in the exercise over these States of all powers whatsoever:

That they will view this as seizing the rights of the States and consolidating them in the hands of the general government with a power assumed to bind the States (not merely in cases made Federal) but in all cases whatsoever, by laws made, not with their consent: That this would be to surrender the form of government we have chosen, and to live under one deriving its powers from its own will, and not from our authority; and that the co-states, recurring to their natural right in cases not made Federal, will concur in declaring these acts void and of no force, and will each unite with this Commonwealth in requesting their repeal at the next session of Congress.

John C. Calhoun, speech in U.S. House of Representatives, February 4, 1817.   Richard K. Crallé, ed., *The Works of John C. Calhoun* (New York, 1851-55), II, 190-93.

. . . We are great, and rapidly—I was about to say fearfully—growing. This is our pride and our danger; our weakness and our strength. Little does he deserve to be intrusted with the liberties of this people, who does not raise his mind to these truths. We are under the most imperious obligation to counteract every tendency to disunion. The strongest of all cements is, undoubtedly, the wisdom, justice, and above all, the moderation of this House; yet the great subject on which we are now deliberating, in this respect deserves the most serious consideration.   Whatever impedes the intercourse of the extremes with this, the centre of the republic, weakens the union.   The more enlarged the sphere of commercial circulation—the more extended that of social intercourse—the more strongly are we bound together—the more inseparable are our destinies.   Those who understand the human heart best know how powerfully distance tends to break the sympathies of our nature.   Nothing—not even dissimilarity of language—tends more to estrange man from man. Let us, then, bind the republic together with a perfect system of roads and canals. Let us conquer space. . . .

Such, then, being the obvious advantages of internal improvements, why should the House hesitate to commence the system?   I understand there are, with some members, constitutional objections.   The power of Congress is objected to: first, that there is none to cut a road or canal through a State, without its consent; and next, that the public moneys can only be appropriated to effect the particular powers enumerated in the constitution. The first of these objections, it is plain, does not apply to this bill. No particular road or canal is proposed to be cut through any State. The bill simply appropriates money to the general purpose of improving the means of intercommunication. When a bill is introduced to apply the money to a particular object in any State, then, and not till then, will the question be fairly before us. I express no opinion on this point. In fact, I scarcely think it worth the discussion, since the good sense of the States may be relied on. They will, in all cases, readily yield their assent. The fear is in a different direction: in too great a solicitude to obtain an undue share to be expended within their respective limits. In fact, as I understand it, this is not the objection insisted on. It is mainly urged, that the Congress can only apply the public money in execution of the enumerated powers. I am no advocate for refined arguments on the constitution. The instrument was not intended as a thesis for the logician to exercise his ingenuity on. It ought to be construed with plain, good sense; and what can be more express than the constitution on this very point?. . . The first power delegated to Congress is comprised in these words: "To lay and collect taxes, duties, imposts, and excises, to pay the debts, and provide for the common defence and general welfare of the United States; but all duties, imposts, and excises, shall be uniform throughout the United States." First, the power is given to lay taxes; next, the objects are enumerated to which the money accruing from the exercise of this power, may be applied—viz., to pay the debts, provide for the defence, and promote the general welfare; and last, the rule for laying the taxes is prescribed—to wit, that all duties, imposts, and excises, shall be uniform. If the framers had intended to limit the use of the money to the powers afterwards enumerated and defined, nothing could have been more easy than to have expressed it plainly. I know it is the opinion of some, that the words "to pay the debts, and provide for the common defence and general welfare," which I have just cited, were not intended to be referred to the power of laying taxes, contained in the first part of the section, but that they are to be understood as distinct and independent powers, granted in general terms; and are qualified by a more detailed enumeration of powers in the subsequent part of the constitution. If such were, in fact, the meaning intended, surely nothing can be conceived more bungling and awkward than the manner in which the framers have communicated their intention. If it were their intention to make a summary of the powers of Congress in general terms, which were afterwards to be particularly defined and enumerated, they should have told us so plainly and distinctly;

and if the words "to pay the debts, and provide for the common defence and general welfare" were intended for this summary, they should have headed the list of our powers, and it should have been stated that, to effect these general objects, the following specific powers were granted. I ask members to read the section with attention; and it will, I conceive, plainly appear that such could not have been the intention. The whole section seemed to me to be about taxes. It plainly commences and ends with it; and nothing could be more strained than to suppose the intermediate words "to pay the debts, and provide for the common defence and general welfare," were to be taken as independent and distinct powers. Forced, however, as such a construction was, I might admit, and urge that the words do constitute a part of the enumerated powers. The constitution gives to Congress the power to establish post-offices and post-roads. I know the interpretation usually given to these words confines our powers to that of designating only the post-roads; but it seems to me that the word "establish" comprehends something more. But suppose the constitution to be silent, why should we be confined in the application of moneys to the enumerated powers? There is nothing in the reason of the thing, that I can perceive, why it should be so restricted; and the habitual and uniform practice of the Government coincides with my opinion. . . .

Concluding protest from John C. Calhoun's "South Carolina Exposition," December 19, 1828. Jonathan Elliot, ed., *Debates in the Several State Conventions on the Adoption of the Federal Constitution*. . . (Philadelphia, 1836), IV, 580-82.

The Senate and House of Representatives of South Carolina, now met, and sitting in General Assembly, through the Hon. William Smith and the Hon. Robert Y. Hayne, their representatives in the Senate of the United States, do, in the name and on behalf of the good people of the said commonwealth, solemnly PROTEST against the system of protecting duties, lately adopted by the federal government, for the following reasons:

1st. *Because* the good people of this commonwealth believe that the powers of Congress were delegated to it in trust for the accomplishment of certain specified objects which limit and control them, and that every exercise of them for any other purposes, is a violation of the Constitution as unwarrantable as the undisguised assumption of substantive, independent powers not granted or expressly withheld.

2d. *Because* the power to lay duties on imports is, and in its very nature can be, only a means of effecting objects specified by the Constitution; since no free government, and least of all a government of enumerated powers, can of right impose any tax, any more than a penalty, which is not at once justified by public necessity, and clearly within the scope and purview of the social compact; and since the right of confining appropriations of the public money to such legitimate and constitutional objects is as essential to the liberty of the people as their unquestionable privilege to be taxed only by their consent.

3d. *Because* they believe that the tariff law passed by Congress at its last session, and all other acts of which the principal object is the protection of manufactures, or any other branch of domestic industry, if they be considered as the exercise of a power in Congress to tax the people at its own good will and pleasure, and to apply the money raised to objects not specified in the Constitution, is a violation of these fundamental principles, a breach of a well-defined trust, and a perversion of the high powers vested in the federal government for federal purposes only.

4th. *Because* such acts, considered in the light of a regulation of commerce, are equally liable to objection; since, although the power to regulate commerce may, like all other powers, be exercised so as to protect domestic manufactures, yet it is clearly distinguishable from a power to do so *eo nomine*, both in the nature of the thing and in the common acception of the terms; and because the confounding of them would lead to the most extravagant results, since the encouragement of domestic industry implies an absolute control over all the interests, resources, and pursuits of a people, and is consistent with the idea of any other than a simple, consolidated government.

5th. *Because*, from the contemporaneous exposition of the Constitution in the numbers of the *Federalist*, (which is cited only because the Supreme Court has recognized its authority,) it is clear that the power to regulate commerce was considered by the Convention as only incidentally connected with the encouragement of agriculture and manufactures; and because the power of laying imposts and duties on imports was not understood to justify in any case, a prohibition of foreign commodities, except as a means of extending commerce, by coercing foreign nations to a fair reciprocity in their intercourse with us, or for some *bona fide* commercial purpose.

6th. *Because*, whilst the power to protect manufactures, is nowhere expressly granted to Congress, nor can be considered as necessary and proper to carry into effect any specified power, it seems to be expressly reserved to the states, by the 10th section of the 1st article of the Constitution.

7th. *Because* even admitting Congress to have a constitutional right to protect manufactures by the imposition of duties, or by regulations of commerce, designed principally for that purpose, yet a tariff of which the operation is grossly unequal and oppressive, is such an abuse of power as is incompatible with the principles of a free government and the great ends of civil society, justice, and equality of rights and protection.

8th. *Finally,* because South Carolina, from her climate, situation, and peculiar institutions, is, and must ever continue to be, wholly dependent upon agriculture and commerce, not only for her prosperity, but for her very existence as a state; because the valuable products of her soil—the blessings by which Divine Providence seems to have designed to compensate for the great disadvantages under which she suffers in other respects—are among the very few that can be cultivated with any profit by slave labor; and if, by the loss of her foreign commerce, these products should be confined to an inadequate market, the fate of this fertile state would be poverty and utter desolation; her citizens, in despair, would emigrate to more fortunate regions, and the whole frame and constitution of her civil policy be impaired and deranged, if not dissolved entirely.

Deeply impressed with these considerations, the representatives of the good people of this commonwealth, anxiously desiring to live in peace with their fellow-citizens, and to do all that in them lies to preserve and perpetuate the union of the states, and liberties of which it is the surest pledge, but feeling it to be their bounden duty to expose and resist all encroachments upon the true spirit of the Constitution, lest an apparent acquiescence in the system of protecting duties should be drawn into precedent—do, in the name of the commonwealth of South Carolina, claim to enter upon the Journal of the Senate their *protest* against it as unconstitutional, oppressive, and unjust.

South Carolina Nullification Ordinance, November 19, 1832. Thomas Cooper, ed., *Statutes at Large of South Carolina* (Columbia, 1836), I, 329-31.

Whereas, The Congress of the United States, by various acts, purporting to be acts laying duties and imposts on foreign imports, but in reality intended for the protection of domestic manufactures, and the giving of bounties to classes and individuals engaged in particular employments, at the expense and to the injury and oppression of other classes and individuals, and by wholly exempting from taxation certain foreign commodities, such as are not produced or manufactured in the United States, to afford a pretext for imposing higher and excessive duties on articles similar to those intended to be protected, hath exceeded its just powers under the Constitution, which confers on it no authority to afford such protection, and hath violated the true meaning and intent of the Constitution, which provides for equality in imposing the burdens of taxation upon the several States and portions of the Confederacy. *And whereas,* the said Congress exceeding its just power to impose taxes and collect revenue for the purpose of effecting and accomplishing the specific objects and purposes which the Constitution of the United States authorizes it to effect and accomplish, hath raised and collected unnecessary revenue for objects unauthorized by the Constitution—

We, therefore, the People of the State of South Carolina in Convention assembled, do Declare and Ordain . . . That the several acts and parts of acts of the Congress of the United States, purporting to be laws for the imposing of duties and imposts on the importation of foreign commodities . . . are unauthorized by the Constitution of the United States, and violate the true meaning and intent thereof, and are null, void, and no law, nor binding upon this State, its officers or citizens; and all promises, contracts and obligations, made or entered into, or to be made or entered into, with purpose to secure the duties imposed by the said acts, and all judicial proceedings which shall be hereafter had in affirmance thereof, are and shall be held utterly null and void.

South Carolina Convention's "Address to the People of the United States," November, 1832. *Statutes of South Carolina,* I, 348-49.

We hold, then, that on their separation from the Crown of Great Britain, the several colonies became free and independent States, each enjoying the separate and independent right of self government; and that no authority can be exercised over them or within their limits, but by their consent, respectively given as States. It is equally true, that the Constitution of the United States is a compact formed between the several States, acting as sovereign communities; that the government created by it is a joint agency of the States, appointed to execute the powers enumerated and granted by that instrument; that all its acts not intentionally authorized are of themselves essentially null and void, and that the States have the right, in the same sovereign capacity in which they adopted the Federal Constitution, to pronounce, in the last resort, authoritative judgment on the usurpations of the Federal Government, and to adopt such measures as they may deem necessary and expedient to arrest the operation of the unconstitutional acts of that Government, within their respective limits. Such we deem to be inherent rights of the States; rights, in the very nature of things, absolutely inseparable from sovereignty. Nor is the duty of a State, to arrest an unconstitutional and oppressive act of the Federal Government less imperative, than the right is incontestible. Each State, by ratifying the Federal Constitution, and becoming a member of the confederacy, contracted an obligation to "protect and defend" that instrument, as well by resisting the usurpations of the Federal Government, as by sustaining that government in the exercise of the powers actually conferred upon it. And the obligation of the oath which is imposed, under the Constitution, on every functionary of the States to "preserve, protect, and defend" the Federal Constitution, as clearly comprehends the duty of protecting and defending it against the usurpations of the Federal Government, as that of protecting and defending it against violation in any other form or from any other quarter.

It is true, that in ratifying the Federal Constitution, the States placed a large and important portion of the rights of their citizens under the joint protection of all the States, with a view to their more effectual security; but it is not less true that they reserved a portion still larger and not less important under their own immediate guardianship, and in relation to which their original obligation to protect their citizens, from whatever quarter assailed, remains unchanged and undiminished.

South Carolina Resolution on Andrew Jackson's Nullification Proclamation, December 17, 1832. *Statutes of South Carolina,* I, 356-57.

Resolved, That the opinions of the President, in regard to the rights of the States, are erroneous and dangerous, leading not only to the establishment of a consolidated government in the stead of our free confederacy, but to the concentration of all power in the chief executive. . . .

Resolved, That each state of the Union has the right, whenever it may deem such a course necessary for the preservation of its liberties or vital interests, to secede peaceably from the Union,

and that there is no constitutional power in the general government, much less in the executive department, of that government,
to retain by force such state in the Union.

Resolved, That the primary and paramount allegiance of the
citizens of this state, native or adopted, is of right due to this
state....

Resolved, That while this legislature has witnessed with sor-
row such a relaxation of the spirit of our institutions, that a President of the United States dare venture upon this highhanded measure, it regards with indignation the menaces which are directed
against it, and the concentration of a standing army on our bor-
ders—that the state will repel force by force, and relying upon the
blessings of God, will maintain its liberty at all hazards.

John C. Calhoun, speech on the Force Bill, January 22, 1833.
Register of Debates in Congress, 22d Cong., 2d Sess., 1832-
33 (Washington, D.C., 1833), Vol IX, Pt. 1, 187-91.

... There are two views of our constitution, going back to its
fundamental principles; one contained in the proclamation and the
message of the President, which have given birth to the bill, and
the other the ordinance and proceedings of the people of South
Carolina. As the one or the other of these views may be correct,
the bill must be pronounced to be constitutional or unconstitutional.
If it be true, as stated by the President, that the people of these
United States are united on the principle of a social compact, as so
many individuals constituting one nation; if they have transferred
to the General Government their allegiance; if they have parted
with the right of judging, in the last resort, what powers are reserved and what delegated; then, indeed, the States are without
sovereignty, without rights; and no other objection can be made to
the bill but what might be made to its expediency. But if, on the
other hand, these positions are utterly false; if, in truth, the constitution is the work of the people forming twenty-four distinct
political communities; if, when adopted, it formed a union of States,
and not of individuals; if the States have not surrendered the right
of judging in the last resort, as to the extent of the reserved, and,
of course, of the delegated powers; then, indeed, there is not a
shadow of foundation in the constitution to authorize the bill; but,
on the contrary, it would be wholly repugnant to its genius, destructive of its very existence; and involve a political sin of the highest
character—of the delegated acting against the sovereign power—of
the creature warring against the creator....

The great question at issue is, where is the paramount power? Where the sovereignty in this complex, but beautiful and admirable system (if well understood) is lodged? for where the sovereignty is, there too must be the paramount power. A few plain, simple, and incontrovertible positions will determine this point. That the people of the States as constituting separate communities, formed the constitution, is as unquestionable as any historical fact whatever. It stands upon the most durable and unquestionable record—as much so as the records of any court in the universe; and that the Union, of which the constitutional compact is the bond, is a union between States, and not between a mere mass of individuals, rests on authority not less high—on the constitution itself, which expressly declares, in the article of ratification, that it shall be binding *between the States ratifying the same* —words more explicit, he would say *technical,* could not be devised; yet, as certain as these facts are, they cannot be admitted without admitting the doctrines for which South Carolina contends. They, by the most certain and direct deduction, conclusively will show where the paramount power of the system is—where its sovereign authority resides.

No one will pretend that the sovereignty is in the Government. To make that assertion would be to go back to the Asiatic idea of government—it is scarcely European, as the most intelligent writers in that section of the globe long since traced sovereignty to a higher source. No, the sovereignty is not in the Government, it is in the people. Any other conception is utterly abhorrent to the ideas of every American. There is not a particle of sovereignty in the Government. If, then, it be in the people, which cannot be denied, unless by extinguishing the lights of political science for more than two thousand years, the only possible question that can remain is, in what people? In the people of the United States collectively, as a mass of individuals, or in the people of the twenty-four States, as forming distinct political communities, confederated in this Union? The facts already published decide this question, and prove the sovereignty to be in the people of the several States. No such community ever existed as the people of the United States, forming a collective body of individuals in one nation; and the idea that they are so united by the present constitution, as a social compact, as alleged by the proclamation, is utterly false and absurd. To call the constitution the social compact, is the greatest possible abuse of language. No two things are more dissimilar; there is not an expression in the whole science of politics more perfectly definite in its meaning than the social compact. It means that association of individuals, founded on the implied assent of all its members, which precedes all Government, and from which Government or the constitutional compact springs; and yet, the President, in the daring attempt to put down our federal system, has ventured to confound things so totally dissimilar. The sovereignty, then, is in the people of the several States, united in this federal Union. It is not only in them, but in them unimpaired; not a particle resides in the Government; not one particle in the American people collectively.

The people of the States have, indeed, delegated a portion of their sovereignty, to be exercised conjointly by a General Government, and have retained the residue to be exercised by their respective State Governments. But to delegate is not to part with or to impair power. The delegated power in the agent is as much the power of the principal as if it remained in the latter, and may, as between him and his agent, be controlled or resumed at pleasure....

... According to our American ideas, sovereignty, instead of lying dormant in the mass of individuals composing a State, and instead of being capable of being called into action by a revolutionary movement only, has a known, organic, and peaceable means of action. That means is a convention of the people. Through its instrumentality all of our constitutions, State and Federal, were formed and ratified. Through the same authentic voice the people of South Carolina spoke in her late ordinance; which, as far as her citizens are concerned, is not less obligatory than the constitution itself.

... High as the authority of the court may be, its powers are but delegated powers; it makes a part of the Government itself; and, like every other portion of the Government, is destitute of the least particle of sovereign power. As delegated powers may be resumed by the sovereign delegating the same, such a resumption may be a breach of compact—a violation of the faith of the State; but, even in that case, the State, as a community, and not its citizens individually, is liable. The State, as a community, can break no law. It can, as a sovereign body, be subject to none. It may pledge its faith; it may delegate its powers; it may break the one and resume the other; but the remedy, in such cases, is not hostile enactments; not law, by which the citizens individually are made responsible—as the bill most assuredly and preposterously proposed; but open force—war itself—unless there be some provision of a remedial and peaceful character provided in the compact.

... He alluded to the provision by which all contests for power between the Federal Government and the States may be virtually decided in a convention of the States. That is the true, wise, and constitutional means of terminating this controversy. Let the States be convened in convention; let the stockholders, if he might be permitted so to express himself, of this great political partnership be called together, that all conflicts of power between the directors and any portion of the stockholders may be determined in conformity to the provisions prescribed in the charter of association.

... viewing the bill on its principles, he conceived it a virtual repeal of the constitution, as much so as if it was expressly drawn on its face with "Be it enacted by the authority of the Senate and House of Representatives, that the constitution be, and the same is hereby repealed." Should it pass, it will effectually and forever put down our beautiful federal system, and rear on its ruins a consolidated Government. The sovereignty of the States would be forever submerged—that sovereignty which constituted ours a federal system, and the loss of which would make it a consolidation.

... But two modes of political existence can long endure in our country; the one that formed, by the framers of our admirable constitution, a federal system, uniting free and independent States in a bond of union for mutual advantages, and to be preserved by the concurrent assent of the parts; or a government of the sword. The choice is before us.

John C. Calhoun, speech on the Force Bill, February 15-16, 1833. *Works of Calhoun,* II, 229-52.

... I proclaim it, that, should this bill pass, and an attempt be made to enforce it, it will be resisted at every hazard, even that of death itself. Death is not the greatest calamity; there are others still more terrible to the free and brave; and among them may be placed the loss of liberty and honor. There are thousands of her brave sons who, if need be, are prepared cheerfully to lay down their lives in defense of the State, and the great principles of constitutional liberty for which she is contending. God forbid that this should become necessary! It never can be, unless this Government is resolved to bring the question to extremity, when her gallant sons will stand prepared to perform their last duty—to die nobly.

... the sovereignty is in the several States, and . . . our system is a union of twenty-four sovereign powers, under a constitutional compact, and not of a divided sovereignty between the States severally and the United States. In spite of all that has been said, he maintained that sovereignty is in its nature indivisible. It is the supreme power in a State; and we might just as well speak of half a square, or half of a triangle, as of half a sovereignty. It is a gross error to confound the exercise of sovereign powers with sovereignty itself; or the delegation of such powers with a surrender of them. A sovereign may delegate his powers to be exercised by as many agents as he may think proper, under such conditions and with such limitations as he may impose; but to surrender any portion of his sovereignty to another is to annihilate the whole....

... according to his (Mr. C.'s) conception, the whole sovereignty was in the several States, while the exercise of sovereign powers was divided, a part being exercised under compact, through this General Government, and the residue through the separate State Governments....

In the same spirit we are told that the Union must be preserved, without regard to the means. And how is it proposed to preserve the Union? By force! Does any man in his senses believe that this beautiful structure, this harmonious aggregate of States, produced by the joint consent of all, can be preserved by force? Its very introduction will be certain destruction of this Federal Union. No, no; you cannot keep the States united in their constitutional and federal bonds by force. Force may, indeed, hold the parts together; but such union would be the bond between master and slave; a union of exaction on one side, and of unqualified obedience on the other....

Disguise it as you may, the controversy is one between power and liberty; and he would tell the gentlemen who are opposed to him, that, strong as might be the love of power on their side, the love of liberty is still stronger on ours. History furnishes many instances of similar struggles, where the love of liberty has prevailed against power, under every disadvantage; and, among them, few more striking than that of our own revolution; where, strong as was the parent country, and feeble as were the colonies, yet, under the impulse of liberty and the blessing of God, they gloriously triumphed in the contest. There were, indeed, many and striking analogies between that and the present controversy....

... others, had relied with great emphasis on the fact, that we are citizens of the United States. I, said Mr. C., do not object to the expression, nor shall I detract from the proud and elevated feelings with which it is associated; but he trusted that he might be permitted to raise the inquiry, in what manner we are citizens of the United States, without weakening the patriotic feeling with which he trusted it would ever be uttered. If, by citizen of the

United States he meant a citizen at large, one whose citizenship extended to the entire geographical limits of the country, without having a local citizenship in some State or Territory, a sort of citizen of the world, all he had to say was, that such a citizen would be a perfect nondescript; that not a single individual of this description could be found in the entire mass of our population. Notwithstanding all the pomp and display of eloquence on the occasion, every citizen is a citizen of some State or Territory, and, as such, under an express provision of the constitution, is entitled to all privileges and immunities of citizens in the several States; and it is in this, and in no other sense, that we are citizens of the United States....

... He knew that it was not only the opinion of a large majority of our country, but it might be said to be the opinion of the age, that the very *beau ideal* of a perfect Government was the Government of a majority, acting through a representative body, without check or limitation in its power; yet if we may test this theory by experience and reason, we will find that, so far from being perfect, the necessary tendency of all Governments, based upon the will of an absolute majority, without constitutional check or limitation of power, is to faction, corruption, anarchy, and despotism; and this, whether the will of the majority be expressed directly through an assembly of the people themselves or by their representatives. I know (said Mr. C.) that in venturing this assertion I utter that which is unpopular, both within and without these walls; but, where truth and liberty are concerned, such considerations should not be regarded. He would place the decision of this point on the fact, that no Government of the kind, among the many attempts which had been made, had ever endured for a single generation. . . . The moment that Government is put into operation, as soon as it begins to collect taxes, and to make appropriations, the different portions of the community must, of necessity, bear different and opposing relations in reference to the action of the Government. There must inevitably spring up two interests—a direction and a stockholder interest; an interest profiting by the action of the Government, and interested in increasing its powers and action; and another at whose expense the political machine is kept in motion....

... The first mistake was, in supposing that the Government of the absolute majority is the Government of this people; that *beau ideal* of a perfect Government, which had been so enthusiastically entertained in every age, by the generous and patriotic, where civilization and liberty had made the smallest progress. There could be no greater error; the Government of the people is the Government of the whole community; of the twenty-four; the self-government of all the parts; too perfect to be reduced to practice in the present, or any past stage of human society. The Government of the absolute majority, instead of the Government of the people, is but the Government of the strongest interests; and when not efficiently checked, is the most tyrannical and oppressive that can be devised....

... Under every circumstance, the majority will ever have its American system—(he meant nothing offensive to any Senator)— but the real meaning of the American system is, that system of plunder which the stronger interest ever waged, and will ever wage, against the weaker, where the latter is not armed with some efficient and constitutional check to arrest its action. Nothing but such check on the part of the weaker interest can arrest it; mere constitutional limitations are wholly inefficient. Whatever interest obtains possession of the Government will, from the nature of things, be in favor of the powers, and against the limitations imposed by the constitution, and will resort to every device that can be imagined to remove those restraints....

Comments on John C. Calhoun in Harriet Martineau's *Retrospect of Western Travel* (London, 1838), 147-48. This English traveler later aroused the South with her public approval of the abolition of slavery.

Our pleasantest evenings were some spent at home in a society of the highest order. Ladies, literary, fashionable, or domestic would spend an hour with us on their way from a dinner or to a ball. Members of Congress would repose themselves by our fireside. Mr. Clay, sitting upright on the sofa, with his snuffbox ever in his hand, would discourse for many an hour in his even, soft, deliberate tone on any one of the great subjects of American policy which we might happen to start, always amazing us with the moderation of estimate and speech which so impetuous a nature has been able to attain. Mr. Webster, leaning back at his ease, telling stories, cracking jokes, shaking the sofa with burst after burst of laughter, or smoothly discoursing to the perfect felicity of the logical part of one's constitution, would illuminate an evening now and then. Mr. Calhoun, the cast-iron man, who looks as if he had never been born and never could be extinguished, would come in sometimes to keep our understandings upon a painful stretch for a short while, and leave us to take to pieces his close, rapid, theoretical, illustrated talk, and see what we could make

of it.   We found it usually more worth retaining as a curiosity
than as either very just or useful. His speech abounds in figures,
truly illustrative, if that which they illustrate were but true also.
But his theories of government (almost the only subject on which
his thoughts are employed), the squarest and compactest that ever
were made, are composed out of limited elements, and are not,
therefore, likely to stand service very well. It is at first extremely
interesting to hear Mr. Calhoun talk; and there is a never-failing
evidence of power in all he says and does which commands
intellectual reverence; but the admiration is too soon turned into
regret, into absolute melancholy.   It is impossible to resist the
conviction that all this force can be at best but useless, and is but
too likely to be very mischievous.   His mind has long lost all
power of communicating with any other.   I know of no man who
lives in such utter intellectual solitude.   He meets men, and
harangues them by the fireside as in the Senate; he is wrought
like a piece of machinery, set agoing vehemently by a weight,
and stops while you answer; he either passes by what you say or
twists it into a suitability with what is in his head, and begins to
lecture again. Of course, a mind like this can have little influence
in the Senate, except by virtue, perpetually wearing out, of what
it did in its less eccentric days; but its influence at home is to
be dreaded.   There is no hope that an intellect so cast in narrow
theories will accommodate itself to varying circumstances; and
there is every danger that it will break up all that it can, in order
to remould the materials in its own way. Mr. Calhoun is as full as
ever of his nullification doctrines; and those who know the force
that is in him, and his utter incapacity of modification by other
minds (after having gone through as remarkable a revolution of
political opinions as perhaps any man ever experienced), will
no more expect repose and self-retention from him than from a
volcano in full force. Relaxation is no longer in the power of his
will.   I never saw anyone who so completely gave me the idea
of possession.   Half an hour's conversation with him is enough
to make a necessarian of anybody.   Accordingly, he is more
complained of than blamed by his enemies.   His moments of
softness in his family, and when recurring to old college days,
are hailed by all as a relief to the vehement working of the intellectual machine; a relief equally to himself and others.   Those
moments are as touching to the observer as tears on the face of
a soldier.

From John C. Calhoun, *A Disquisition on Government,* printed in *Works of Calhoun,* I, 5-45. Calhoun worked on the *Disquisition* and on the *Discourse on the Constitution and Government of the United States* during the last five years of his life, and it is unlikely that he had entirely completed the corrections when he died in the spring of 1850.

. . . while man is so constituted as to make the social state necessary to his existence and the full development of his faculties, this state itself cannot exist without government. . . .

But government, although intended to protect and preserve society, has itself a strong tendency to disorder and abuse of its powers, as all experience and almost every page of history testify. . . . They must be administered by men in whom, like others, the individual are stronger than the social feelings. And hence the powers vested in them to prevent injustice and oppression on the part of others will, if left unguarded, be by them converted into instruments to oppress the rest of the community. That by which this is prevented, by whatever name called, is what is meant by *constitution,* in its most comprehensive sense, when applied to *government.*

. . . without a constitution—something to counteract the strong tendency of government to disorder and abuse and to give stability to political institutions—there can be little progress or permanent improvement.

. . . Such an organism, then, as will furnish the means by which resistance may be systematically and peaceably made on the part of the ruled to oppression and abuse of power on the part of the rulers is the first and indispensable step toward *forming* a constitutional government. . . .

. . . the very uncertainty of the tenure, combined with the violent party warfare which must ever precede a change of parties under such governments, would rather tend to increase than diminish the tendency to oppression.

As, then, the right of suffrage, without some other provision, cannot counteract this tendency of government, the next question for consideration is—What is that other provision? This demands the most serious consideration; for of all the questions embraced in the science of government, it involves a principle, the most important, and the least understood; and when understood, the most difficult of application in practice. It is, indeed, emphatically, that principle which *makes* the constitution, in its strict and limited sense.

From what has been said, it is manifest, that this provision must be of a character calculated to prevent any one interest, or combination of interests, from using the powers of government to aggrandize itself at the expense of the others. Here lies the evil: and just in proportion as it shall prevent, or fail to prevent it, in the same degree it will effect, or fail to effect the end intended to be accomplished. There is but one certain mode in which this result can be secured; and that is, by the adoption of some restriction or limitation, which shall so effectually prevent any one interest, or combination of interests, from obtaining the exclusive control of the government, as to render hopeless all attempts directed to that end. There is, again, but one mode in which this can be effected; and that is, by taking the sense of each interest or portion of the community, which may be unequally and injuriously affected by the action of the government, separately, through its own majority, or in some other way by which its voice may be fairly expressed; and to require the consent of each interest, either to put or to keep the government in action. This, too, can be accomplished only in one way,—and that is, by such an organism of the government,—and, if necessary for the purpose, of the community also,—as will, by dividing and distributing the powers of government, give to each division or interest, through its appropriate organ, either a concurrent voice in making and executing the laws, or a veto on their execution. It is only by such an organism, that the assent of each can be made necessary to put the government in motion; or the power made effectual to arrest its action, when put in motion;—and it is only by the one or the other that the different interests, orders, classes, or portions, into which the community may be divided, can be protected, and all conflict and struggle between them prevented,—by rendering it impossible to put or to keep it in action, without the concurrent consent of all.

Such an organism as this, combined with the right of suffrage, constitutes, in fact, the elements of constitutional government. The one, by rendering those who make and execute the laws responsible to those on whom they operate, prevents the rulers from oppressing the ruled; and the other, by making it impossible for any one interest or combination of interests or class, or order, or portion of the community, to obtain exclusive control, prevents any one of them from oppressing the other. It is clear, that oppression and abuse of power must come, if at all, from the one or the other quarter. From no other can they come. It follows, that the two, suffrage and proper organism combined, are sufficient to counteract the tendency of government to oppression and abuse of power; and to restrict it to the fulfilment of the great ends for which it is ordained.

In coming to this conclusion, I have assumed the organism to be perfect, and the different interests, portions, or classes of the community, to be sufficiently enlightened to understand its character and object, and to exercise, with due intelligence, the right of suffrage. To the extent that either may be defective, to the same extent the government would fall short of fulfilling its end. But this does not impeach the truth of the principles on which it rests. In reducing them to proper form, in applying them to practical uses, all elementary principles are liable to difficulties; but they are not, on this account, the less true, or valuable. Where the organism is perfect, every interest will be truly and fully represented, and of course the whole community must be so. It may be difficult, or even impossible, to make a perfect organism,—but, although this be true, yet even when, instead of the sense of each and of all, it takes that of a few great and prominent interests only, it would still, in a great measure, if not altogether, fulfil the end intended by a constitution. For, in such case, it would require so large a portion of the community, compared with the whole, to concur, or acquiesce in the action of the government, that the number to be plundered would be too few, and the number to be aggrandized too many, to afford adequate motives to oppression and the abuse of its powers. Indeed, however imperfect the organism, it must have more or less effect in diminishing such tendency.

It may be readily inferred, from what has been stated, that the effect of organism is neither to supersede nor diminish the importance of the right of suffrage; but to aid and perfect it. The object of the latter is, to collect the sense of the community. The more fully and perfectly it accomplishes this, the more fully and perfectly it fulfils its end. But the most it can do, of itself, is to collect the sense of the greater number; that is, of the stronger interests, or combination of interests; and to assume this to be the sense of the community. It is only when aided by a proper organism, that it can collect the sense of the entire community,—of each and all its interests; of each, through its appropriate organ, and of the whole, through all of them united. This would truly be the sense of the entire community; for whatever diversity each interest might have within itself,—as all would have the same interest in reference to the action of the government, the individuals composing each would be fully and truly represented by its own majority or appropriate organ, regarded in reference to the other interests. In brief, every individual of every interest might trust, with confidence, its majority or appropriate organ, against that of every other interest.

It results, from what has been said, that there are two different modes in which the sense of the community may be taken; one, simply by the right of suffrage, unaided; the other, by the right through a proper organism. Each collects the sense of the majority. But one regards numbers only, and considers the whole community as a unit, having but one common interest throughout; and collects the sense of the greater number of the whole, as that of the community. The other, on the contrary, regards interests as well as numbers;—considering the community as made up of different and conflicting interests, as far as the action of the government is concerned; and takes the sense of each, through its majority or appropriate organ, and the united sense of all, as the sense of the entire community. The former of these I shall call the numerical, or absolute majority; and the latter, the concurrent, or constitutional majority. I call it the constitutional majority, because it is an essential element in every constitutional government,—be its form what it may. So great is the difference, politically speaking, between the two majorities, that they cannot be confounded, without leading to great and fatal errors; and yet the distinction between them has been so entirely overlooked, that when the term *majority* is used in political discussions, it is applied exclusively to designate the numerical,—as if there were no other. Until this distinction is recognized, and better understood, there will continue to be great liability to error in properly constructing constitutional governments, especially of the popular form, and of preserving them when properly constructed. Until then, the latter will have a strong tendency to slide, first, into the government of the numerical majority, and, finally, into absolute government of some other form. To show that such must be the case, and at the same time to mark more strongly the difference between the two, in order to guard against the danger of overlooking it, I propose to consider the subject more at length.

The first and leading error which naturally arises from overlooking the distinction referred to, is, to confound the numerical majority with the people; and this so completely as to regard them as identical. This is a consequence that necessarily results from considering the numerical as the only majority. All admit, that a popular government, or democracy, is the government of the people; for the terms imply this. A perfect government of the kind would be one which would embrace the consent of every citizen or member of the community; but as this is impracticable, in the opinion of those who regard the numerical as the only majority, and who can perceive no other way by which the sense of the people can be taken,—they are compelled to adopt this as the only true basis of popular government, in contradistinction to governments of the aristocratical or monarchical form. Being thus constrained, they are, in the next place, forced to regard the numerical majority, as, in effect, the entire people; that is, the greater part as the whole; and the government of the greater part as the government of the whole. It is thus the two come to be confounded, and a part made identical with the whole. And it is thus, also, that all the rights, powers, and immunities of the whole people come to be attributed to the numerical majority; and, among others, the supreme, sovereign authority of establishing and abolishing governments at pleasure.

This radical error, the consequence of confounding the two, and of regarding the numerical as the only majority, has contributed more than any other cause, to prevent the formation of popular constitutional governments,—and to destroy them even when they have been formed. It leads to the conclusion that, in their formation and establishment nothing more is necessary than the right of suffrage,—and the allotment to each division of the community a representation in the government, in proportion to numbers. If the numerical majority were really the people; and if, to take its sense truly, were to take the sense of the people truly, a government so constituted would be a true and perfect model of a popular constitutional government; and every departure from it would detract from its excellence. But, as such is not the case,—as the numerical majority, instead of being the people, is only a portion of them.—such a government, instead of being a true and perfect model of the people's government, that is, a people self-governed, is but the government of a part, over a part,—the major over the minor portion.

But this misconception of the true elements of constitutional government does not stop here. It leads to others equally false and fatal, in reference to the best means of preserving and perpetuating them, when, from some fortunate combination of circumstances, they are correctly formed. For they who fall into these errors regard the restrictions which organism imposes on the will of the numerical majority as restrictions on the will of the people, and, therefore, as not only useless, but wrongful and mischievous. And hence they endeavor to destroy organism, under the delusive hope of making government more democratic.

Such are some of the consequences of confounding the two, and of regarding the numerical as the only majority. And in this may be found the reason why so few popular governments have been properly constructed, and why, of these few, so small a number have proved durable. Such must continue to be the result, so long as these errors continue to be prevalent.

There is another error, of a kindred character, whose influence contributes much to the same results: I refer to the prevalent opinion, that a written constitution, containing suitable restrictions on the powers of government, is sufficient, of itself, without the aid of any organism,—except such as is necessary to separate its several departments, and render them independent of each other,—to counteract the tendency of the numerical majority to oppression and the abuse of power.

A written constitution certainly has many and considerable advantages; but it is a great mistake to suppose, that the mere insertion of provisions to restrict and limit the powers of the government, without investing those for whose protection they are inserted with the means of enforcing their observance, will be sufficient to prevent the major and dominant party from abusing its powers.   Being the party in possession of the government, they will, from the same constitution of man which makes government necessary to protect society, be in favor of the powers granted by the constitution, and opposed to the restrictions intended to limit them.   As the major and dominant party, they will have no need of these restrictions for their protection. The ballot-box, of itself, would be ample protection to them. Needing no other, they would come, in time, to regard these limitations as unnecessary and improper restraints;—and endeavor to elude them, with the view of increasing their power and influence.

The minor, or weaker party, on the contrary, would take the opposite direction;—and regard them as essential to their protection against the dominant party.   And, hence, they would endeavor to defend and enlarge the restrictions, and to limit and contract the powers.   But where there are no means by which they could compel the major party to observe the restrictions, the only resort left them would be, a strict construction of the constitution,—that is, a construction which would confine these powers to the narrowest limits which the meaning of the words used in the grant would admit.

To this the major party would oppose a liberal construction,— one which would give to the words of the grant the broadest meaning of which they were susceptible.   It would then be construction against construction; the one to contract, and the other to enlarge the powers of the government to the utmost.   But of what possible avail could the strict construction of the minor party be, against the liberal interpretation of the major, when the one would have all the powers of the government to carry its construction into effect,—and the other be deprived of all means of enforcing its construction?   In a contest so unequal, the result would not be doubtful.   The party in favor of the restrictions would be overpowered.   At first, they might command some respect, and do something to stay the march of encroachment; but they would, in the progress of the contest, be regarded as mere abstractionists; and, indeed, deservedly, if they should indulge the folly of supposing that the party in possession of the ballot-box and the physical force of the country, could be successfully resisted by an appeal to reason, truth, justice, or the obligations imposed by the constitution.   For when these, of themselves, shall exert sufficient influence to stay the hand of power, then government will be no longer necessary to protect society, nor constitutions needed to prevent government from abusing its powers.   The end of the contest would be the subversion of the constitution, either by the undermining process of construction, —where its meaning would admit of possible doubt,—or by substituting in practice what is called party-usage, in place of its provisions;—or, finally, when no other contrivance would subserve the purpose, by openly and boldly setting them aside.   By the one or the other, the restrictions would ultimately be annulled, and the government be converted into one of unlimited powers.

Nor would the division of government into separate, and, as it regards each other, independent departments, prevent this result.   Such a division may do much to facilitate its operations, and to secure to its administration greater caution and deliberation; but as each and all the departments,—and, of course, the entire government,—would be under the control of the numerical majority, it is too clear to require explanation, that a mere distribution of its powers among its agents or representatives, could do little or nothing to counteract its tendency to oppression and abuse of power.   To effect this, it would be necessary to go one step further, and make the several departments the organs of the distinct interests or portions of the community; and to clothe each with a negative on the others.   But the effect of this would be to change the government from the numerical into the concurrent majority.

Having now explained the reasons why it is so difficult to form and preserve popular constitutional government, so long as the distinction between the two majorities is overlooked, and the opinion prevails that a written constitution, with suitable restrictions and a proper division of its powers, is sufficient to counteract the tendency of the numerical majority to the abuse of its power,—I shall next proceed to explain, more fully, why the concurrent majority is an indispensable element in forming constitutional governments; and why the numerical majority, of itself, must, in all cases, make governments absolute.

The necessary consequence of taking the sense of the community by the concurrent majority is, as has been explained, to give to each interest or portion of the community a negative on the others. It is this mutual negative among its various conflicting interests, which invests each with the power of protecting itself;—and places the rights and safety of each, where only they can be securely placed, under its own guardianship. Without this there can be no systematic, peaceful, or effective resistance to the natural tendency of each to come into conflict with the others: and without this there can be no constitution. It is this negative power,—the power of preventing or arresting the action of the government,—be it called by what term it may,—veto, interposition, nullification, check, or balance of power,—which, in fact, forms the constitution. They are all but different names for the negative power. In all its forms, and under all its names, it results from the concurrent majority. Without this there can be no negative; and, without a negative, no constitution. The assertion is true in reference to all constitutional governments, be their forms what they may. It is, indeed, the negative power which makes the constitution,—and the positive which makes the government. The one is the power of acting;—and the other the power of preventing or arresting action. The two, combined, make constitutional governments.

But, as there can be no constitution without the negative power, and no negative power without the concurrent majority; —it follows, necessarily, that where the numerical majority has the sole control of the government, there can be no constitution; as constitution implies limitation or restriction,—and, of course, is inconsistent with the idea of sole or exclusive power. And hence, the numerical, unmixed with the concurrent majority, necessarily forms, in all cases, absolute government.

It is, indeed, the single, or *one power*, which excludes the negative, and constitutes absolute government; and not the *number* in whom the power is vested. The numerical majority is as truly a *single power*, and excludes the negative as completely as the absolute government of one, or of the few. The former is as much the absolute government of the democratic, or popular form, as the latter of the monarchical or aristocratical. It has, accordingly, in common with them, the same tendency to oppression and abuse of power.

Constitutional governments, of whatever form, are, indeed, much more similar to each other, in their structure and character, than they are, respectively, to the absolute governments, even of their own class. All constitutional governments, of whatever

class they may be, take the sense of the community by its parts,
—each through its appropriate organ; and regard the sense of all
its parts, as the sense of the whole. They all rest on the right of
suffrage, and the responsibility of rulers, directly or indirectly.
On the contrary, all absolute governments, of whatever form,
concentrate power in one uncontrolled and irresponsible individual or body, whose will is regarded as the sense of the community. And, hence, the great and broad distinction between
governments is,—not that of the one, the few, or the many,—
but of the constitutional and the absolute.

From this there results another distinction, which, although
secondary in its character, very strongly marks the difference
between these forms of government. I refer to their respective
conservative principle;—that is, the principle by which they are
upheld and preserved. This principle, in constitutional governments, is *compromise;*—and in absolute governments, is *force;*—
as will be next explained.

It has been already shown, that the same constitution of man
which leads those who govern to oppress the governed,—if not
prevented,—will, with equal force and certainty, lead the latter
to resist oppression, when possessed of the means of doing so
peaceably and successfully. But absolute governments, of all
forms, exclude all other means of resistance to their authority,
than that of force; and, of course, leave no other alternative to
the governed, but to acquiesce in oppression, however great it
may be, or to resort to force to put down the government. But
the dread of such a resort must necessarily lead the government
to prepare to meet force in order to protect itself; and hence, of
necessity, force becomes the conservative principle of all such
governments.

On the contrary, the government of the concurrent majority,
where the organism is perfect, excludes the possibility of oppression, by giving to each interest, or portion, or order,—where
there are established classes,—the means of protecting itself, by
its negative, against all measures calculated to advance the peculiar interests of others at its expense. Its effect, then, is, to cause
the different interests, portions, or orders,—as the case may be,—
to desist from attempting to adopt any measure calculated to promote the prosperity of one, or more, by sacrificing that of others;
and thus to force them to unite in such measures only as would
promote the prosperity of all, as the only means to prevent the
suspension of the action of the government;—and, thereby, to
avoid anarchy, the greatest of all evils. It is by means of such
authorized and effectual resistance, that oppression is prevented,

and the necessity of resorting to force superseded, in governments of the concurrent majority;—and, hence, compromise, instead of force, becomes their conservative principle.

It would, perhaps, be more strictly correct to trace the conservative principle of constitutional governments to the necessity
which compels the different interests, or portions, or orders, to
compromise,—as the only way to promote their respective prosperity, and to avoid anarchy,—rather than to the compromise
itself. No necessity can be more urgent and imperious, than that
of avoiding anarchy. It is the same as that which makes government indispensable to preserve society; and is not less imperative
than that which compels obedience to superior force. Traced to
this source, the voice of a people,—uttered under the necessity of
avoiding the greatest of calamities, through the organs of a government so constructed as to suppress the expression of all partial
and selfish interests, and to give a full and faithful utterance to
the sense of the whole community, in reference to its common welfare,—may, without impiety, be called *the voice of God*. To call any
other so, would be impious.

In stating that force is the conservative principle of absolute,
and compromise of constitutional governments, I have assumed
both to be perfect in their kind; but not without bearing in mind,
that few or none, in fact, have ever been so absolute as not to be
under some restraint, and none so perfectly organized as to represent fully and perfectly the voice of the whole community. Such
being the case, all must, in practice, depart more or less from
the principles by which they are respectively upheld and preserved; and depend more or less for support, on force, or compromise, as the absolute or the constitutional form predominates
in their respective organizations.

Nor, in stating that absolute governments exclude all other
means of resistance to its authority than that of force, have I
overlooked the case of governments of the numerical majority,
which form, apparently, an exception. It is true that, in such governments, the minor and subject party, for the time, have the
right to oppose and resist the major and dominant party, for the
time, through the ballot-box; and may turn them out, and take
their place, if they can obtain a majority of votes. But, it is no
less true, that this would be a mere change in the relations of the
two parties. The minor and subject party would become the major
and dominant party, with the same absolute authority and tendency
to abuse power; and the major and dominant party would become
the minor and subject party, with the same right to resist through
the ballot-box; and, if successful, again to change relations, with

like effect. But such a state of things must necessarily be temporary. The conflict between the two parties must be transferred,
sooner or later, from an appeal to the ballot-box to an appeal to
force;—as I shall next proceed to explain.

The conflict between the two parties, in the government of the
numerical majority, tends necessarily to settle down into a struggle for the honors and emoluments of the government; and each, in
order to obtain an object so ardently desired, will, in the process
of the struggle, resort to whatever measure may seem best calculated to effect this purpose. The adoption, by the one, of any measure, however objectionable, which might give it an advantage,
would compel the other to follow its example. In such case, it
would be indispensable to success to avoid division and keep
united;—and hence, from a necessity inherent in the nature of such
governments, each party must be alternately forced, in order to
insure victory, to resort to measures to concentrate the control
over its movements in fewer and fewer hands, as the struggle became more and more violent. This, in process of time, must lead
to party organization, and party caucuses and discipline; and these,
to the conversion of the honors and emoluments of the government
into means of rewarding partisan services, in order to secure the
fidelity and increase the zeal of the members of the party. The
effect of the whole combined, even in the earlier stages of the
process, when they exert the least pernicious influence, would be
to place the control of the two parties in the hands of their respective majorities; and the government itself, virtually, under the
control of the majority of the dominant party, for the time, instead
of the majority of the whole community;—where the theory of this
form of government vests it. Thus, in the very first stage of the
process, the government becomes the government of a minority
instead of a majority;—a minority, usually, and under the most
favorable circumstances, of not much more than one-fourth of the
whole community.

But the process, as regards the concentration of power, would
not stop at this stage. The government would gradually pass from
the hands of the majority of the party into those of its leaders; as
the struggle became more intense, and the honors and emoluments
of the government the all-absorbing objects. At this stage, principles and policy would lose all influence in the elections; and cunning, falsehood, deception, slander, fraud, and gross appeals to
the appetites of the lowest and most worthless portions of the
community, would take the place of sound reason and wise debate.
After these have thoroughly debased and corrupted the community,
and all the arts and devices of party have been exhausted, the gov-

ernment would vibrate between the two factions (for such will parties have become) at each successive election. Neither would be able to retain power beyond some fixed term; for those seeking office and patronage would become too numerous to be rewarded by the offices and patronage at the disposal of the government; and these being the sole objects of pursuit, the disappointed would, at the next succeeding election, throw their weight into the opposite scale, in the hope of better success at the next turn of the wheel. These vibrations would continue until confusion, corruption, disorder, and anarchy, would lead to an appeal to force;—to be followed by a revolution in the form of the government. Such must be the end of the government of the numerical majority; and such, in brief, the process through which it must pass, in the regular course of events, before it can reach it.

This transition would be more or less rapid, according to circumstances. The more numerous the population, the more extensive the country, the more diversified the climate, productions, pursuits and character of the people, the more wealthy, refined, and artificial their condition,—and the greater the amount of revenues and disbursements,—the more unsuited would the community be to such a government, and the more rapid would be the passage. On the other hand, it might be slow in its progress amongst small communities, during the early stages of their existence, with inconsiderable revenues and disbursements, and a population of simple habits; provided the people are sufficiently intelligent to exercise properly, the right of suffrage, and sufficiently conversant with the rules necessary to govern the deliberations of legislative bodies. It is, perhaps, the only form of popular government suited to a people, while they remain in such a condition. Any other would be not only too complex and cumbersome, but unnecessary to guard against oppression, where the motive to use power for that purpose would be so feeble. And hence, colonies, from countries having constitutional governments, if left to themselves, usually adopt governments based on the numerical majority. But as population increases, wealth accumulates, and, above all, the revenues and expenditures become large,—governments of this form must become less and less suited to the condition of society; until, if not in the mean time changed into governments of the concurrent majority, they must end in an appeal to force, to be followed by a radical change in its structure and character; and, most probably, into monarchy in its absolute form,—as will be next explained.

Such, indeed, is the repugnance between popular governments and force,—or, to be more specific,—military power,—that the almost necessary consequence of a resort to force, by such governments, in order to maintain their authority, is, not only a change of their form, but a change into the most opposite,—that of absolute monarchy. The two are the opposites of each other. From the nature of popular governments, the control of its powers is vested in the many; while military power, to be efficient, must be vested in a single individual. When, then, the two parties, in governments of the numerical majority, resort to force, in their struggle for supremacy, he who commands the successful party will have the control of the government itself. And, hence, in such contests, the party which may prevail, will usually find, in the commander of its forces, a master, under whom the great body of the community will be glad to find protection against the incessant agitation and violent struggles of two corrupt factions,—looking only to power as the means of securing to themselves the honors and emoluments of the government.

From the same cause, there is a like tendency in aristocratical to terminate in absolute governments of the monarchical form; but by no means as strong, because there is less repugnance between military power and aristocratical, than between it and democratical governments.

A broader position may, indeed, be taken; viz., that there is a tendency, in constitutional governments of every form, to degenerate into their respective absolute forms; and, in all absolute governments, into that of the monarchical form. But the tendency is much stronger in constitutional governments of the democratic form to degenerate into their respective absolute forms, than in either of the others; because, among other reasons, the distinction between the constitutional and absolute forms of aristocratical and monarchical governments, is far more strongly marked than in democratic governments. The effect of this is, to make the different orders or classes in an aristocracy, or monarchy, far more jealous and watchful of encroachment on their respective rights; and more resolute and persevering in resisting attempts to concentrate power in any one class or order. On the contrary, the line between the two forms, in popular governments, is so imperfectly understood, that honest and sincere friends of the constitutional form not unfrequently, instead of jealously watching and arresting their tendency to degenerate into their absolute forms, not only regard it with approbation, but employ all their powers to add to its strength and to increase its impetus, in the vain hope of making the government more perfect and popular. The numerical majority, perhaps, should usually be one of the elements of a constitutional democracy; but to make it the sole element, in order to perfect the constitution and make the government more popular, is one of the greatest and most fatal of political errors.

From John C. Calhoun, *Discourse on the Constitution*, in *Works of Calhoun*, I, 392-95.

How the Constitution could best be modified, so as to effect the object, can only be authoritatively determined by the amending power. It may be done in various ways. Among others, it might be effected through a reorganization of the executive department; so that its powers, instead of being vested, as they now are, in a single officer, should be vested in two; to be so elected as that the two should be constituted the special organs and representatives of the respective sections in the executive department of the government, and requiring each to approve all the acts of Congress before they shall become laws. One might be charged with the administration of matters connected with the foreign relations of the country, and the other of such as were connected with its domestic institutions, the selection to be decided by lot. It would thus effect, more simply, what was intended by the original provisions of the Constitution, in giving to one of the majorities composing the government a decided preponderance in the Electoral College, and to the other majority a still more decided influence in the eventual choice in case the College failed to elect a President. It was intended to effect an equilibrium between the larger and smaller States in this department, but which, in practice, has entirely failed, and, by its failure, done much to disturb the whole system and to bring about the present dangerous state of things.

Indeed, it may be doubted whether the framers of the Constitution did not commit a great mistake in constituting a single instead of a plural executive. Nay, it may even be doubted whether a single chief magistrate—invested with all the power properly appertaining to the executive department of the government, as is the President—is compatible with the permanence of a popular government, especially in a wealthy and populous community, with a large revenue and a numerous body of officers and employees. Certain it is that there is no instance of a popular government so constituted which has long endured. Even ours, thus far, furnishes no evidence in its favor, and not a little against it; for to it the present disturbed and dangerous state of things, which threatens the country with monarchy or disunion, may be justly attributed. On the other hand, the two most distinguished constitutional governments of antiquity, both in respect to permanence and power, had a dual executive. I refer to those of Sparta and of Rome. The former had two hereditary, and the latter two elective chief magistrates. It is true that England, from which ours, in this respect, is copied, has a single hereditary head of the executive department of her government; but it is not less true that she has had many and arduous struggles to prevent her chief magistrate from becoming absolute, and that, to guard against it effectually, she was finally compelled to divest him substantially of the power of administering the government by transferring it, practically, to a cabinet of responsible ministers, who, by established custom, cannot hold office unless supported by a majority of the two houses of Parliament. She has thus avoided the danger of the chief magistrate becoming absolute and contrived to unite, substantially, a single with a plural executive, in constituting that department of her government. We have no such guard, and can have none such without an entire change in the character of our government; and her example, of course, furnishes no evidence in favor of a single chief magistrate in a popular form of government like ours—while the example of former times, and our own thus far, furnish strong evidence against it.

But it is objected that a plural executive necessarily leads to intrigue and discord among its members, and that it is inconsistent with prompt and efficient action. This may be true when they are all elected by the same constituency and may be a good reason, where this is the case, for preferring a single executive, with all its objections, to a plural executive. But the case is very different where they are elected by different constituencies having conflicting and hostile interests, as would be the fact in the case under consideration. Here the two would have to act concurringly in approving the acts of Congress and separately in the sphere of their respective departments. The effect, in the latter case, would be to retain all the advantages of a single executive, as far as the administration of the laws were concerned; and, in the former, to insure harmony and concord between the two sections and, through them, in the government. For as no act of Congress could become a law without the assent of the chief magistrates representing both sections, each, in the elections, would choose the candidate who, in addition to being faithful to its interests, would best command the esteem and confidence of the other section. And thus the Presidential election, instead of dividing the Union into hostile geographical parties—the stronger struggling to enlarge its powers, and the weaker to defend its rights, as is now the case—would become the means of restoring harmony and concord to the country and the government. It would make the Union a union in truth—a bond of mutual affection and brotherhood—and not a mere connection used by the stronger as the instrument of dominion and aggrandizement, and submitted to by the weaker only from the lingering remains of former attachment and the fading hope of being able to restore the government to what it was originally intended to be, a blessing to all.

John C. Calhoun, speech on the Compromise of 1850, U.S. Senate, March 4, 1850. *Works of Calhoun*, IV, 559-73.

... How can the Union be saved? To this I answer, there is but one way by which it can be, and that is, by adopting such measures as will satisfy the States belonging to the southern section that they can remain in the Union consistently with their honor and their safety. There is, again, only one way by which that can be effected, and that is, by removing the causes by which this belief has been produced....

It cannot, then, be saved by eulogies on the Union, however splendid or numerous. The cry of "Union, Union, the glorious Union!" can no more prevent disunion than the cry of "Health, health, glorious health!" on the part of the physician can save a patient lying dangerously ill....

... How can the Union be saved? There is but one way by which it can with any certainty; and that is, by a full and final settlement, on the principle of justice, of all the questions at issue between the two sections. The South asks for justice, simple justice, and less she ought not to take. She has no compromise to offer but the Constitution, and no concession or surrender to make. She has already surrendered so much that she has little left to surrender. Such a settlement would go to the root of the evil, and remove all cause of discontent, by satisfying the South she could remain honorably and safely in the Union, and thereby restore the harmony and fraternal feelings between the sections which existed anterior to the Missouri agitation. Nothing else can, with any certainty, finally and forever settle the questions at issue, terminate agitation, and save the Union.

But can this be done? Yes, easily; not by the weaker party, for it can of itself do nothing—not even protect itself—but by the stronger. The North has only to will it to accomplish it ....

... the responsibility of saving the Union rests on the North, and not the South. The South cannot save it by any act of hers, and the North may save it without any sacrifice whatever, unless to do justice, and to perform her duties under the Constitution, should be regarded by her as a sacrifice.

... If you, who represent the stronger portion, cannot agree to settle them on the broad principle of justice and duty, say so; and let the States we both represent agree to separate and part in peace. If you are unwilling we should part in peace, tell us so, and we shall know what to do, when you reduce the question to submission or resistance....

Jefferson Davis, speech before the Mississippi Legislature, Jackson, November 16, 1858. Dunbar Rowland, ed., *Jefferson Davis: Constitutionalist, His Letters Papers and Speeches* (Jackson, 1923), III, 358.

Now, as in 1851, I hold separation from the Union by the State of Mississippi to be the last remedy—the final alternative. In the language of the venerated Calhoun I consider the disruption of the Union as a great though not the greatest calamity. I would cling tenaciously to our constitutional Government, seeing as I do in the fraternal Union of equal States the benefit to all and the fulfillment of that high destiny which our fathers hoped for and left it for their sons to attain. I love the flag of my country with even more than a filial affection. Mississippi gave me in my boyhood to her military service. For many of the best years of my life I have followed that flag and upheld it on fields where if I had fallen it might have been claimed as my winding sheet. When I have seen it surrounded by the flags of foreign countries, the pulsations of my heart have beat quicker with every breeze which displayed its honored stripes and brilliant constellation. I have looked with veneration on those stripes as recording the original size of our political family and with pride upon that constellation as marking the family's growth; I glory in the position which Mississippi's star holds in the group; but sooner than see its lustre dimmed—sooner than see it degraded from its present equality—would tear it from its place to be set even on the perilous ridge of battle as a sign round which Mississippi's best and bravest should gather to the harvest-home of death.

Jefferson Davis to R. B. Rhett, Jr., November 10, 1860. *Jefferson Davis*, IV, 541.

... interest controls the policy of States, and finally all the planting communities must reach the same conclusion. *My opinion is, therefore, as it has been, in favor of seeking to bring those*

States into cooperation before asking for a popular decision upon a new policy and relation to the nations of the earth. If South Carolina should resolve to secede before that cooperation can be obtained,.... there appears to me to be no advantage in waiting until the government has passed into hostile hands, and men have become familiarized to that injurious and offensive perversion of the general government from the ends for which it was established....

South Carolina Ordinance of Secession, December 20, 1860. Frank Moore, ed., *The Rebellion Record: A Diary of American Events* (New York, 1869), I, 2.

We, the people of the State of South Carolina, in Convention assembled, do declare and ordain, and it is hereby declared and ordained, that the ordinance adopted by us in Convention, on the 23d day of May, in the year of our Lord 1788, whereby the Constitution of the United States of America was ratified, and also all Acts and parts of Acts of the General Assembly of this State ratifying the amendments of the said Constitution, are hereby repealed, and that the union now subsisting between South Carolina and other States under the name of the United States of America is hereby dissolved.

Jefferson Davis, speech on retiring from the Senate, January 21, 1861. *Jefferson Davis*, V, 41-42.

It is known to Senators who have served with me here, that I have for many years advocated, as an essential attribute of State sovereignty, the right of a State to secede from the Union....

I hope none who hear me will confound this expression of mind with the advocacy of the right of a State to remain in the Union, and to disregard its constitutional obligations by the nullification of the law. Such is not my theory. Nullification and secession, so often confounded, are indeed antagonistic principles. Nullification is a remedy which it is sought to apply within the Union, and against the agent of the States. It is only to be justified when the agent has violated his constitutional obligation, and a State, assuming to judge for itself, denies the right of the agent thus to act, and appeals to the other States of the Union for a decision; but when the States themselves, and when the people of the States, have so acted as to convince us that they will not regard our constitutional rights, then, and then for the first time, arises the doctrine of secession in its practical application....

Secession belongs to a different class of remedies. It is to be justified upon the basis that the States are sovereign. There was a time when none denied it. I hope the time may come again, when a better comprehension of the theory of our Government, and the inalienable rights of the people of the States, will prevent any one from denying that each State is a sovereign, and thus may reclaim the grants which it has made to any agent whomsoever.

Jefferson Davis, First Inaugural Address, February 18, 1861. James D. Richardson, ed., *Messages and Papers of the Confederacy* (Nashville, Tenn., 1905), I, 32-36.

Called to the difficult and responsible station of Chief Magistrate of the Provisional Government which you have instituted, I approach the discharge of the duties assigned to me with humble distrust of my abilities, but with a sustaining confidence in the wisdom of those who are to guide and aid me in the administration of public affairs, and an abiding faith in the virtue and patriotism of the people. Looking forward to the speedy establishment of a permanent government to take the place of this, which by its greater moral and physical power will be better able to combat with many difficulties that arise from the conflicting interests of separate nations, I enter upon the duties of the office to which I have been chosen with the hope that the beginning of our career, as a Confederacy, may not be obstructed by hostile opposition to our enjoyment of the separate existence and independence we have asserted, and which, with the blessing of Providence, we intend to maintain.

Our present political position has been achieved in a manner unprecedented in the history of nations. It illustrates the American idea that governments rest on the consent of the governed, and that it is the right of the people to alter or abolish them at will whenever they become destructive of the ends for which they were established. The declared purpose of the compact of the Union from which we have withdrawn was to "establish justice, insure domestic tranquillity, provide for the common defense, promote the general welfare, and secure the blessings of liberty to ourselves and our posterity;" and when, in the judgment of the sovereign States composing this Confederacy, it has been perverted from the purposes for which it was ordained, and ceased to answer the ends for which it was established, a peaceful appeal to the ballot box declared that, so far as they are concerned, the Government created by that compact should cease to exist. In this they merely asserted the right which the Declaration of Independence of July 4, 1776, defined to be "inalienable." Of the time and occasion of its exercise they as sovereigns were the final judges, each for itself. The impartial and enlightened verdict of mankind will vindicate the rectitude of our conduct; and He who knows the hearts of men will judge of the sincerity with which we have labored to preserve the Government of our fathers in its spirit.

The right solemnly proclaimed at the birth of the United States, and which has been solemnly affirmed and reaffirmed in the Bills of Rights of the States subsequently admitted into the Union of 1789, undeniably recognizes in the people the power to resume the authority delegated for the purposes of government. Thus the sovereign States here represented have proceeded to form this Confederacy; and it is by abuse of language that their act has been denominated a revolution. They formed a new alliance, but within each State its government has remained; so that the rights of person and property have not been disturbed. . . . [Therefore,] if we may not hope to avoid war, we may at least expect that posterity will acquit us of having needlessly engaged in it. Doubly justified by the absence of wrong on our part, and by wanton aggression on the part of others, there can be no cause to doubt that the courage and patriotism of the people of the Confederate States will be found equal to any measure of defense which their honor and security may require.

An agricultural people, whose chief interest is the export of commodities required in every manufacturing country, our true policy is peace, and the freest trade which our necessities will permit. . . .

We have entered upon the career of independence, and it must be inflexibly pursued. Through many years of controversy with our late associates of the Northern States, we have vainly endeavored to secure tranquillity and obtain respect for the rights to which we were entitled. As a necessity, not a choice, we have resorted to the remedy of separation, and henceforth our energies must be directed to the conduct of our own affairs, and the perpetuity of the Confederacy which we have formed. If a just perception of mutual interest shall permit us peaceably to pursue our separate political career, my most earnest desire will have been fulfilled. But if this be denied to us, and the integrity of our territory and jurisdiction be assailed, it will but remain for us with firm resolve to appeal to arms and invoke the blessing of Providence on a just cause. . . .

With a Constitution differing only from that of our fathers in so far as it is explanatory of their well-known intent, freed from sectional conflicts, which have interfered with the pursuit of the general welfare, it is not unreasonable to expect that States from which we have recently parted may seek to unite their fortunes to ours under the Government which we have instituted. For this your Constitution makes adequate provision; but beyond this, if I mistake not the judgment and will of the people, a reunion with the States from which we have separated is neither practicable nor desirable. To increase the power, develop the resources and promote the happiness of the Confederacy, it is requisite that there should be so much of homogeneity that the welfare of every portion shall be the aim of the whole. When this does not exist, antagonisms are engendered which must and should result in separation. . . .

We have changed the constituent parts, but not the system of government. The Constitution framed by our fathers is that of these Confederate States. In their exposition of it, and in the judicial construction it has received, we have a light which reveals its true meaning.

Thus instructed as to the true meaning and just interpretation of that instrument, and ever remembering that all offices are but trusts held for the people, and that powers delegated are to be strictly construed, I will hope by due diligence in the performance of my duties, though I may disappoint your expectations, yet to retain, when retiring, something of the good will and confidence which welcome my entrance into office.

Jefferson Davis, *The Rise and Fall of the Confederate Government* (1881), quoted in Henry Steele Commager, ed., *Living Ideas in America* (New York, 1951), 287-88.

Looking back for a moment at the ground over which we have gone, I think it may be fairly asserted that the following propositions have been clearly and fully established:

1. That the states of which the American union was formed, from the moment when they emerged from their colonial or provincial condition, became severally sovereign, free, and independent States—not one State, or nation.

2. That the union formed under the Articles of Confederation was a compact between the States, in which these attributes of "sovereignty, freedom, and independence," were expressly asserted and guaranteed.

3. That, in forming the "more perfect union" of the Constitu-

tion, afterward adopted, the same contracting powers formed an *amended compact,* without any surrender of these attributes of sovereignty, freedom, and independence, either expressed or implied: on the contrary, that, by the tenth amendment to the Constitution, limiting the power of the Government to its express grants, they distinctly guarded against the presumption of a surrender of anything by implication.

4. That political sovereignty resides, neither in individual citizens, nor in unorganized masses, nor in fractional subdivisions of a community, but in the people of an organized political body.

5. That no "republican form of government," in the sense in which that expression is used in the Constitution, and was generally understood by the founders of the Union—whether it be the government of a State or of a confederation of States—is possessed of any sovereignty whatever, but merely exercises certain powers delegated by the sovereign authority of the people, and subject to recall and reassumption by the same authority that conferred them.

6. That the "people" who organized the first confederation, the people who dissolved it, the people who ordained and established the Constitution which succeeded it, the only people, in fine, known or referred to in the phraseology of that period—whether the term was used collectively or distributively—were the people of the respective States, each acting separately and with absolute independence of the others.

7. That, in forming and adopting the Constitution, the States, or the people of the States—terms which, when used with reference to acts performed in a sovereign capacity, are precisely equivalent to each other—forming a new *Government,* but no new *people;* and that, consequently, no new sovereignty was created—for sovereignty in an American republic can belong only to a people, never to a government—and that the Federal Government is entitled to exercise only the powers delegated to it by the people of the respective States.

8. That the term "people," in the preamble to the Constitution and in the tenth amendment, is used distributively; that the only "people of the United States" known to the Constitution are the people of each State in the Union; that no such political community or corporate unit as one people of the United States then existed, has ever been organized, or yet exists; that no political action by the people of the United States in the aggregate has ever taken place, or ever can take place, under the Constitution.

The fictitious idea of *one* people of the United States, contradicted in the last paragraph, has been so impressed upon the popular mind by false teaching, by careless and vicious phraseology, and by the ever-present spectacle of a great Government, with its army and navy, its custom-houses and post-offices, its multitude of office-holders, and the splendid prizes which it offers to political ambition, that the tearing away of these illusions and presentation of the original fabric, which they have overgrown and hidden from view, have no doubt been unwelcome, distasteful, and even repellent to some of my readers. The artificial splendor which makes the deception attractive is even employed as an argument to prove its reality.

Jefferson Davis to R. C. Holland, July 25, 1881. *Jefferson Davis*, IX, 6.

Force may prevail over right, but cannot destroy truth. The exercise of a power to coerce a State cannot give to that act constitutional authority, but it has been so acquiesced in, that the remedy of secession by an oppressed minority must be considered impracticable.

SPOKESMEN FOR THE UNION

Daniel Webster, "Second Reply to Hayne," U.S. Senate, January 26, 1830. Fletcher Webster, ed., *The Writings and Speeches of Daniel Webster* (Boston, 1903), VI, 74-75.

... The people of the United States have chosen to impose comment, made for the people, made by the people, and answerable to the people. The people of the United States have declared that this Constitution shall be supreme law. We must either admit the proposition, or deny their authority. The States are, unquestionably, sovereign, so far as their sovereignty is not affected by this supreme law. But the State Legislatures, as political bodies, however sovereign, are yet not sovereign over the people.... The National Government possesses those powers which it can be shown the people have conferred on it, and no more. All the rest belongs to the State Governments, or to the people themselves. . . .[W]e the people of the United States have chosen to impose control on State sovereignties. There are those, doubtless, who wish they had been left without restraint; but the Constitution has ordered the matter differently. To make war, for instance, is an exercise of sovereignty; but the Constitution declares that no State shall make war. To coin money is another exercise of sovereign power; but no State is at liberty to coin money. Again, the Constitution says that no sovereign State shall be so sovereign as to make a treaty....

... I profess, sir, in my career hitherto, to have kept steadily in view the prosperity and honor of the whole country and the preservation of our federal Union. It is to that Union we owe our safety at home and our consideration and dignity abroad. It is to that Union that we are chiefly indebted for whatever makes us most proud of our country. That Union we reached only by the discipline of our virtues in the severe school of adversity. It had its origin in the necessities of disordered finance, prostrate commerce, and ruined credit. Under its benign influence, these great interests immediately awoke as from the dead and sprang forth with newness of life. Every year of its duration has teemed with fresh proofs of its utility and its blessings, and although our territory has stretched out wider and wider and our population spread farther and farther, they have not outrun its protection or its benefits. It has been to us all a copious fountain of national, social, and personal happiness. I have not allowed myself, sir, to look beyond the Union, to see what might lie hidden in the dark recess behind. I have not cooly weighed the chances of preserving liberty when the bonds that unite us together shall be broken asunder. I have not accustomed myself to hang over the precipice of disunion, to see whether, with my short sight, I can fathom the depth of the abyss below; nor could I regard him as a safe counselor, in the affairs of this government, whose thoughts should be mainly bent on considering, not how the Union should be best preserved, but how tolerable might be the condition of the people when it shall be broken up and destroyed. While the Union lasts, we have high, exciting, gratifying prospects spread out before us, for us and our children. Beyond that, I seek not to penetrate the veil. God grant that in my day, at least, that curtain may not rise. God grant that, on my vision, never may be opened what lies behind. When my eyes shall be turned to behold for the last times the sun in heaven, may I not see him shining on the broken and dishonored fragments of a once glorious Union; on states dissevered, discordant, belligerent; on a land rent with civil feuds, or drenched, it may be, in fraternal blood! Let their last feeble and lingering glance rather behold the gorgeous ensign of the republic, now known and honored throughout the earth, still full high advanced, its arms and trophies streaming in their original luster, not a stripe erased or polluted, nor a single star obscured, bearing for its motto no

such miserable interrogatory as, What is all this worth? nor those
other words of delusion and folly, Liberty first, and Union afterward; but everywhere, spread all over in characters of living light,
blazing on all its ample folds, as they float over the sea and over
the land, and in every wind upon the whole heavens, that other
sentiment, dear to every true American heart—Liberty *and* Union,
now and forever, one and inseparable!

Andrew Jackson, Proclamation on Nullification, December 10,
1832.   James D. Richardson, ed., *A Compilation of the
Messages and Papers of the Presidents*. . . (New York,
1897-1917), II, 1204-18.

The ordinance is founded, not on the indefeasible right of resisting acts which are plainly unconstitutional and too oppressive
to be endured, but on the strange position that any one State may
not only declare an act of Congress void, but prohibit its execution; that they may do this consistently with the Constitution; that
the true construction of that instrument permits a State to retain
its place in the Union and yet be bound by no other of its laws than
those it may choose to consider as constitutional.... There are two
appeals from an unconstitutional act passed by Congress—one to the
judiciary, the other to the people and the States. There is no appeal
from the State decision in theory, and the practical illustration
shows that the courts are closed against an application to review
it, both judges and jurors being sworn to decide in its favor. But
reasoning on this subject is superfluous when our social compact,
in express terms, declares that the laws of the United States, its
Constitution, and treaties made under it are the supreme law of
the land, and, for greater caution, adds "that the judges in every
State shall be bound thereby, anything in the constitution or laws
of any State to the contrary notwithstanding." And it may be asserted without fear of refutation that no federative government
could exist without a similar provision....
   If this doctrine had been established at an earlier day, the
Union would have been dissolved in its infancy. The excise law in
Pennsylvania, the embargo and nonintercourse law in the Eastern
States, the carriage tax in Virginia, were all deemed unconstitutional, and were more unequal in their operation than any of the
laws now complained of; but, fortunately, none of those States discovered that they had the right now claimed by South Carolina....
   If the doctrine of a State veto upon the laws of the Union car-
ries with it internal evidence of its impracticable absurdity, our
constitutional history will also afford abundant proof that it would
have been repudiated with indignation had it been proposed to form
a feature in our Government.

...can it be conceived that an instrument made for the purpose of *"forming a more perfect union"* than that of the Confederation could be so constructed by the assembled wisdom of our country as to substitute for that Confederation a form of government dependent for its existence on the local interest, the party spirit, of a State, or of a prevailing faction in a State?...

I consider, then, the power to annul a law of the United States, assumed by one State, *incompatible with the existence of the Union, contradicted expressly by the letter of the Constitution, unauthorized by its spirit, inconsistent with every principle on which it was founded, and destructive of the great object for which it was formed.*

...nothing can be more dangerous than to admit the position that an unconstitutional purpose entertained by the members who assent to a law enacted under a constitutional power shall make that law void. For how is that purpose to be ascertained? Who is to make the scrutiny?...

The next objection is that the laws in question operate unequally. This objection may be made with truth to every law that has been or can be passed. The wisdom of man never yet contrived a system of taxation that would operate with perfect equality. . . . No; we have not erred. The Constitution is still the object of our reverence, the bond of our Union, our defense in danger, the source of our prosperity in peace. It shall descend, as we have received it, uncorrupted by sophistical construction, to our posterity; and the sacrifices of local interest, of State prejudices, of personal animosities, that were made to bring it into existence, will again be patriotically offered for its support. . . .

This right to secede is deduced from the nature of the Constitution, which, they say, is a compact between sovereign States who have preserved their whole sovereignty and therefore are subject to no superior; that because they made the compact they can break it when in their opinion it has been departed from by the other States. . . .

The people of the United States formed the Constitution, acting through the State legislatures in making the compact, to meet and discuss its provisions, and acting in separate conventions when they ratified those provisions; but the terms used in all its construction show it to be a Government in which the people of all the States, collectively, are represented. . . . The people, then, and not the States, are represented in the executive branch. . . .

The Constitution of the United States, then, forms a *government*, not a league; and whether it be formed by compact between the States or in any other manner, its character is the same. It is a Government in which all the people are represented, which operates directly on the people individually, not upon the States;

they retained all the power they did not grant. But each State, having expressly parted with so many powers as to constitute, jointly with the other States, a single nation, can not, from that period, possess any right to secede, because such secession does not break a league, but destroys the unity of a nation; and any injury to that unity is not only a breach which would result from the contravention of a compact, but it is an offense against the whole Union. To say that any State may at pleasure secede from the Union is to say that the United States are not a nation, because it would be a solecism to contend that any part of a nation might dissolve its connection with the other parts, to their injury or ruin, without committing any offense. Secession, like any other revolutionary act, may be morally justified by the extremity of oppression; but to call it a constitutional right is confounding the meaning of terms, and can only be done through gross error or to deceive those who are willing to assert a right, but would pause before they made a revolution or incur the penalties consequent on a failure.

Because the Union was formed by a compact, it is said the parties to that compact may, when they feel themselves aggrieved, depart from it; but it is precisely because it is a compact that they can not. A compact is an agreement or binding obligation. It may by its terms have a sanction or penalty for its breach, or it may not. If it contains no sanction, it may be broken with no other consequence than moral guilt; if it have a sanction, then the breach incurs the designated or implied penalty.... An attempt, by force of arms, to destroy a government is an offense, by whatever means the constitutional compact may have been formed; and such government has the right by the law of self-defense to pass acts for punishing the offender, unless that right is modified, restrained, or resumed by the constitutional act....

[Secession] rests, as we have seen, on the alleged undivided sovereignty of the States and on their having formed in this sovereign capacity a compact which is called the Constitution, from which, because they made it, they have the right to secede. Both of these positions are erroneous, and some of the arguments to prove them so have been anticipated.

The States severally have not retained their entire sovereignty. It has been shown that in becoming parts of a nation, not members of a league, they surrendered many of their essential parts of sovereignty. The right to make treaties, declare war, levy taxes, exercise exclusive judicial and legislative powers, were all of them functions of sovereign power. The States, then, for all these important purposes were no longer sovereign. The allegiance of their citizens was transferred, in the first instance, to the Government of the United States; they became American citizens and owed obedience to the Constitution of the United States and to laws made in conformity with the powers it vested in Congress. This last position has not been and can not be denied. How, then, can that State be said to be sovereign and independent whose citizens owe obedience to laws not made by it and whose magistrates are sworn to disregard those laws when they come in conflict with those passed by another?... The unity of our political character ...commenced with its very existence. Under the royal Government we had no separate character; our opposition to its oppressions began as *united colonies*. We were the *United States* under the Confederation, and the name was perpetuated and the Union rendered more perfect by the Federal Constitution. In none of these stages did we consider ourselves in any other light than as forming one nation.... It would not do to say that our Constitution was only a league, but it is labored to prove it a compact (which in one sense it is) and then to argue that as a league is a compact every compact between nations must of course be a league, and that from such an engagement every sovereign power has a right to secede. But it has been shown that in this sense the States are not sovereign, and that even if they were, and the national Constitution had been formed by compact, there would be no right in any one State to exonerate itself from its obligations.

... it is the intent of this instrument to *proclaim*, not only that the duty imposed on me by the Constitution "to take care that the laws be faithfully executed" shall be performed to the extent of the powers already vested in me by law, or of such others as the wisdom of Congress shall devise and intrust to me for that purpose, but to warn the citizens of South Carolina who have been deluded into an opposition to the laws of the danger they will incur by obedience to the illegal and disorganizing ordinance of the convention; to exhort those who have refused to support it to persevere in their determination to uphold the Constitution and laws of their country; and to point out to all the perilous situation into which the good people of that State have been led, and that the course they are urged to pursue is one of ruin and disgrace to the very State whose rights they affect to support.

... The laws of the United States must be executed. I have no discretionary power on the subject; my duty is emphatically pronounced in the Constitution. Those who told you that you might peaceably prevent their execution deceived you; they could not have been deceived themselves. They know that a forcible opposition could alone prevent the execution of the laws, and they know that such opposition must be repelled. Their object is disunion. But be not deceived by names. Disunion by armed force is *treason*.

Are you really ready to incur its guilt? If you are, on the heads of the instigators of the act be the dreadful consequences; on their heads be the dishonor, but on yours may fall the punishment. On your unhappy State will inevitably fall all the evils of the conflict you force upon the Government of your country. It can not accede to the mad project of disunion, of which you would be the first victims. Its First Magistrate can not, if he would, avoid the performance of his duty. The consequence must be fearful for you, distressing to your fellow-citizens here and to the friends of good government throughout the world. Its enemies have beheld our prosperity with a vexation they could not conceal; it was a standing refutation of their slavish doctrines, and they will point to our discord with the triumph of malignant joy. It is yet in your power to disappoint them. . . . Declare that you will never take the field unless the star-spangled banner of your country shall float over you; that you will not be stigmatized when dead, and dishonored and scorned while you live, as the authors of the first attack on the Constitution of your country. Its destroyers you can not be. You may disturb its peace, you may interrupt the course of its prosperity, you may cloud its reputation for stability; but its tranquillity will be restored, its prosperity will return, and the stain upon its national character will be transferred and remain an eternal blot on the memory of those who caused the disorder.

Andrew Jackson, Second Inaugural Address, March 4, 1833, *Messages of the Presidents*, III, 1222-24.

In the domestic policy of this Government there are two objects which especially deserve the attention of the people and their representatives, and which have been and will continue to be the subjects of my increasing solicitude. They are the preservation of the rights of the several States and the integrity of the Union.

These great objects are necessarily connected, and can only be attained by an enlightened exercise of the powers of each within its appropriate sphere in conformity with the public will constitutionally expressed. To this end it becomes the duty of all to yield a ready and patriotic submission to the laws constitutionally enacted. . . .

My experience in public concerns and the observation of a life somewhat advanced confirm the opinions long since imbibed by me, that the destruction of our State governments or the annihilation of their control over the local concerns of the people would lead directly to revolution and anarchy, and finally to despotism and military domination. In proportion, therefore, as the General Government encroaches upon the rights of the States, in the same proportion does it impair its own power and detract from its ability to fulfill the purposes of its creation. Solemnly impressed with these considerations, my countrymen will ever find me ready to exercise my constitutional powers in arresting measures which may directly or indirectly encroach upon the rights of the States or tend to consolidate all political power in the General Government. But of equal, and, indeed, of incalculable, importance is the union of these States, and the sacred duty of all to contribute to its preservation by a liberal support of the General Government in the exercise of its just powers.... Without union our independence and liberty would never have been achieved; without union they never can be maintained.... The loss of liberty, of all good government, of peace, plenty, and happiness, must inevitably follow a dissolution of the Union. In supporting it, therefore, we support all that is dear to the freeman and the philanthropist.

...I shall continue to exert all my faculties to maintain the just powers of the Constitution and to transmit unimpaired to posterity the blessings of our Federal Union. At the same time, it will be my aim to inculcate by my official acts the necessity of exercising by the General Government those powers only that are clearly delegated; to encourage simplicity and economy in the expenditures of the Government; to raise no more money from the people than may be requisite for these objects, and in a manner that will best promote the interests of all classes of the community and of all portions of the Union. Constantly bearing in mind that in entering into society "individuals must give up a share of liberty to preserve the rest," it will be my desire so to discharge my duties as to foster with our brethren in all parts of the country a spirit of liberal concession and compromise, and, by reconciling our fellow-citizens to those partial sacrifices which they must unavoidably make for the preservation of a greater good, to recommend our invaluable Government and Union to the confidence and affections of the American people.

Abraham Lincoln, speech at Galena, Illinois, July 23, 1856. Paul M. Angle and Earl Schenck Miers, eds., *The Living Lincoln,* (New Brunswick, N. J., 1955), 196.

We, the majority, would not strive to dissolve the Union; and if any attempt is made it must be by you, who so loudly stigmatize us as Disunionists. But the Union, in any event, won't be dissolved. We don't want to dissolve it, and if you attempt it, we *won't let you.* With the purse and sword, the army and navy and treasury in our hands and at our command, you *couldn't do it.* This government would be very weak, indeed, if a majority, with a disciplined army and navy, and a well-filled treasury, could not preserve itself, when attacked by an unarmed, undisciplined, unorganized minority.

All this talk about the dissolution of the Union is humbug—nothing but folly. *We won't* dissolve the Union, and *you shan't.*

Abraham Lincoln, First Inaugural Address, March 4, 1861. *Living Lincoln,* 381-89.

In compliance with a custom as old as the government itself, I appear before you to address you briefly, and to take, in your presence, the oath prescribed by the Constitution of the United States, to be taken by the President "before he enters on the execution of his office."

I do not consider it necessary, at present, for me to discuss those matters of administration about which there is no special anxiety, or excitement.

Apprehension seems to exist among the people of the Southern states, that by the accession of a Republican administration, their property, and their peace, and personal security, are to be endangered. There has never been any reasonable cause for such apprehension. Indeed, the most ample evidence to the contrary has all the while existed, and been open to their inspection. It is found in nearly all the published speeches of him who now addresses you. I do but quote from one of those speeches when I declare that "I have no purpose, directly or indirectly, to interfere with the institution of slavery in the states where it exists. I believe I have no lawful right to do so, and I have no inclination to do so." Those who nominated and elected me did so with full knowledge that I had made this, and many similar declarations, and had never recanted them. And more than this, they placed in the platform, for my acceptance, and as a law to themselves, and to me, the clear and emphatic resolution which I now read:

"*Resolved,* That the maintenance inviolate of the rights of the states, and especially the right of each state to order and control its own domestic institutions according to its own judgment exclusively, is essential to that balance of power on which the perfection and endurance of our political fabric depend; and we denounce the lawless invasion by armed force of the soil of any state or territory, no matter under what pretext, as among the gravest of crimes."

I now reiterate these sentiments: and in doing so, I only press upon the public attention the most conclusive evidence of which the case is susceptible, that the property, peace and security of no section are to be in anywise endangered by the now incoming administration. I add too, that all the protection which, consistently with the Constitution and the laws, can be given, will be cheerfully given to all the states when lawfully demanded, for whatever cause—as cheerfully to one section, as to another.

There is much controversy \about the delivering up of fugitives from service or labor. The clause I now read is as plainly written in the Constitution as any other of its provisions:

"No person held to service or labor in one state, under the laws thereof, escaping into another, shall, in consequence of any law or regulation therein, be discharged from such service or labor, but shall be delivered up on claim of the party to whom such service or labor may be due."

It is scarcely questioned that this provision was intended by those who made it, for the reclaiming of what we call fugitive slaves; and the intention of the law-giver is the law. All members of Congress swear their support to the whole Constitution—to this provision as much as to any other. To the proposition, then, that slaves whose cases come within the terms of this clause, "shall be delivered up," their oaths are unanimous. Now, if they would make the effort in good temper, could they not, with nearly equal unanimity, frame and pass a law, by means of which to keep good that unanimous oath?

There is some difference of opinion whether this clause should be enforced by national or by state authority; but surely that difference is not a very material one. If the slave is to be surrendered, it can be of but little consequence to him, or to others, by which authority it is done. And should anyone, in any case, be content that his oath shall go unkept, on a merely unsubstantial controversy as to *how* it shall be kept?

Again, in any law upon this subject, ought not all the safeguards of liberty known in civilized and humane jurisprudence to be introduced, so that a free man be not, in any case, surrendered as a slave? And might it not be well, at the same time, to provide by law for the enforcement of that clause in the Constitution which guarantees that "The citizens of each state shall be entitled to all privileges and immunities of citizens in the several states?"

I take the official oath today, with no mental reservations, and with no purpose to construe the Constitution or laws, by any hypercritical rules. And while I do not choose now to specify particular acts of Congress as proper to be enforced, I do suggest, that it will be much safer for all, both in official and private stations, to conform to, and abide by, all those acts which stand unrepealed, than to violate any of them, trusting to find impunity in having them held to be unconstitutional.

It is seventy-two years since the first inauguration of a President under our national Constitution. During that period fifteen different and greatly distinguished citizens, have, in succession, administered the executive branch of the government. They have conducted it through many perils; and, generally, with great success. Yet, with all this scope for precedent, I now enter upon the same task for the brief constitutional term of four years, under great and peculiar difficulty. A disruption of the Federal Union heretofore only menaced, is now formidably attempted.

I hold, that in contemplation of universal law, and of the Constitution, the Union of these states is perpetual. Perpetuity is implied, if not expressed, in the fundamental law of all national governments. It is safe to assert that no government proper, ever had a provision in its organic law for its own termination. Continue to execute all the express provisions of our national Constitution, and the Union will endure forever—it being impossible to destroy it, except by some action not provided for in the instrument itself.

Again, if the United States be not a government proper, but an association of states in the nature of contract merely, can it, as a contract, be peaceably unmade, by less than all the parties who made it? One party to a contract may violate it—break it, so to speak; but does it not require all to lawfully rescind it?

Descending from these general principles, we find the proposition that, in legal contemplation, the Union is perpetual, confirmed by the history of the Union itself. The Union is much older than the Constitution. It was formed in fact, by the Articles of Association in 1774. It was matured and continued by the Declaration of Independence in 1776. It was further matured and the faith of all the then thirteen states expressly plighted and engaged that it should be perpetual, by the Articles of Confederation in 1778. And finally, in 1787, one of the declared objects for ordaining and establishing the Constitution, was *"to form a more perfect union."*

But if destruction of the Union, by one, or by a part only, of the states, be lawfully possible, the Union is *less* perfect than before the Constitution, having lost the vital element of perpetuity.

It follows from these views that no state, upon its own mere motion, can lawfully get out of the Union,—that *resolves* and *ordinances* to that effect are legally void; and that acts of violence, within any state or states, against the authority of the United States, are insurrectionary or revolutionary, according to circumstances.

I therefore consider that, in view of the Constitution and the laws, the Union is unbroken; and, to the extent of my ability, I shall take care, as the Constitution itself expressly enjoins upon me, that the laws of the Union be faithfully executed in all the states. Doing this I deem to be only a simple duty on my part; and I shall perform it, so far as practicable, unless my rightful masters, the American people, shall withhold the requisite means, or, in some authoritative manner, direct the contrary. I trust this will not be regarded as a menace, but only as the declared purpose of the Union that it *will* constitutionally defend, and maintain itself.

In doing this there needs to be no bloodshed or violence; and there shall be none, unless it be forced upon the national authority. The power confided to me, will be used to hold, occupy, and possess the property, and places belonging to the government, and to collect the duties and imposts; but beyond what may be necessary for these objects, there will be no invasion—no using of force against, or among the people anywhere. Where hostility to the United States, in any interior locality, shall be so great and so universal, as to prevent competent resident citizens from holding the federal offices, there will be no attempt to force obnoxious strangers among the people for that object. While the strict legal right may exist in the government to enforce the exercise of these offices, the attempt to do so would be so irritating, and so nearly impracticable with all, that I deem it better to forego, for the time, the uses of such offices.

The mails, unless repelled, will continue to be furnished in all parts of the Union. So far as possible, the people everywhere shall have that sense of perfect security which is most favorable to calm thought and reflection. The course here indicated will be followed, unless current events, and experience, shall show a modification, or change, to be proper; and in every case and exigency, my best discretion will be exercised, according to circumstances actually existing, and with a view and a hope of a peaceful solution of the national troubles, and the restoration of fraternal sympathies and affections.

That there are persons in one section, or another who seek to destroy the Union at all events, and are glad of any pretext to do it, I will neither affirm or deny; but if there be such, I need address no word to them. To those, however, who really love the Union, may I not speak?

Before entering upon so grave a matter as the destruction of our national fabric, with all its benefits, its memories, and its hopes, would it not be wise to ascertain precisely why we do it? Will you hazard so desperate a step, while there is any possibility that any portion of the ills you fly from, have no real existence? Will you, while the certain ills you fly to, are greater than all the real ones you fly from? Will you risk the commission of so fearful a mistake?

All profess to be content in the Union, if all constitutional rights can be maintained. Is it true, then, that any right, plainly written in the Constitution, has been denied? I think not. Happily the human mind is so constituted, that no party can reach to the audacity of doing this. Think, if you can, of a single instance in which a plainly written provision of the Constitution has ever been denied. If, by the mere force of numbers, a majority should deprive a minority of any clearly written constitutional right, it might, in a moral point of view, justify revolution—certainly would, if such right were a vital one. But such is not our case. All the vital rights of minorities, and of individuals, are so plainly assured to them, by affirmations and negations, guarantees and prohibitions, in the Constitution, that controversies never arise concerning them. But no organic law can ever be framed with a provision specifically applicable to every question which may occur in practical administration. No foresight can anticipate, nor any document of reasonable length contain express provisions for all possible questions. Shall fugitives from labor be surrendered by national or by state authority? The Constitution does not expressly say. *May* Congress prohibit slavery in the territories? The Constitution does not expressly say. *Must* Congress protect slavery in the territories? The Constitution does not expressly say.

From questions of this class spring all our constitutional controversies, and we divide upon them into majorities and minorities. If the minority will not acquiesce, the majority must, or the government must cease. There is no other alternative; for continuing the government, is acquiescence on one side or the other. If a minority, in such case, will secede rather than acquiesce, they make a precedent which, in turn, will divide and ruin them; for a minority of their own will secede from them, whenever a majority refuses to be controlled by such minority. For instance, why may not any portion of a new confederacy, a year or two hence, arbitrarily secede again, precisely as portions of the present Union now claim to secede from it. All who cherish disunion sentiments, are now being educated to the exact temper of doing this. Is there such perfect identity of interests among the states to compose a new Union, as to produce harmony only, and prevent renewed secession?

Plainly, the central idea of secession, is the essence of anarchy. A majority, held in restraint by constitutional checks, and limitations, and always changing easily, with deliberate changes of popular opinions and sentiments, is the only true sovereign of a free people. Whoever rejects it, does, of necessity, fly to anarchy or to despotism. Unanimity is impossible; the rule of a minority, as a permanent arrangement, is wholly inadmissible; so that, rejecting the majority principle, anarchy, or despotism in some form, is all that is left.

I do not forget the position assumed by some, that constitutional questions are to be decided by the Supreme Court; nor do I deny that such decisions must be binding in any case, upon the parties to a suit, as to the object of that suit, while they are also entitled to very high respect and consideration, in all parallel cases, by all other departments of the government. And while it is obviously possible that such decision may be erroneous in any given case, still the evil effect following it, being limited to that particular case, with the chance that it may be overruled, and never become a precedent for other cases, can better be borne than could the evils of a different practice. At the same time the candid citizen must confess that if the policy of the government, upon vital questions, affecting the whole people, is to be irrevocably fixed by decisions of the Supreme Court, the instant they are made, in ordinary litigation between parties, in personal actions, the people will have ceased to be their own rulers, having, to that extent, practically resigned their government, into the hands of that eminent tribunal. Nor is there, in this view, any assault upon the court, or the judges. It is a duty, from which they may not shrink, to decide cases properly brought before them; and it is no fault of theirs, if others seek to turn their decisions to political purposes.

One section of our country believes slavery is *right*, and ought to be extended, while the other believes it is *wrong*, and ought not to be extended. This is the only substantial dispute. The fugitive slave clause of the Constitution, and the law for the suppression of the foreign slave trade, are each as well enforced, perhaps, as any law can ever be in a community where the moral sense of the people imperfectly supports the law itself. The great body of the people abide by the dry legal obligation in both cases, and a few break over in each. This, I think, cannot be perfectly cured; and it would be worse in both cases *after* the separation of the sections, than before. The foreign slave trade, now imperfectly suppressed, would be ultimately revived without restriction, in one section; while fugitive slaves, now only partially surrendered, would not be surrendered at all, by the other.

Physically speaking we cannot separate. We cannot remove our respective sections from each other, nor build an impassable wall between them. A husband and wife may be divorced, and go out of the presence, and beyond the reach of each other; but the different parts of our country cannot do this. They cannot but remain face to face; and intercourse, either amicable or hostile, must continue between them. Is it possible then to make that intercourse more advantageous, or more satisfactory, *after* separation than *before?* Can aliens make treaties easier than friends can make laws? Can treaties be more faithfully enforced between aliens, than laws can among friends? Suppose you go to war, you cannot fight always; and when, after much loss on both sides, and no gain on either, you cease fighting, the identical old questions, as to terms of intercourse, are again upon you.

This country, with its institutions, belongs to the people who inhabit it. Whenever they shall grow weary of the existing government, they can exercise their *constitutional* right of amending it, or their *revolutionary* right to dismember, or overthrow it. I cannot be ignorant of the fact that many worthy, and patriotic citizens are desirous of having the national Constitution amended. While I make no recommendation of amendments, I fully recognize the rightful authority of the people over the whole subject, to be exercised in either of the modes prescribed in the instrument itself; and I should, under existing circumstances, favor, rather than oppose, a fair opportunity being afforded the people to act upon it.

I will venture to add that, to me, the convention mode seems preferable, in that it allows amendments to originate with the people themselves, instead of only permitting them to take, or reject, propositions, originated by others, not especially chosen for the purpose, and which might not be precisely such, as they would wish to either accept or refuse. I understand a proposed amendment to the Constitution—which amendment, however, I have not seen, has passed Congress, to the effect that the federal government, shall never interfere with the domestic institutions of the states, including that of persons held to service. To avoid misconstruction of what I have said, I depart from my purpose not to speak of particular amendments, so far as to say that, holding such a provision to now be implied constitutional law, I have no objection to its being made express, and irrevocable.

The chief magistrate derives all his authority from the people, and they have conferred none upon him to fix terms for the separation of the states. The people themselves can do this also if they choose; but the executive, as such, has nothing to do with it. His duty is to administer the present government, as it came to his hands, and to transmit it, unimpaired by him, to his successor.

Why should there not be a patient confidence in the ultimate justice of the people? Is there any better, or equal hope, in the world? In our present differences, is either party without faith of being in the right? If the Almighty Ruler of nations, with his eternal truth and justice, be on your side of the North, or on yours of the South, that truth, and that justice, will surely prevail, by the judgment of this great tribunal, the American people.

By the frame of the government under which we live, this same people have wisely given their public servants but little power for mischief; and have, with equal wisdom, provided for the return of that little to their own hands at very short intervals.

While the people retain their virtue, and vigilance, no administration, by any extreme of wickedness or folly, can very seriously injure the government, in the short space of four years.

My countrymen, one and all, think calmly and *well,* upon this whole subject. Nothing valuable can be lost by taking time. If there be an object to *hurry* any of you, in hot haste, to a step which you would never take *deliberately,* that object will be frustrated by taking time; but no good object can be frustrated by it. Such of you as are now dissatisfied, still have the old Constitution unimpaired, and, on the sensitive point, the laws of your own framing under it; while the new administration will have no immediate power, if it would, to change either. If it were admitted that you who are dissatisfied, hold the right side in the dispute, there still is no single good reason for precipitate action. Intelligence, patriotism, Christianity, and a firm reliance on Him, who has never yet forsaken this favored land, are still competent to adjust, in the best way, all our present difficulty.

In *your* hands, my dissatisfied fellow-countrymen, and not in *mine,* is the momentous issue of civil war. The government will not assail *you.* You can have no conflict, without being yourselves the aggressors. *You* have no oath registered in Heaven to destroy the government, while *I* shall have the most solemn one to "preserve, protect and defend" it.

I am loath to close. We are not enemies but friends. We must not be enemies. Though passion may have strained, it must not break our bonds of affection. The mystic chords of memory, stretching from every battlefield, and patriot grave, to every living heart and hearthstone, all over this broad land, will yet swell the chorus of the Union, when again touched, as surely they will be, by the better angels of our nature.

Abraham Lincoln, Special Message to Congress, July 4, 1861. *Living Lincoln,* 418-21.

It might seem, at first thought, to be of little difference whether the present movement at the South be called "secession" or "rebellion." The movers, however, well understand the difference. At the beginning, they knew they could never raise their treason to any respectable magnitude, by any name which implies *violation* of law. They knew their people possessed as much of moral sense, as much of devotion to law and order, and as much pride in, and reverence for, the history, and government, of their common country, as any other civilized, and patriotic people. They knew they could make no advancement directly in the teeth of these strong and noble sentiments. Accordingly they commenced by an insidious debauching of the public mind. They invented an ingenious sophism, which, if conceded, was followed by perfectly logical steps, through all the incidents, to the complete destruction of the Union. The sophism itself is, that any state of the Union may, *consistently* with the national Constitution, and therefore *lawfully*, and *peacefully*, withdraw from the Union, without the consent of the Union, or of any other state. The little disguise that the supposed right is to be exercised only for just cause, themselves to be the sole judge of its justice, is too thin to merit any notice.

With rebellion thus sugar-coated, they have been drugging the public mind of their section for more than thirty years; and, until at length, they have brought many good men to a willingness to take up arms against the government the day *after* some assemblage of men have enacted the farcical pretence of taking their state out of the Union, who could have been brought to no such thing the day *before*.

This sophism derives much—perhaps the whole—of its currency, from the assumption, that there is some omnipotent, and sacred supremacy, pertaining to a *state*—to each state of our federal Union. Our states have neither more, nor less power, than that reserved to them, in the Union, by the Constitution—no one of them ever having been a state *out* of the Union. The original ones passed into the Union even *before* they cast off their British colonial dependence; and the new ones each came into the Union directly from a condition of dependence, excepting Texas. And even Texas, in its temporary independence, was never designated a state. The new ones only took the designation of states, on coming into the Union, while that name was first adopted for the old ones, in, and by, the Declaration of Independence. Therein the

"United Colonies" were declared to be "Free and Independent States"; but, even then, the object plainly was not to declare their independence of *one another*, or of the *Union;* but directly the contrary, as their mutual pledge, and their mutual action, before, at the time, and afterwards, abundantly show. The express plighting of faith, by each and all of the original thirteen, in the Articles of Confederation, two years later, that the Union shall be perpetual, is most conclusive. Having never been states, either in substance, or in name, *outside* of the Union, whence this magical omnipotence of "state rights," asserting a claim of power to lawfully destroy the Union itself? Much is said about the "sovereignty" of the states; but the word, even, is not in the national Constitution; nor, as is believed, in any of the state constitutions. What is a "sovereignty," in the political sense of the term? Would it be far wrong to define it "A political community, without a political superior"? Tested by this, no one of our states, except Texas, ever was a sovereignty. And even Texas gave up the character on coming into the Union; by which act, she acknowledged the Constitution of the United States, and the laws and treaties of the United States made in pursuance of the Constitution, to be, for her, the supreme law of the land. The states have their *status in* the Union, and they have no other *legal status*. If they break from this, they can only do so against law, and by revolution. The Union, and not themselves separately, procured their independence, and their liberty. By conquest, or purchase, the Union gave each of them, whatever of independence, and liberty, it has. The Union is older than any of the states; and, in fact it created them as states. Originally, some dependent colonies made the Union; and, in turn, the Union threw off their old dependence, for them, and made them states, such as they are. Not one of them ever had a state constitution, independent of the Union. Of course, it is not forgotten that all the new states framed their constitutions, before they entered the Union; nevertheless, dependent upon, and preparatory to, coming into the Union.

Unquestionably the states have the powers, and rights, reserved to them in, and by the national Constitution; but among these, surely, are not included all conceivable powers, however mischievous, or destructive; but, at most, such only, as were known in the world, at the time, as governmental powers; and certainly, a power to destroy the government itself, had never been known as a governmental—as a merely administrative power. This relative matter of national power, and state rights, as a principle, is no other than the principle of *generality*, and *locality*. Whatever concerns the whole, should be confided to the whole—to the general government; while, whatever concerns *only* the state, should be left exclusively, to the state. This is all there is of original principle about it. Whether the national Constitution, in defining boundaries between the two, has applied the principle with exact accuracy, is not to be questioned. We are all bound by that defining, without question.

What is now combatted, is the position that secession is *consistent* with the Constitution—is *lawful*, and *peaceful*. It is not contended that there is any express law for it; and nothing should ever be implied as law, which leads to unjust, or absurd consequences. . . .

The seceders insist that our Constitution admits of secession. They have assumed to make a national constitution of their own, in which, of necessity, they have either *discarded,* or *retained,* the right of secession, as they insist, it exists in ours. If they have discarded it, they thereby admit that, on principle, it ought not to be in ours. If they have retained it, by their own construction of ours they show that to be consistent they must secede from one another, whenever they shall find it the easiest way of settling their debts, or effecting any other selfish, or unjust object. The principle itself is one of disintegration, and upon which no government can possibly endure. . . .

It may be affirmed, without extravagance, that the free institutions we enjoy, have developed the powers, and improved the condition, of our whole people, beyond any example in the world. Of this we now have a striking, and an impressive illustration. So large an army as the government has now on foot, was never before known, without a soldier in it, but who had taken his place there, of his own free choice. But more than this: there are many single regiments whose members, one and another, possess full practical knowledge of all the arts, sciences, professions, and whatever else, whether useful or elegant, is known in the world; and there is scarcely one, from which there could not be selected, a president, a cabinet, a congress, and perhaps a court, abundantly competent to administer the government itself. Nor do I say this is not true, also, in the army of our late friends, now adversaries, in this contest; but if it is, so much better the reason why the government, which has conferred such benefits on both them and us, should not be broken up. Whoever, in any section, proposes to abandon such a government, would do well to consider, in deference to what principle it is, that he does it—what better he is likely to get in its stead—whether the substitute will give, or be intended to give, so much of good to the people. There are some foreshadowings on this subject. Our adversaries have adopted some Declarations of Independence; in which, unlike the good old one, penned by Jefferson, they omit the words "all men are created equal." Why? They have adopted a temporary national constitution, in the preamble of which, unlike our good old one, signed by Washington, they omit "We, the people," and substitute "We, the deputies of the sovereign and independent states." Why? Why this deliberate pressing out of view, the rights of men, and the authority of the people?

Abraham Lincoln to Horace Greeley, August 22, 1862. *Living Lincoln*, 495-96.

As to the policy I "seem to be pursuing" as you say, I have not meant to leave any one in doubt.

I would save the Union. I would save it the shortest way under the Constitution. The sooner the national authority can be restored; the nearer the Union will be "the Union as it was." If there be those who would not save the Union, unless they could at the same time *save* slavery, I do not agree with them. If there be those who would not save the Union unless they could at the same time *destroy* slavery, I do not agree with them. My paramount object in this struggle *is* to save the Union, and is *not* either to save or to destroy slavery. If I could save the Union without freeing *any* slave I would do it, and if I could save it by freeing *all* the slaves I would do it; and if I could save it by freeing some and leaving others alone I would also do that. What I do about slavery, and the colored race, I do because I believe it helps to save the Union; and what I forbear, I forbear because I do *not* believe it would help to save the Union. I shall do *less* whenever I shall believe what I am doing hurts the cause, and I shall do *more* whenever I shall believe doing more will help the cause. I shall try to correct errors when shown to be errors; and I shall adopt new views so fast as they shall appear to be true views.

I have here stated my purpose according to my view of *official* duty; and I intend no modification of my oft-expressed *personal* wish that all men everywhere could be free.

Abraham Lincoln, Second Inaugural Address, March 4, 1865. *Living Lincoln*, 638-40.

At this second appearing to take the oath of the presidential office, there is less occasion for an extended address than there was at the first. Then a statement, somewhat in detail, of a course to be pursued, seemed fitting and proper. Now, at the expiration of four years, during which public declarations have been constantly called forth on every point and phase of the great contest which still absorbs the attention, and engrosses the energies of the nation, little that is new could be presented. The progress of our arms, upon which all else chiefly depends, is as well known to the public as to myself; and it is, I trust, reasonably satisfactory and encouraging to all. With high hope for the future, no prediction in regard to it is ventured.

On the occasion corresponding to this four years ago, all thoughts were anxiously directed to an impending civil war. All dreaded it—all sought to avert it. While the inaugural address was being delivered from this place, devoted altogether to *saving* the Union without war, insurgent agents were in the city seeking to *destroy* it without war—seeking to dissolve the Union, and divide effects, by negotiation. Both parties deprecated war; but one of them would *make* war rather than let the nation survive; and the other would *accept* war rather than let it perish. And the war came.

One eighth of the whole population were colored slaves, not distributed generally over the Union, but localized in the southern part of it. These slaves constituted a peculiar and powerful interest. All knew that this interest was, somehow, the cause of the war. To strengthen, perpetuate, and extend this interest was the object for which the insurgents would rend the Union, even by war; while the government claimed no right to do more than to restrict the territorial enlargement of it. Neither party expected for the war, the magnitude, or the duration, which it has already attained. Neither anticipated that the *cause* of the conflict might cease with, or even before, the conflict itself should cease. Each looked for an easier triumph, and a result less fundamental and astounding. Both read the same Bible, and pray to the same God; and each invokes His aid against the other. It may seem strange that any men should dare to ask a just God's assistance in wringing their bread from the sweat of other men's faces; but let us judge not that we be not judged. The prayers of both could not be answered; that of neither has been answered fully. The Almighty has His own purposes. "Woe unto the world because of offences! for it must needs be that offences come; but woe to that man by whom the offence cometh!" If we shall suppose that American slavery is one of those offences which, in the providence of God, must needs come, but which, having continued through His appointed time, He now wills to remove, and that He gives to both North and South, this terrible war, as the woe due to those by whom the offence came, shall we discern therein any departure from those divine attributes which the believers in a Living God always ascribe to Him? Fondly do we hope—fervently do we pray—that this mighty scourge of war may speedily pass away. Yet, if God wills that it continue, until all the wealth piled by the bondman's two hundred and fifty years of unrequited toil shall be sunk, and until every drop of blood drawn with the lash, shall be paid by another drawn with the sword, as was said three thousand years ago, so still it must be said, "the judgments of the Lord, are true and righteous altogether."

With malice toward none; with charity for all; with firmness in the right, as God gives us to see the right, let us strive on to finish the work we are in; to bind up the nation's wounds; to care for him who shall have borne the battle, and for his widow, and his orphan—to do all which may achieve and cherish a just, and a lasting peace, among ourselves, and with all nations.

Varied Views of Slavery

CRITICS OF SLAVERY

THOMAS JEFFERSON

Notes on the State of Virginia, reprinted in H. A. Washington, ed., *The Writings of Thomas Jefferson* (Washington, D.C., 1854), VIII, 404.

The whole commerce between mâster ând slave is a perpetual exercise of the most boisterous passions, the most unremitting despotism on the one part and degrading submissions on the other. . . . The man must be a prodigy who can retain his manners and morals undepraved by such circumstances. And with what execration should the statesman be loaded who, permitting one half the citizens thus to trample on the rights of the other, transforms those into despots and these into enemies, destroys the morals of the one part and the *amor patriae* of the other! . . . Indeed I tremble for my country when I reflect that God is just; that His justice cannot sleep forever; that, considering numbers, nature, and natural means only, a revolution of the wheel of fortune, an exchange of situation is among possible events. . .

Proposed Constitution for Virginia, 1783. Paul Leicester Ford, ed., *The Writings of Thomas Jefferson* (New York, 1892-99), III, 325.

The General Assembly shall not have power. . . to permit the introduction of any more slaves to reside in this State, or the continuance of slavery beyond the generation which shall be living on the thirty-first day of December, One Thousand Eight Hundred— all persons born after that day being hereby declared free. . . .

Letter to John Holmes, April 22, 1820. *Writings of Jefferson* (Ford ed.), X, 157.

. . . I can say, with conscious truth, that there is not a man on earth who would sacrifice more than I would to relieve us from this heavy reproach[slavery] in any *practicable* way. The cession of that kind of property (for so it is misnamed) is a bagatelle which would not cost me a second thought if, in that way, a general emancipation and *expatriation* could be effected; and gradually and with due sacrifices, I think it might be. But as it is, we have the wolf by the ears, and we can neither hold him nor safely let him go. Justice is in one scale and self-preservation in the other. . . .

ALEXANDER HAMILTON

Letter to John Jay, March 14, 1779. Richard B. Morris, ed., *The Basic Ideas of Alexander Hamilton* (New York, 1957), 343-44.

. . . I have frequently heard it objected to the scheme of em-bodying Negroes, that they are too stupid to make soldiers. This is so far from appearing to me a valid objection, that I think their want of cultivation (for their natural faculties are as good as ours), joined to that habit of subordination which they acquire from a life of servitude, will enable them sooner to become soldiers than our white inhabitants. Let officers be men of sense and sentiment; and the nearer the soldiers approach to machines, perhaps the better.
. . . The contempt we have been taught to entertain for the blacks, makes us fancy many things that are founded neither in reason nor experience. . . . An essential part of the plan is to give them their freedom with their swords. This will secure their fidelity, animate their courage, and, I believe, will have a good influence upon those who remain, by opening a door to their eman-cipation. This circumstance, I confess, has no small weight in in-ducing me to wish the success of the project; for the dictates of humanity, and true policy, equally interest me in favor of this un-fortunate class of men.

"Camillus" Essay No. 3, July 30, 1795. *Basic Ideas of Hamil-ton*, 344-45.

In the interpretation of treaties, things *odious* or *immoral* are not to be presumed. The abandonment of Negroes, who had been induced to quit their masters on the faith of official proclamations, promising them liberty, to fall again under the yoke of their masters, and into slavery, is as *odious* and *immoral* a thing as can be conceived. It is odious, not only as it imposes an act of perfidy on one of the contracting parties, but as it tends to bring back to servitude men once made free. The general interests of humanity conspire with the obligation which Great Britain had contracted towards the Negroes, to repel this construction of the treaty, if another can be found.

HENRY CLAY

Speech at meeting of American Colonization Society, January 1, 1818. James F. Hopkins, ed., *The Papers of Henry Clay* (Lexington, Ky., 1959—), II, 420, 422.

... It was proper again and again to repeat, that it was far from the intention of the Society to affect, in any manner, the tenure by which a certain species of property is held. He was himself a slaveholder; and he considered that kind of property as inviolable as any other in the country. He would resist as soon, and with as much firmness, encroachments upon it as he would encroachments upon any other property which he held. . . .

... This word happiness, Mr. C. said, comprised many items. It comprehended what were hardly less important than subsistence, political and social considerations. These the men of color never can enjoy here, but are what he would find in the contemplated colony. And can there be any thing, to a reflecting freeman, (and some among the class of persons to whom he alluded were doubtless capable of reflection) more humiliating, more dark and cheerless, than to see himself, and to trace in imagination his posterity, through all succeeding time, degraded and debased, aliens to the society of which they are members, and cut off from all its higher blessings?

Speech at meeting of American Colonization Society, January 20, 1827. Calvin Colton, ed., *The Life, Correspondence, and Speeches of Henry Clay*. . . (New York, 1857), I, 189.

If I could be instrumental in eradicating this deepest stain from the character of our country, and removing all cause of reproach on account of it, by foreign nations; if I could only be instrumental in ridding of this foul blot that revered state that gave me birth, or that not less beloved state which kindly adopted me as her son; I would not exchange the proud satisfaction which I should enjoy, for the honor of all the triumphs ever decreed to the most successful conqueror.

Speech at Frankfort, Kentucky, December 17, 1829. *Life, Correspondence, Speeches of Clay*, I, 191.

If we were to invoke the greatest blessing on earth, which Heaven, in its mercy, could now bestow on this nation, it would be the separation of the two most numerous races of its population, and their comfortable establishment in distinct and distant countries. . . . Who, if this promiscuous residence of whites and blacks, of freemen and slaves, is for ever to continue, can imagine the servile wars, the carnage and the crimes, which will be its probable consequences, without shuddering with horror?

WILLIAM LLOYD GARRISON

The most famous of the reformers demanding an immediate end to Southern slavery was William Lloyd Garrison (1805-1879). The following policy statement appeared in the first issue of *The Liberator*, the abolitionist newspaper which he began publishing in Boston on January 1, 1831. Wendell Phillips Garrison and Francis Jackson Garrison, *William Lloyd Garrison, 1805-1879: The Story of His Life Told by His Children* (New York, 1885), I, 224-25.

. . . I determined, at every hazard, to lift up the standard of emancipation in the eyes of the nation, *within sight of Bunker Hill and in the birth place of liberty*. That standard is now unfurled; and long may it float, unhurt by the spoliations of time or the missiles of a desperate foe—yea, till every chain be broken, and every bondman set free! Let Southern oppressors tremble—let their secret abettors tremble—let their Northern apologists tremble—let all the enemies of the persecuted blacks tremble.
. . . I shall strenuously contend for the immediate enfranchisement of our slave population. In Park-Street Church, on the Fourth of July, 1829, in an address on slavery, I unreflectingly assented to the popular but pernicious doctrine of *gradual* abolition. I seize this opportunity to make a full and unequivocal recantation, and thus publicly to ask pardon of my God, of my country, and of my brethren the poor slaves, for having uttered a sentiment so full of timidity, injustice and absurdity. . . .

I am aware, that many object to the severity of my language; but is there not cause for severity? I *will be* as harsh as truth, and as uncompromising as justice. On this subject, I do not wish to think, or speak, or write, with moderation. No! no! Tell a man whose house is on fire, to give a moderate alarm; tell him to moderately rescue his wife from the hands of the ravisher; tell the mother to gradually extricate her babe from the fire into which it has fallen;—but urge me not to use moderation in a cause like the present. I am in earnest—I will not equivocate—I will not excuse—I will not retreat a single inch—*AND I WILL BE HEARD.* The apathy of the people is enough to make every statue leap from its pedestal, and to hasten the resurrection of the dead.

It is pretended, that I am retarding the cause of emancipation by the coarseness of my invective and the precipitancy of my measures. *The charge is not true.* On this question my influence, —humble as it is,—is felt at this moment to a considerable extent, and shall be felt in coming years—not perniciously, but beneficially—not as a curse, but as a blessing; and posterity will bear testimony that I was right. I desire to thank God, that He enables me to disregard "the fear of man which bringeth a snare," and to speak His truth in its simplicity and power.

ABRAHAM LINCOLN

Speech attacking Kansas-Nebraska Act, Peoria, Illinois, October 16, 1854. *Living Lincoln*, 161-78.

When southern people tell us they are no more responsible for the origin of slavery than we, I acknowledge the fact. When it is said that the institution exists, and that it is very difficult to get rid of it, in any satisfactory way, I can understand and appreciate the saying. I surely will not blame them for not doing what I should not know how to do myself. If all earthly power were given me, I should not know what to do, as to the existing institution. My first impulse would be to free all the slaves, and send them to Liberia,— to their own native land. But a moment's reflection would convince me, that whatever of high hope, (as I think there is) there may be in this, in the long run, its sudden execution is impossible. If they were all landed there in a day, they would all perish in the next ten days; and there are not surplus shipping and surplus money enough in the world to carry them there in many times ten days. What then? Free them all, and keep them among us as underlings?

Is it quite certain that this betters their condition? I think I would not hold one in slavery, at any rate; yet the point is not clear enough for me to denounce people upon. What next? Free them, and make them politically and socially, our equals? My own feelings will not admit of this; and if mine would, we well know that those of the great mass of white people will not. Whether this feeling accords with justice and sound judgment, is not the sole question, if indeed, it is any part of it. A universal feeling, whether well or ill-founded, cannot be safely disregarded. We cannot, then, make them equals. It does seem to me that systems of gradual emancipation might be adopted; but for their tardiness in this, I will not undertake to judge our brethren of the South.

When they remind us of their constitutional rights, I acknowledge them, not grudgingly, but fully, and fairly; and I would give them any legislation for the reclaiming of their fugitives, which should not, in its stringency, be more likely to carry a free man into slavery, than our ordinary criminal laws are to hang an innocent one.

But all this, to my judgment, furnishes no more excuse for permitting slavery to go into our own free territory, than it would for reviving the African slave-trade by law. The law which forbids the bringing of slaves *from* Africa; and that which has so long forbid the taking them *to* Nebraska, can hardly be distinguished on any moral principle; and the repeal of the former could find quite as plausible excuses as that of the latter. . . .

Equal justice to the South, it is said, requires us to consent to the extending of slavery to new countries. That is to say, inasmuch as you do not object to my taking my hog to Nebraska, therefore I must not object to you taking your slave. Now, I admit this is perfectly logical, if there is no difference between hogs and Negroes. But while you thus require me to deny the humanity of the Negro, I wish to ask whether you of the South yourselves, have ever been willing to do as much? . . . The great majority, south as well as north, have human sympathies, of which they can no more divest themselves than they can of their sensibility to physical pain. These sympathies, in the bosoms of the Southern people, manifest in many ways, their sense of the wrong of slavery, and their consciousness that, after all, there is humanity in the Negro. . . .

. . . if the Negro is a man, is it not to that extent, a total destruction of self-government, to say that he too shall not govern *himself*? When the white man governs himself that is self-government; but when he governs himself, and also governs *another* man, that is *more* than self-government—that is despotism. If the Negro is a *man,* why then my ancient faith teaches me that "all men are created equal;" and that there can be no moral right in connection with one man's making a slave of another.

... I too, go for saving the Union. Much as I hate slavery, I would consent to the extension of it rather than see the Union dissolved, just as I would consent to any *great* evil, to avoid a *greater* one. ...

Our republican robe is soiled, and trailed in the dust. Let us re-purify it. Let us turn and wash it white, in the spirit, if not the blood, of the Revolution. Let us turn slavery from its claims of "moral right," back upon its existing legal rights, and its arguments of "necessity." Let us return it to the position our fathers gave it; and there let it rest in peace. ...

Letter to Joshua F. Speed, August 24, 1855. *Living Lincoln,* 189-90.

... You know I dislike slavery; and you fully admit the abstract wrong of it. So far there is no cause of difference. But you say that sooner than yield your legal right to the slave—especially at the bidding of those who are not themselves interested, you would see the Union dissolved. I am not aware that *any one* is bidding you to yield that right; very certainly *I* am not. I leave that matter entirely to yourself. I also acknowledge *your* rights and *my* obligations, under the Constitution, in regard to your slaves. I confess I hate to see the poor creatures hunted down, and caught, and carried back to their stripes, and unrewarded toils; but I bite my lip and keep quiet. In 1841 you and I had together a tedious low-water trip, on a steamboat from Louisville to St. Louis. You may remember, as I well do, that from Louisville to the mouth of the Ohio there were, on board, ten or a dozen slaves, shackled together with irons. That sight was a continual torment to me; and I see something like it every time I touch the Ohio, or any other slave-border. It is hardly fair for you to assume, that I have no interest in a thing which has, and continually exercises, the power of making me miserable. You ought rather to appreciate how much the great body of the Northern people do crucify their feelings, in order to maintain their loyalty to the Constitution and the Union.

I do oppose the extension of slavery, because my judgment and feelings so prompt me; and I am under no obligation to the contrary. If for this you and I must differ, differ we must. ...

You say if Kansas fairly votes herself a free state, as a Christian you will rather rejoice at it. All decent slave-holders *talk* that way; and I do not doubt their candor. But they never *vote* that way. Although in a private letter, or conversation, you will express your preference that Kansas shall be free, you would *vote* for no man for Congress who would say the same thing publicly. No such man could be elected from any district in any slave state. . . .

. . . Our progress in degeneracy appears to me to be pretty rapid. As a nation, we began by declaring that *"all men are created equal."* We now practically read it "all men are created equal, *except Negroes."* When the Know-Nothings get control, it will read "all men are created equal, except Negroes, *and foreign-ers, and Catholics."* When it comes to this I should prefer emigrating to some country where they make no pretence of loving liberty—To Russia, for instance, where despotism can be taken pure, and without the base alloy of hyprocrisy.

Speech accepting Senatorial nomination, Springfield, Illinois, June 16, 1858. *Living Lincoln,* 212.

We are now far into the *fifth* year, since a policy was initiated, with the *avowed* object, and *confident* promise, of putting an end to slavery agitation.

Under the operation of that policy, that agitation has not only, *not ceased,* but has *constantly augmented.*

In *my* opinion, it *will* not cease, until a *crisis* shall have been reached, and passed.

"A house divided against itself cannot stand."

I believe this government cannot endure, permanently half-*slave* and half-*free.*

I do not expect the Union to be *dissolved*—I do not expect the house to *fall*—but I *do* expect it will cease to be divided.

It will become *all* one thing, or *all* the other.

Either the *opponents* of slavery, will arrest the further spread of it, and place it where the public mind shall rest in the belief that it is in course of ultimate extinction; or its *advocates* will push it forward, till it shall become alike lawful in *all* the states, *old* as well as *new—North* as well as *South.*

Have we no tendency to the latter condition?

The Lincoln-Douglas Debates took place in the late summer and autumn of 1858, when Lincoln ran for the Senate seat of Stephen A. Douglas. These extracts are from Douglas' speech at Freeport, Illinois, on August 27 and from Lincoln's reply at Jonesboro, Illinois, on September 15. Paul M. Angle, ed., *Created Equal? The Complete Lincoln-Douglas Debates of 1858* (Chicago, 1958), 152-55, 216-18.

The next question propounded to me by Mr. Lincoln is: Can the people of a territory in any lawful way, against the wishes of any citizen of the United States, exclude slavery from their limits prior to the formation of a state constitution? I answer emphatically, as Mr. Lincoln has heard me answer a hundred times from every stump in Illinois, that in my opinion the people of a territory can, by lawful means, exclude slavery from their limits prior to the formation of a state constitution. . . . It matters not what way the Supreme Court may question. It matters not what way the Supreme Court may hereafter decide as to the abstract question whether slavery may or may not go into a territory under the Constitution, the people have the lawful means to introduce it or exclude it as they please, for the reason that slavery cannot exist a day or an hour anywhere unless it is supported by local police regulations. Those police regulations can only be established by the local legislature, and, if the people are opposed to slavery, they will elect representatives to that body who will by unfriendly legislation effectually prevent the introduction of it into their midst. If, on the contrary, they are for it, their legislation will favor its extension. Hence, no matter what the decision of the Supreme Court may be on that abstract question, still the right of the people to make a slave territory or a free territory is perfect and complete under the Nebraska Bill. . . .

The fourth question of Mr. Lincoln is: Are you in favor of acquiring additional territory, in disregard as to how such acquisition may affect the Union on the slavery questions? This question is very ingeniously and cunningly put.

The Black Republican creed lays it down expressly, that under no circumstances shall we acquire any more territory unless slavery is first prohibited in the country. I ask Mr. Lincoln whether he is in favor of that proposition. Are you [addressing Mr. Lincoln] opposed to the acquisition of any more territory, under any circumstances, unless slavery is prohibited in it? That he does not like to answer. When I ask him whether he stands up to that article in the platform of his party, he turns, Yankee-fashion, and without answering it, asks me whether I am in favor of acquiring territory without regard to how it may affect the Union on the slavery question. I answer that whenever it becomes necessary, in our growth and progress, to acquire more territory, that I am in favor of it, without reference to the question of slavery, and, when we have acquired it, I will leave the people free to do as they please, either to make it slave or free territory, as they prefer. . . .

[Lincoln's response:]

. . . Judge Douglas answered that they [the territories] can lawfully exclude slavery from the territory prior to the formation of a constitution. He goes on to tell us how it can be done. As I understand him, he holds that it can be done by the territorial legislature refusing to make any enactments for the protection of slavery in the territory, and especially by adopting unfriendly legislation to it. . . .

In the first place, the Supreme Court of the United States has decided that any congressional prohibition of slavery in the territories is unconstitutional—that they have reached this proposition as a conclusion from their former proposition, that the Constitution of the United States expressly recognizes property in slaves, and from that other constitutional provision that no person shall be deprived of property without due process of law. Hence they reach the conclusion that as the Constitution of the United States expressly recognizes property in slaves, and prohibits any person from being deprived of property without due process of law, to pass an act of Congress by which a man who owned a slave on one side of a line would be deprived of him if he took him on the other side, is depriving him of that property without due process of law. That I understand to be the decision of the Supreme Court. I understand also that Judge Douglas adheres most firmly to that decision; and the difficulty is: How is it possible for any power to exclude slavery from the territory unless in violation of that decision? That is the difficulty. . . .

I hold that the proposition that slavery cannot enter a new country without police regulations is historically false. It is not true at all. I hold that the history of this country shows that the institution of slavery was originally planted upon this continent *without* these "police regulations" which the Judge now thinks necessary for the actual establishment of it. Not only so, but is there not another fact—how came this Dred Scott decision to be made? It was made upon the case of a Negro being taken and actually held in slavery in Minnesota Territory, claiming his freedom because the act of Congress prohibited his being so held there. . . . This shows that there is vigor enough in slavery to plant itself in a new country even against unfriendly legislation. It takes not only law but the enforcement of law to keep it out. That is the history of this country upon the subject. . . .

Address at Cooper Union, New York, February 27, 1860. *Living Lincoln*, 318-19. This was Lincoln's first major address in the East.

. . . Holding, as they do, that slavery is morally right, and socially elevating, they cannot cease to demand a full national recognition of it, as a legal right, and a social blessing.

Nor can we justifiably withhold this on any ground save our conviction that slavery is wrong. If slavery is right, all words, acts, laws, and constitutions against it, are themselves wrong, and should be silenced, and swept away. If it is right, we cannot justly object to its nationality—its universality; if it is wrong, they cannot justly insist upon its extension—its enlargement. All they ask, we could readily grant, if we thought slavery right; all we ask, they could as readily grant, if they thought it wrong. Their thinking it right, and our thinking it wrong, is the precise fact upon which depends the whole controversy. Thinking it right, as they do, they are not to blame for desiring its full recognition, as being right; but, thinking it wrong, as we do, can we yield to them? Can we cast our votes with their view, and against our own? In view of our moral, social, and political responsibilities, can we do this?

Wrong as we think slavery is, we can yet afford to let it alone where it is, because that much is due to the necessity arising from its actual presence in the nation; but can we, while our votes will prevent it, allow it to spread into the national Territories, and to overrun us here in these free States? If our sense of duty forbids this, then let us stand by our duty, fearlessly and effectively. Let us be diverted by none of these sophistical contrivances wherewith we are so industriously plied and belabored—contrivances such as groping for some middle ground between the right and the wrong, vain as the search for a man who should be neither a living man nor a dead man—such as a policy of "don't care" on a question about which all true men do care—

such as Union appeals beseeching true Union men to yield to Disunionists, reversing the divine rule, and calling, not the sinners, but the righteous to repentance—such as invocations to Washington, imploring men to unsay what Washington said, and undo what Washington did.

Neither let us be slandered from our duty by false accusations against us, nor frightened from it by menaces of destruction to the government nor of dungeons to ourselves. LET US HAVE FAITH THAT RIGHT MAKES MIGHT, AND IN THAT FAITH, LET US, TO THE END, DARE TO DO OUR DUTY AS WE UNDERSTAND IT.

Message to Congress, March 6, 1862. *Living Lincoln*, 464-66.

I recommend the adoption of a Joint Resolution by your honorable bodies which shall be substantially as follows:

"Resolved that the United States ought to co-operate with any state which may adopt gradual abolishment of slavery, giving to such state pecuniary aid, to be used by such state in its discretion, to compensate for the inconveniences public and private, produced by such change of system."

... The federal government would find its highest interest in such a measure, as one of the most efficient means of self-preservation. The leaders of the existing insurrection entertain the hope that this government will ultimately be forced to acknowledge the independence of some part of the disaffected region, and that all the slave states north of such part will then say "the Union, for which we have struggled, being already gone, we now choose to go with the southern section." To deprive them of this hope, substantially ends the rebellion; and the initiation of emancipation completely deprives them of it, as to all the states initiating it. . . . I say "initiation" because, in my judgment, gradual, and not sudden emancipation, is better for all. In the mere financial, or pecuniary view, any Member of Congress, with the census tables and Treasury reports before him, can readily see for himself how very soon the current expenditures of this war would purchase, at fair valuation, all the slaves in any named state. Such a proposition, on the part of the general government, sets up no claim of a right, by federal authority, to interfere with slavery within state limits, referring, as it does, the absolute control of the subject, in each case, to the state and its people, immediately interested. It is proposed as a matter of perfectly free choice with them.

Appeal to border state Representatives, July 12, 1862. *Living Lincoln*, 489.

... How much better for you, as seller, and the nation as buyer, to sell out, and buy out, that without which the war could never have been, than to sink both the thing to be sold, and the price of it, in cutting one another's throats.

I do not speak of emancipation *at once*, but of a *decision* at once to emancipate *gradually*. Room in South America for colonization, can be obtained cheaply, and in abundance; and when numbers shall be large enough to be company and encouragement for one another, the freed people will not be so reluctant to go.

Emancipation Proclamation, January 1, 1863. *Living Lincoln*, 525-26.

... I, Abraham Lincoln, President of the United States, by virtue of the power in me vested as Commander-in-Chief, of the Army and Navy of the United States in time of actual armed rebellion against authority and government of the United States, and as a fit and necessary war measure for suppressing said rebellion, do, on this first day of January, in the year of our Lord one thousand eight hundred and sixty-three, and in accordance with my purpose so to do publicly proclaimed for the full period of one hundred days . . . order and designate as the States and parts of States wherein the people thereof respectively, are this day in rebellion against the United States, the following: . . .

And by virtue of the power, and for the purpose aforesaid, I do order and declare that all persons held as slaves within said designated States, and parts of States, are, and henceforward shall be free; and that the executive government of the United States, including the military and naval authorities thereof, will recognize and maintain the freedom of said persons.

And I hereby enjoin upon the people so declared to be free to abstain from all violence, unless in necessary self-defence; and I recommend to them that, in all cases when allowed, they labor faithfully for reasonable wages.

And I further declare and make known, that such persons of suitable condition, will be received into the armed service of the United States to garrison forts, positions, stations, and other places, and to man vessels of all sorts in said service.

And upon this act, sincerely believed to be an act of justice, warranted by the Constitution, upon military necessity, I invoke the considerate judgment of mankind, and the gracious favor of Almighty God.

Letter to Albert G. Hodges, April 4, 1864. *Living Lincoln*, 600-601.

I am naturally anti-slavery. If slavery is not wrong, nothing is wrong. I cannot remember when I did not so think, and feel. And yet I have never understood the Presidency conferred upon me an unrestricted right to act officially upon this judgment and feeling. It was in the oath I took that I would, to the best of my ability, preserve, protect, and defend the Constitution of the United States. . . . I could not feel that, to the best of my ability, I had even tried to preserve the Constitution, if, to save slavery, or any minor matter, I should permit the wreck of government, country, and Constitution all together. . . . I was, in my best judgment, driven to the alternative of either surrendering the Union, and with it, the Constitution, or of laying strong hand upon the colored element. I chose the latter. . . .

Reply to notification of nomination for second term, Washington, D.C., June 9, 1864. *Living Lincoln*, 607-8.

I will say now . . . that I approve the declaration in favor of so amending the Constitution as to prohibit slavery throughout the nation. When the people in revolt, with a hundred days of explicit notice, that they could, within those days, resume their allegiance, without the overthrow of their institution, and that they could not so resume it afterwards, elected to stand out, such an amendment of the Constitution as is now proposed, became a fitting, and necessary conclusion to the final success of the Union cause. . . .

Speech to Indiana Regiment, Washington, D.C., March 17, 1865. *Living Lincoln*, 641.

. . . I have always thought that all men should be free; but if any should be slaves it should be first those who desire it for *themselves*, and secondly those who *desire* it for *others*. Whenever I hear anyone arguing for slavery I feel a strong impulse to see it tried on him personally.

DEFENDERS OF SLAVERY

JOHN C. CALHOUN

Speech in U.S. Senate against the reading of abolitionist petitions, February 6, 1837. *Works of Calhoun*, II, 630-33.

... But let me not be understood as admitting, even by implication, that the existing relations between the two races in the slaveholding States is an evil:—far otherwise; I hold it to be a good, as it has thus far proved itself to be to both, and will continue to prove so if not disturbed by the fell spirit of abolition. I appeal to facts. Never before has the black race of Central Africa, from the dawn of history to the present day, attained a condition so civilized and so improved, not only physically, but morally and intellectually. It came among us in a low, degraded, and savage condition, and in the course of a few generations it has grown up under the fostering care of our institutions, reviled as they have been, to its present comparatively civilized condition. This, with the rapid increase of numbers, is conclusive proof of the general happiness of the race, in spite of all the exaggerated tales to the contrary.

In the mean time, the white or European race has not degenerated. It has kept pace with its brethren in other sections of the Union where slavery does not exist. It is odious to make comparison; but I appeal to all sides whether the South is not equal in virtue, intelligence, patriotism, courage, disinterestedness, and all the high qualities which adorn our nature. I ask whether we have not contributed our full share of talents and political wisdom in forming and sustaining this political fabric; and whether we have not constantly inclined most strongly to the side of liberty, and been the first to see and first to resist the encroachments of power. In one thing only are we inferior—the arts of gain; we acknowledge that we are less wealthy than the Northern section of this Union, but I trace this mainly to the fiscal action of this Government, which has extracted much from, and spent little among us. Had it been the reverse,—if the exaction had been from the other section, and the expenditure with us, this point of superiority would not be against us now, as it was not at the formation of this Government.

But I take higher ground. I hold that in the present state of civilization, where two races of different origin, and distinguished by color, and other physical differences, as well as intellectual, are brought together, the relation now existing in the slaveholding States between the two, is, instead of an evil, a good—a positive good. I feel myself called upon to speak freely upon the subject where the honor and interests of those I represent are involved. I hold then, that there never has yet existed a wealthy and civilized society in which one portion of the community did not, in point of fact, live on the labor of the other. . . . I may say with truth, that in few countries so much is left to the share of the laborer, and so little exacted from him, or where there is more kind attention paid to him in sickness or infirmities of age. Compare his condition with the tenants of the poor houses in the more civilized portions of Europe—look at the sick, and the old and infirm slave, on one hand, in the midst of his family and friends, under the kind superintending care of his master and mistress, and compare it with the forlorn and wretched condition of the pauper in the poor house. But I will not dwell on this aspect of the question; I turn to the political; and here I fearlessly assert that the existing relations between the two races in the South, against which these blind fanatics are waging war, forms the most solid and durable foundation on which to rear free and stable political institutions. It is useless to disguise the fact. There is and always has been in an advanced stage of wealth and civilization, a conflict between labor and capital. The condition of society in the South exempts us from the disorders and dangers resulting from this conflict; and which explains why it is that the political condition of the slaveholding States has been so much more stable and quiet than that of the North. . . . Be assured that emancipation itself would not satisfy these fanatics:—that gained, the next step would be to raise the negroes to a social and political equality with the whites; and that being effected, we would soon find the present condition of the two races reversed. They and their northern allies would be the masters, and we the slaves; the condition of the white race in the British West India Islands, bad as it is, would be happiness to ours. There the mother country is interested in sustaining the supremacy of the European race. It is true that the authority of the former master is destroyed, but the African will there still be a slave, not to individuals but to the community,—forced to labor, not by the authority of the overseer, but by the bayonet of the soldiery and the rod of the civil magistrate.

JEFFERSON DAVIS

Speech before the Mississippi Legislature, Jackson, November 16, 1858. *Jefferson Davis*, III, 357.

... by interest, if not by higher motive, slave labor bears to capital as kind a relation as can exist between them anywhere; that it removes from us all that controversy between the laborer and the capitalist, which has filled Europe with starving millions and made their poorhouses an onerous charge. ...

Speech before the Democractic State Convention, Jackson, Mississippi, July 6, 1859. *Jefferson Davis*, IV, 63.

... Though the defense of African slavery (thus it is commonly called) is left to the South, the North are jointly benefited by it. Deduct from their trade and manufactures all which is dependent upon the products of slave labor, their prosperity would fade, and poverty would come upon them "as one that travaileth."

Message to the Confederate Congress, Montgomery, Alabama, April 29, 1861. *Rebellion Record*, I, 168-69.

... under the mild and genial climate of the Southern States, and the increasing care for the well being and comfort of the laboring classes, dictated alike by interest and humanity, the African slaves had augmented in number from about six hundred thousand, at the date of the adoption of the constitutional compact, to upwards of four millions.

In moral and social condition they had been elevated from brutal savages into docile, intelligent, and civilized agricultural laborers, and supplied not only with bodily comforts, but with careful religious instruction, under the supervision of a superior race. Their labor had been so directed as not only to allow a gradual and marked amelioration of their own condition, but to convert hundreds of thousands of square miles of the wilderness into cultivated lands covered with a prosperous people. Towns and cities had sprung into existence, and had rapidly increased in wealth and population under the social system of the South.

Message on the Emancipation Proclamation, January 12, 1863. *Messages and Papers of the Confederacy*, I, 290.

We may well leave it to the instincts of that common humanity which a beneficent Creator has implanted in the breasts of our fellow men of all countries to pass judgment on a measure by which several millions of human beings of an inferior race, peaceful and contented laborers in their sphere, are doomed to extermination, while at the same time they are encouraged to a general assassination of their masters by the insidious recommendation "to abstain from violence unless in necessary self-defense." Our own detestation of those who have attempted the most execrable measure recorded in the history of guilty man is tempered by profound contempt for the impotent rage which it discloses. . . .

The Economy in a Divided Nation

THE REPUBLICANS

The Republican Platform of 1860. *The Chicago Tribune's History of the National Conventions of Both Parties* (Chicago, 1892), 10-11.

12. That, while providing revenue for the support of the general government by duties upon imports, sound policy requires such an adjustment of these imports as to encourage the development of the industrial interests of the whole country; and we commend that policy of natural exchanges, which secures to the workingmen liberal wages, to agriculture remunerative prices, to mechanics and manufacturers an adequate reward for their skill, labor, and enterprise, and to the nation commercial prosperity and independence.

13. That we protest against any sale or alienation to others of the public lands held by actual settlers, and against any view of the free homestead policy which regards the settlers as paupers or suppliants for public bounty; and we demand the passage by Congress of the complete and satisfactory homestead measure which has already passed the House.

15. That appropriations by Congress for river and harbor improvements of a national character, required for the accommodation and security of an existing commerce, are authorized by the Constitution, and justified by the obligation of Government to protect the lives and property of its citizens.

16. That a railroad to the Pacific Ocean is imperatively demanded by the interests of the whole country; that the federal government ought to render immediate and efficient aid to its construction; and that, as a preliminary thereto, a daily overland mail should be promptly established.

From the beginning of his political career in 1832 Lincoln advocated government aid to the economy. The following is a newspaper account of a speech given at Peoria on September

17, 1852. Roy P. Basler, ed., *The Collected Works of Abraham Lincoln* (New Brunswick, N.J., 1953), II, 158.

The people of this city were addressed at the court house on Friday evening last, by Hon. A. Lincoln, of Springfield. He showed up the inconsistency of the sham democracy on the question of internal improvements in such a manner that it is not to be wondered at that the friends of [Franklin] Pierce. . . were dissatisfied. On the subject of the tariff he advocated the American side of the question, asking why, instead of sending a distance of 4,000 miles for our railroad iron, the immense iron beds of Missouri were not worked, affording a better article than that of English manufacture, and giving employment to American labor. . . .

Lincoln's Third Annual Message, December 8, 1863. *Works of Lincoln*, VII, 41-47.

The operations of the treasury during the last year have been successfully conducted. The enactment by Congress of a national banking law has proved a valuable support of the public credit. . . .

[Our wise land] policy has received its most signal and beneficent illustration in the recent enactment granting home-steads to actual settlers.

Since the first day of January last the before-mentioned quantity of one million four hundred and fifty-six thousand five hundred and fourteen acres of land have been taken up under its provisions. This fact and the amount of sales furnish gratifying evidence of increasing settlement upon the pubic lands. . . .

THE DEMOCRATS

The Douglas platform of 1860 concentrated almost exclusively upon the slavery question, taking time only to "declare our affirmance of the resolutions unanimously adopted and de-clared as a platform of principles by the Democratic Con-vention at Cincinnati, in the year 1856, believing that Demo-cratic principles are unchangeable in their nature, when applied to the same subject matters. . . . "The following economic planks were in the 1856 platform. *Tribune's Conventions*, 86-87.

1. That the Federal Government is one of limited power, derived solely from the Constitution; and the grants of power made therein ought to be strictly construed by all the departments and agents of the government; and that it is inexpedient and dangerous to exercise doubtful constitutional powers.

2. That the Constitution does not confer upon the general government the power to commence and carry on a general system of internal improvements.

3. That the Constitution does not confer authority upon the Federal Government, directly or indirectly, to assume the debts of the several States, contracted for local and internal improvements, or other State purposes; nor would such assumption be just or expedient.

4. That justice and sound policy forbid the Federal Government to foster one branch of industry to the detriment of any other, or to cherish the interest of one portion to the injury of another portion of our common country; that every citizen and every section of the country has a right to demand and insist upon an equality of rights and privileges, and to complete and ample protection of persons and property from domestic violence or foreign aggression.

5. That it is the duty of every branch of the Government to enforce and practice the most rigid economy in conducting our public affairs, and that no more revenue ought to be raised than is required to defray the necessary expenses of the Government, and for the gradual but certain extinction of the public debt.

6. That the proceeds of the public lands ought to be sacredly applied to the national objects specified in the Constitution; and that we are opposed to any law for the distribution of such proceeds among the States, as alike inexpedient in policy and repugnant to the Constitution.

7. That Congress has no power to charter a national bank; that we believe such an institution one of deadly hostility to the best interests of the country, dangerous to our republican institutions and the liberties of the people, and calculated to place the business of the country within the control of a concentrated money power, and above the laws and the will of the people. . . .

8. That the separation of the moneys of the Government from banking institutions is indispensible for the safety of the funds of the Government and the rights of the people.

9. That we are decidedly opposed to taking from the President the qualified veto power, by which he. . . has saved the American people from the corrupt and tyrannical domination of the Bank of the United States, and from a corrupting system of general internal improvements.

The Breckinridge faction of the Democratic Party in 1860 concentrated its platform on the slave issue, with only one economic clause. *Tribune's Conventions*, 93.

WHEREAS, One of the greatest necessities of the age, in a political, commercial, postal and military point of view, is a speedy communication between the Pacific and Atlantic coasts. Therefore be it

Resolved, That the National Democratic party do hereby pledge themselves to use every means in their power to secure the passage of some bill, to the extent of the constitutional authority of Congress, for the construction of a Pacific Rail Road from the Mississippi River to the Pacific Ocean, at the earliest practicable moment.

Jefferson Davis' speech in the Senate on the Pacific Railroad Bill, January 19, 1859. *Jefferson Davis*, III, 388-89.

. . .I say, then, the consent of a State can give no power to the Federal Government which it could exercise for the construction of a railroad within the limits of a State. It might be very convenient as a means of military defense; it might be necessary as a means of military defense; and still I say this government has no power, even when you prove the necessity to exist, to invade the limits of a sovereign State, there to set up its artificial creature, and exercise a jurisdiction which the Constitution does not give. Over the territories I hold the case to be widely different. . . .I say, they hold powers in a Territory which they could not possess within the limits of a State. Therefore my opinion is, that we may exercise the power to construct a railroad as we do other roads within the limits of a Territory, without thence deriving the power to do the same thing within the limits of a State.

Jefferson Davis' speech in the Senate on internal improvements, February 6, 1860. *Jefferson Davis*, IV, 190.

I think, then, if I be right, that the Senator from Michigan properly desires to know how improvements can be made; and I answer him, by tolls, by taxes, by wharfage duties, by light taxes, by all of those taxes which the sovereignty of a State may impose, or joint sovereignties, having equal control of the river, by the consent of Congress, may impose, upon the commerce which passes over it. . . . I hold, in one place as well as another, at home, as well as in any other portion of the United States, that this power to tax the whole people of the United States to improve the navigation of one locality, is an offense against the Constitution, and not to be drawn from any of its specific grants.

Jefferson Davis, speech in the Senate, June 20, 1860. *Jefferson Davis*, IV, 530.

I do not propose to go into a discussion of the general question of the tariff, but I may be permitted just now and here to say that I look upon all duties imposed on imposts as a mode of taxation, and as the most expensive mode in which a given amount of money can be raised. It imposes a large amount of tax upon the consumer which does not go into the public Treasury, and because of the indirect manner in which the money is raised, it encourages profligacy of expenditure. I think, therefore, the whole system a bad one. . . .

The Role of the People in a Divided Nation

JOHN C. CALHOUN

Speech on the admission of Michigan, U.S. Senate, January 5, 1837. *Works of Calhoun,* II, 613-14.

... I understood the Senator from Pennsylvania (Mr. Buchanan) as holding language countenancing the principle, that the will of a mere numerical majority is paramount to the authority of law and constitution. He did not, indeed, announce distinctly this principle, but it might fairly be inferred from what he said; for he told us the people of a State, where the constitution gives the same weight to a smaller as to a greater number, might take the remedy into their own hands; meaning, as I understood him, that a mere majority might, at their pleasure, subvert the constitution and government of a State,—which he seemed to think was the essence of democracy. ... We call our State a Republic—a Commonwealth, not a Democracy; and let me tell the Senator it is a far more popular government than if it had been based on the simple principle of the numerical majority. It takes more voices to put the machine of government in motion, than in those that the Senator would consider more popular. It represents all the interests of the State,—and is in fact the government of the people, in the true sense of the term, and not that of the mere majority, or the dominant interests.

... while I thus openly avow myself a conservative, God forbid I should ever deny the glorious right of rebellion and revolution. Should corruption and oppression become intolerable, and not otherwise be thrown off—if liberty must perish, or the government be overthrown, I would not hesitate, at the hazard of life, to resort to revolution, and to tear down a corrupt government that could neither be reformed nor borne by freemen. . . .

Extracts from *A Disquisition* (1845-50). *Works of Calhoun,* I, 22-58.

... the dominant majority, for the time, would have the same tendency to oppression and abuse of power which, without the right of suffrage, irresponsible rulers would have. No reason, indeed, can be assigned why the latter would abuse their power, which would not apply, with equal force, to the former. The dominant majority, for the time, would in reality, through the right of suffrage, be the rulers—the controlling, governing, and irresponsible power; and those who make and execute the laws would, for the time, be in reality but *their* representatives and agents.

... there must, of necessity, be a governing and a governed— a ruling and a subject portion. . . . [The] minority, for the time, will be as much the governed or subject portion as are the people in an aristocracy or the subjects in a monarchy.

... as the community becomes populous, wealthy, refined, and highly civilized, the difference between the rich and the poor will become more strongly marked, and the number of the ignorant and dependent greater in proportion to the rest of the community. With the increase of this difference, the tendency to conflict between them will become stronger; and as the poor and dependent become more numerous in proportion, there will be in governments of the numerical majority no want of leaders among the wealthy and ambitious to excite and direct them in their efforts to obtain the control.

... in governments of the concurrent majority ... the wealthy and intelligent, being identified in interest with the poor and ignorant of their respective portions or interests of the community, become their leaders and protectors. . . .

... it is a great and dangerous error to suppose that all people are equally entitled to liberty. It is a reward to be earned, not a blessing to be gratuitously lavished on all alike—a reward reserved for the intelligent, the patriotic, the virtuous and deserving, and not a boon to be bestowed on a people too ignorant, degraded, and vicious to be capable either of appreciating or of enjoying it. Nor is it any disparagement to liberty that such is and ought to be the case. On the contrary, its greatest praise—its proudest distinction is that an all-wise Providence has reserved it as the noblest and highest reward for the development of our faculties, moral and intellectual. A reward more appropriate than liberty could not be conferred on the deserving, nor a punishment inflicted on the undeserving more just than to be subject to lawless and despotic rule. . . . The progress of a people rising from a lower to a higher point in the scale of liberty is necessarily slow; and by attempting to precipitate, we either retard or permanently defeat it.

... that equality of citizens, in the eyes of the law, is essential to liberty in a popular government is conceded. But to go further and make equality of *condition* essential to liberty would be to destroy both liberty and progress. The reason is that inequality of condition, while it is a necessary consequence of liberty, is at the same time indispensable to progress. . . . It is, indeed, this inequality of condition between the front and rear ranks, in the march of progress, which gives so strong an impulse to the former to maintain their position, and to the latter to press forward into their files. This gives to progress its greatest impulse. To force the front rank back to the rear or attempt to push forward the rear into line with the front, by the interposition of the government, would put an end to the impulse and effectually arrest the march of progress.

These great and dangerous errors have their origin in the prevalent opinion that all men are born free and equal—than which nothing can be more unfounded and false. It rests upon the assumption of a fact which is contrary to universal observation, in whatever light it may be regarded. It is, indeed, difficult to explain how an opinion so destitute of all sound reason ever could have been so extensively entertained. . . .

JAMES HENRY HAMMOND

Speech in the Senate, March 4, 1858. *Congressional Globe,* 35th Cong., 1st Session, pp. 961-962. The South Carolina senator (1807-1864) here introduced the "mud-sill" theory, which Lincoln was later to attack.

In all special systems there must be a class to do the menial duties, to perform the drudgery of life. That is, a class requiring but a low order of intellect and but little skill. Its requisites are vigor, docility, fidelity. Such a class you must have, or you would not have that other class which leads progress, civilization, and refinement. It constitutes the very mud-sill of society and of political government; and you might as well attempt to build a house in the air, as to build either the one or the other, except on this mud-sill. Fortunately for the South, she found a race adapted to that purpose to her hand. A race inferior to her own, but eminently qualified in temper, in vigor, in docility, in capacity to stand the climate, to answer all her purposes. We use them for our purpose, and call them slaves. We found them slaves by the common "consent of mankind," which, according to Cicero, *"lex naturae est."* The highest proof of what is Nature's law. We are old-fashioned at the South yet; slave is a word discarded now by "ears polite;" I will not characterize that class at the North by that term; but you have it; it is there; it is everywhere; it is eternal.

The Senator from New York said yesterday that the whole world had abolished slavery. Aye, the *name*, but not the *thing;* all the powers of the earth cannot abolish that. God only can do it when he repeals the *fiat*, "the poor ye always have with you;" for the man who lives by daily labor, and scarcely lives at that, and who has to put out his labor in the market, and take the best he can get for it; in short, your whole hireling class of manual laborers and "operatives," as you call them, are essentially slaves. The difference between us is, that our slaves are hired for life and well compensated; there is no starvation, no begging, no want of employment among our people, and not too much employment either. Yours are hired by the day, not cared for, and scantily compensated, which may be proved in the most painful manner, at any hour in any street in any of your large towns. Why, you meet more beggars in one day, in any single street of the city of New York, than you would meet in a lifetime in the whole South. We do not think that whites should be slaves either by law or necessity. Our slaves are black, of another and inferior race. The *status* in which we have placed them is an elevation. They are elevated from the condition in which God first created them, by being made our slaves. None of that race on the whole face of the globe can be compared with the slaves of the South. They are happy, content, unaspiring, and utterly incapable, from intellectual weakness, ever to give us any trouble by their aspirations. Yours are white, of your own race; you are brothers of one blood. They are your equals in natural endowment of intellect, and they feel galled by their degradation. Our slaves do not vote. We give them no political power. Yours do vote, and, being the majority, they are the depositaries of all your political power. If they knew the tremendous secret, that the ballot-box is stronger than "an army with banners," and could combine, where would you be? Your society would be reconstructed, your government overthrown, your property divided, not as they have mistakenly attempted to initiate such proceedings by meeting in parks, with arms in their hands, but by the quiet process of the ballot-box. You have been making war upon us to our very hearthstones. How would you like for us to send lecturers and agitators North, to teach these people this, to aid in combining, and to leading them?

JEFFERSON DAVIS

Remarks on slavery, U.S. Senate, March 2, 1859. *Jefferson Davis*, IV, 49-50.

... the lower race of human beings that constitute the substratum of what is termed the slave population of the South, elevates every white man in our community. I say it is there true that every mechanic assumes among us the position which only a master workman holds among you. Hence it is that the mechanic in our southern States is admitted to the table of his employer, converses with him on terms of equality—not merely political equality, but an actual equality—wherever the two men come in contact. The white laborers of the South are all of them men who are employed in what you would term the higher pursuits of labor among you. It is the presence of a lower caste, those lower by their mental and physical organization, controlled by the higher intellect of the white man, that gives this superiority to the white laborer. Menial services are not there performed by the white man. We have none of our brethren sunk to the degradation of being menials. That belongs to the lower race—the descendants of Ham, who, under the judgment of God speaking to the prophet Noah, were condemned to be servants. To propose that we should change our industrial system, that we should bring the negroes up to a level with the white man, would be such an offense that the lecturer who would come to teach such philosophy would be fortunate indeed if he should escape without some public indignity. One of the reconciling features in the existence of that particular institution called domestic slavery of African bondsmen, is the fact that it raises white men to the same general level, that it dignifies and exalts every white man by the presence of a lower race. I say it in no terms of disparaging comparison with others. I say but what has been with me a deliberate conviction, that it is promotive of, if not essential to, the preservation of the higher orders of republican civilization.

ABRAHAM LINCOLN

Letter to the *Sangamo Journal*, New Salem, Illinois, June 13, 1836. *Living Lincoln*, 11.

I go for all sharing the privileges of the government, who

assist in bearing its burthens.   Consequently I go for admitting all whites to the right of suffrage, who pay taxes or bear arms, (by no means excluding females).

Fragment on government, July, 1854. *Living Lincoln,* 155.

The legitimate object of government, is to do for a community of people, whatever they need to have done, but cannot do, *at all,* or cannot, *so well do,* for themselves—in their separate, and individual capacities.

In all that the people can individually do as well for themselves, government ought not to interfere.

The desirable things which the individuals of a people cannot do, or cannot well do, for themselves, fall into two classes: those which have relation to *wrongs,* and those which have not. Each of these branch off into an infinite variety of subdivisions.

The first—that in relation to wrongs—embraces all crimes, misdemeanors, and non-performance of contracts. The other embraces all which, in its nature, and without wrong, requires combined action, as public roads and highways, public schools, charities, pauperism, orphanage, estates of the deceased, and the machinery of government itself.

From this it appears that if all men were just, there still would be *some,* though not *so much,* need of government.

Definition of democracy, August 1, 1858 [?]. *Works of Lincoln,* II, 532.

As I would not be a *slave,* so I would not be a *master.* This expresses my idea of democracy. Whatever differs from this, to the extent of the difference, is no democracy.

Address at the Wisconsin State Fair, Madison, September 30, 1859. *Living Lincoln,* 299-301.

... another class of reasoners hold the opinion... that labor is prior to, and independent of, capital; that, in fact, capital is the fruit of labor, and could never have existed if labor had not *first* existed—that labor can exist without capital, but that capital could never have existed without labor. Hence they hold that labor is the superior—greatly the superior of capital.

... the opponents of the *"mud-sill"* theory insist that there is not, of necessity, any such thing as the free hired laborer being fixed to that condition for life. There is demonstration for saying this. Many independent men, in this assembly, doubtless a few years ago were hired laborers. And their case is almost if not quite the general rule.

The prudent, penniless beginner in the world, labors for wages awhile, saves a surplus from which to buy tools or land, for himself; then labors on his own account another while, and at length hires another new beginner to help him. This, say its advocates, is free labor—the just and generous, and prosperous system, which opens the way for all—gives hope to all, and energy, and progress, and improvement of condition to all. If any continue through life in the condition of the hired laborer, it is not the fault of the system, but because of either a dependent nature which prefers it, or improvidence, folly, or singular misfortune. . . . [But] *now*, especially in these free states, nearly all are educated— quite too nearly all, to leave the labor of the uneducated, in any wise adequate to the support of the whole. It follows from this that henceforth educated people must labor. Otherwise, education itself would become a positive and intolerable evil. No country can sustain, in idleness, more than a small percentage of its numbers. The free at majority must labor at something productive. From these premises the problem springs, "How can *labor* and *education* be the most satisfactorily combined?"

By the *"mud-sill"* theory it is assumed that labor and education are incompatible; and any practical combination of them impossible. According to that theory, a blind horse upon a treadmill, is a perfect illustration of what a laborer should be—all the better for being blind, that he could not tread out of place, or kick understandingly. According to that theory, the education of laborers, is not only useless, but pernicious, and dangerous. In fact, it is, in some sort, deemed a misfortune that laborers should have heads at all. Those same heads are regarded as explosive materials, only to be safely kept in damp places, as far as possible from that peculiar sort of fire which ignites them. A Yankee who could invent a strong *handed* man without a head would receive the everlasting gratitude of the *"mud-sill"* advocates.

But free labor says "no!" Free labor argues that, as the Author of man makes every individual with one head and one pair of hands, it was probably intended that heads and hands should cooperate as friends; and that that particular head, should direct and control that particular pair of hands. . . . [Thus] every head should be cultivated, and improved, by whatever will add to its capacity for performing its charge. In one word free labor insists on universal education. . . .

Speech at Independence Hall, Philadelphia, February 22, 1861. *Living Lincoln*, 379.

. . . I have never had a feeling politically that did not spring from the sentiments embodied in the Declaration of Independence. . . . I have often inquired of myself, what great principle or idea it was that kept this confederacy so long together. It was not the mere matter of the separation of the colonies from the mother land; but something in that Declaration giving liberty, not alone to the people of this country, but hope to the world for all future time. It was that which gave promise that in due time the weights should be lifted from the shoulders of all men, and that *all* should have an equal chance. This is the sentiment embodied in that Declaration of Independence.

Message to Congress, July 4, 1861. *Living Lincoln*, 421.

This is essentially a people's contest. On the side of the Union, it is a struggle for maintaining in the world, that form, and substance of government, whose leading object is, to elevate the condition of men—to lift artificial weights from all shoulders—to clear the paths of laudable pursuit for all—to afford all, an unfettered start, and a fair chance, in the race of life. Yielding to partial, and temporary departures, from necessity, this is the leading object of the government for whose existence we contend.

The Gettysburg Address, November 19, 1863. *Living Lincoln*, 591.

Four score and seven years ago our fathers brought forth on this continent, a new nation, conceived in liberty, and dedicated to the proposition that all men are created equal.

Now we are engaged in a great civil war, testing whether that nation, or any nation so conceived and so dedicated, can long endure. We are met on a great battlefield of that war. We have come to dedicate a portion of that field, as a final resting place for those who here gave their lives that that nation might live. It is altogether fitting and proper that we should do this.

But, in a larger sense, we cannot dedicate—we cannot consecrate—we cannot hallow—this ground. The brave men, living and dead, who struggled here, have consecrated it, far above our poor power to add or detract. The world will little note, nor long remember what we say here, but it can never forget what they did here. It is for us the living, rather, to be dedicated here to the unfinished work which they who fought here have thus far so nobly advanced. It is rather for us to be here dedicated to the great task remaining before us—that from these honored dead we take increased devotion to that cause for which they gave the last full measure of devotion—that we here highly resolve that these dead shall not have died in vain—that this nation, under God, shall have a new birth of freedom—and that government of the people, by the people, for the people, shall not perish from the earth.

Response to an election victory serenade, November 10, 1864. *Living Lincoln,* 623-24.

We cannot have free government without elections; and if the rebellion could force us to forego, or postpone a national election, it might fairly claim to have already conquered and ruined us. The strife of the election is but human nature practically applied to the facts of the case. . . .

But the election, along with its incidental, and undesirable strife, has done good too. It has demonstrated that a people's government can sustain a national election, in the midst of a great civil war. Until now it has not been known to the world that this was a possibility. It shows also how *sound,* and how *strong* we still are. . . .